LATIN@S' PRESENCE
IN THE FOOD INDUSTRY

FOOD AND FOODWAYS

SERIES EDITOR:
JENNIFER JENSEN WALLACH

OTHER TITLES
IN THIS SERIES

Latin@s' Presence in the Food Industry

CHANGING HOW WE THINK ABOUT FOOD

EDITED BY
MEREDITH E. ABARCA
AND CONSUELO
CARR SALAS

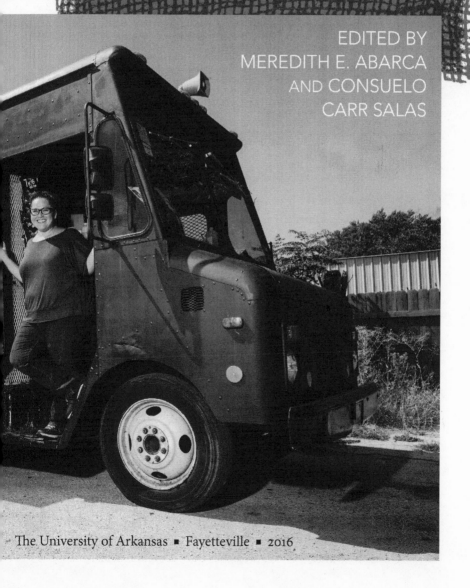

The University of Arkansas ▪ Fayetteville ▪ 2016

ISBN: 978-1-55728-693-2
e-ISBN: 978-1-61075-579-5

20   19   18   17   16   5   4   3   2   1

Designed by Liz Lester

⊖ The paper used in this publication meets the minimum requirements
of the American National Standard for Permanence of Paper for Printed
Library Materials Z39.48-1984.

LIBRARY OF CONGRESS CONTROL NUMBER: 2015948064

Cover image: © Tino Soriano/National Geographic Creative/Corbis

To those who help us up the mountain

Salt of the earth

—MATTHEW 5:13

CONTENTS

SERIES EDITOR'S PREFACE

The University of Arkansas Press series on Food and Foodways explores historical and contemporary issues in global food studies. We are committed to telling lesser-known food stories and to representing a diverse set of voices. Our strength is works in the humanities and social sciences that use food as a lens to examine broader, social, cultural, environmental, ethical, and economic issues. However, we recognize that food—perhaps the most central of all human concerns— is not only a barometer by which to gauge social, cultural, and environmental conditions, it can also be a source of pleasure. In addition to scholarly books, we publish creative nonfiction that explores the sensory dimensions of consumption and celebrates food as evidence of human creativity and innovation.

This essay collection, *Latin@s' Presence in the Food Industry: Changing How We Think about Food*, edited by groundbreaking food studies scholar Meredith E. Abarca and Consuelo Carr Salas represents the current state of the growing subfield of Latin@ food studies. The eleven essays collected here represent a wide variety of methodological perspectives ranging from history to anthropology to literary studies. Collectively, the authors explore the role of Latin@s as "active creators of food-based communities, as self-cultural representations, and as professionals rather than just laborers (i.e., 'braceros': the reduction of people to 'arms' for picking fruits and vegetables)." The diverse set of voices and nuanced approaches represented here help fulfill the Food and Foodways series mandate to publish research on rich but underexplored topics. They survey the abundant but still understudied subject of Latin@ food studies and establish an ongoing research agenda that should animate scholars of American food culture for years to come.

—JENNIFER JENSEN WALLACH

ACKNOWLEDGMENTS

To Jennifer Wallach, editor of the book series Food and Foodways published by the University of Arkansas Press, we extend our appreciation for the opportunity of compiling this collection. We offer our thanks to the contributors to this volume, and to the anonymous readers for their insightful comments. We are indebted to Jalaine Weller for her careful editing of the final manuscript.

We express our gratitude to those who champion our intellectual passions with their steadfast nourishment. I, Meredith, would like to say *gracias* to my mother, Liduvina Vélez, whose faith keeps me going, and to my four-legged companions whose tail wagging keeps me sane. I, Consuelo, would like to acknowledge my parents, Armando Salas Jr. and Norma Carr Salas, and my sister, Angelica Maria Carr Salas, for their continuing love and support in all that I do, and David Juarez for his "lottle" love and encouragement. Last, but not least, together we thank Lucy Fischer-West for feeding us chocolates when we most needed them.

INTRODUCTION

MEREDITH E. ABARCA
AND CONSUELO CARR SALAS

Margarita Juarez,[1] also known as Doña Margie, fed strangers who stopped and knocked at her front door on their way to *el norte* (the United States) searching for a job. Doña Margie (October 8, 1918–December 8, 2013) lived most of her life in El Paso, Texas, which is a site of historical significance as it, first, marked the pass to northern New Spain and, later, an international border between Mexico and the United States. El Paso del Norte continued to be a highly used port of entry to el norte for legal and undocumented crossings; however, in the 1990s much of the flow of undocumented crossing moved to the Sonora-Arizona desert crossing. Historically, the influx of those crossing the international border of Ciudad Juárez–El Paso without documents was of working-class Mexicans in search of paying jobs.[2] What has been at the root of this northern journey, especially for those taking the risk of crossing without documents, is that people often lack the means to provide food for their families in their home country. Once in the United States, food also marks their lives as many find employment in the lowest-paying sectors within the food industry.

During the late 1980s and into the 1990s, a period when Mexico faced substantial economic crises,[3] Doña Margie's front porch became a stop for nourishment to those who had just crossed the international border without documents in search of a job. The frequency of strangers eating at Doña Margie's was such that it became common for her grandson David Juarez to see them on his return home from Crockett Elementary School. These strangers somehow knew to go to Doña Margie's house, which was some two miles away from the border crossing, where they were certain to receive a meal. While family and friends used the side kitchen door as the main entrance, unfamiliar people knocked on the front door and asked to speak to *la señora* Juarez. After acknowledging their presence, she would return to her kitchen to prepare a plate of food using whatever food she had cooked for her own family to serve the passerby. While the porch marked a distinction between strangers and family, Doña Margie's nourishing act blurred this divide as she served strangers the food she cooked for her loved ones.

Doña Margie's family found her willingness to feed whoever knocked at her door odd. Her grandson states,

> I used to think that my grandmother was part of an "underground railroad." Was she the first stop or was she the third stop, was she a stop? On their way to wherever they were going, were they aware of other places [to stop for a meal]? Maybe my grandmother didn't know if she was part of a larger network, but people knew when they crossed over that they could come to this address [because someone had told them]: "*La señora que vive alli le va dar comida. Si ella no tiene comida le va a dar agua.*" (The lady who lives there will give you something to eat. If she does not have anything to eat she will give you water.)

While Doña Margie's family still, to this day, does not know why or how complete strangers knew to stop at her house, they do know why she fed them. Doña Margie's grandson once asked her, and he recalls her answer in this manner: "God guides people. He is going to guide them to others who are going to help them. I just happened to be on the path; I just happened to be that house, on that path, to help. So who am I to not help these people?"

Doña Margie's "underground railroad" practice, as her grandson David called it, is part of a food system network that generally goes unnoticed except by those who need it. Her home became a visible center point for those who had to render themselves invisible due to the circumstances of their crossing. Her front porch and her food were part of a food system that we might consider calling circumstantial or situational as opposed to global or local. Unlike a globalized food industry often motivated by efficiency, consistency, and profit, or even its counterpart, the localized food system grounded in concerns of cultural preservation, environment issues, and sustainability, this circumstantial or situational food system is one driven by the values of hospitality and the ethics of kindness and compassion.

We begin with Doña Margie's story for three reasons. First, actions such as hers are rarely, if ever, thought of as a food system network. As a single moment in someone's life, this action can easily be dismissed as not affecting the systemic problems embedded in the food industry. Yet, her action of feeding strangers marks a single moment of food security at a time when it is most needed. We also see this food giving as a form of food system network because Doña Margie's story, while particular to her, is not uncommon. Second, it makes visible food narratives—ways in which people use food to define cultural, social, and economic aspects of their lives—that would otherwise go unnoticed. For Doña Margie, this food narrative is based on cultural and religious beliefs of a Good Samaritan and hospitality. Finally, Doña Margie's story reminds us that individuals' daily realities become the map by which they navigate the maze of practices and policies of the global food industry in order to create their own micro-communities, which are yet another example of a food system.

Latin@s' Presence in the Food Industry: Changing How We Think about Food presents our effort to continue to map ways Latin@s navigate the food industry. The relationship between Latin@s and the US food industry is multifaceted and multilayered. We intend to show this complexity through the ways in which the chapters in this volume complement and complicate how Latin@s negotiate their roles within this industry to insert themselves as active creators of food-based communities, as self-cultural representations, and as professionals rather than just laborers (i.e., "braceros": the reduction of people to "arms" for picking fruits and vegetables).

Before we go any further, we need to explain our use of the term Latin@s as it is central to the collection as a whole and to the individual chapters. Generally speaking, Latin@ is used as a gender inclusive noun that stands for both Latina and Latino. But beyond this gender neutrality, we are using Latin@s to stress both a transnational *Latinidad* as well as the national/ethnic demographic changes taking place within the United States. In the realm of ethnic identity politics, the term Latin@ has a relatively short history and it is often juxtaposed to the history and use of the term Hispanic.[4] While we are not interested in getting into the polemics embedded within these terms, we use Latin@s as a way to speak of people living in Latin America, including the Caribbean, and those of Latin American and Caribbean origins living in the United States.

While the majority of chapters in this collection focus on Mexican and Mexican American food-related experiences, we use Latin@s to bring attention to a few facts. For example, the food industry, through its need for laborers and consumers, affects the lives of everyone, regardless of specific ethnicities. Dairies in the Northeast equally employ immigrants from Mexico, Central and South America, as well as the Caribbean. Puerto Ricans, Cubans, Dominicans, and Central and South Americas often find themselves working in diverse aspects of the food industry on the West Coast. Food items such as genetically modified corn exported from the United States to different nations of the Global South affect these native economies and food cultures. Our use of Latin@, then, is our way of capturing the interlocking effects various people of Latin American and the Caribbean face within the structure of our modern food industry. But most important, our goal is to demonstrate the different ways in which many Latin@s work at carving out a place and space to renegotiate their own participation within the food industry while simultaneously creating their own versions of circumstantial or situational food systems.[5]

This collection speaks beyond issues of labor conditions, economic politics, and immigration laws that create what is known as structural vulnerability. Such vulnerability is the result of "class-based economic exploitation and cultural, gender/sexual, and racialized discrimination, as well as complementary processes of depreciated subjectivity formation."[6] The social sciences have contributed much to reveal how labor economic policies and practices are designed with the intentional result to hide the daily conditions experienced by workers on the front lines of food production.[7] While the working conditions that cause such vulnerabilities cannot be ignored, it is equally important to underscore the active and self-conscious ways in which Latin@s create spaces to maneuver food systems, both global and local, in order to establish communities guided by their own food-based professionalism.

By speaking of Latin@s' presence in the food industry, we showcase the ways in which Latin@s express forms of professionalism based on their cultural food knowledge. The term professionalism underscores people's knowledge as vendors, producers, providers, and consumers. For example, selling food on the streets, in the market, from home, or in a food establishment is perhaps the oldest profession of most working-class people, particularly women. This way of making a living or assisting in making a living, however, is not always conceived of as a profession. Yet, this informal economy requires a vast knowledge of food in terms of production, purchase, and resale value; it often necessitates maneuvering a network between producers and consumers.[8] It also requires the ability to create a loyal customer base, and when this is done successfully, a community network is developed as Norma Cárdenas's and Lidia Marte's chapters included in this collection demonstrate. Our use of professionalism reflects an extension of a paradigm shift presented in a special issue for Food and Foodways edited by Meredith E. Abarca and Ramona Lee Pérez, "*Cocinas Públicas: Food and Border Consciousness in Greater Mexico*."[9] In the introduction, the editors define *cocinas públicas* (public kitchens) as reflecting a multitude of social, political, economic, and cultural values by addressing three meanings of *cocina*:

> *Cocina* has three literal and symbolic translations that show how private and public spaces blend into each other to transform them both. First, cocina . . . denot[es] cooking as an activity, a set of tasks performed for food preparation [that is] predicated on knowledge and skills . . . Second, cocina as [a home] kitchen defines a focal point of making meaning in household life. [It] is a critical space where people congregate not just to prepare and consume food, but to share in each other, thus enacting the connective tissue of kinship. This domestic emotional economy can also function within the public market place as the physical site of the family kitchen develops into a place and space for social, economic, and cultural activity both in and out of the home. . . . Third, cocina as cuisine or cookery is a system [that] denotes the rules for making a culturally appropriate set of substances. . . . Cocina as cuisine can also contribute substances for emotional growth, linking feeder and eater through ties of affect.[10]

The skillful, cultural-based knowledge and affective aspects evoked and preformed within la cocina, as the site of cooking, are not limited to the private/domestic space of a home's kitchen.

Abarca and Pérez conceptualize cocinas públicas as spatial, cultural, social, and economic sites within multiple localities. While these sites usually are not looked to as spaces of professionalism, their analytical model creates a "paradigmatic distinction" that views the work being done as professions. The function of this model is that it serves to analyze "the entire field of food and cooking in public space. From agriculture to food processing and shipping, from markets [to] eateries . . . a cocina pública approach can help reveal linkages within and between food chains. Full consideration of cocina[s] pública[s] would also incorporate multiple culinary discourses."[11] Latin@s' Presence in the Food Industry reflects some of the results that a cocina pública analytical model can produce.

Professionalism, in the contexts we are using it, showcases certain performative acts that demonstrate how Latin@s constantly enact and recreate their cultural as well as socioeconomic subjectivities. The enactment of this form of professionalism expresses a cultural and economic network that subverts the social and spatial divisions such as domestic/public, local/global, and producer/consumer. By blurring these dichotomies, Latin@s in the food industry literally and symbolically create and promote their cultural identities. Furthermore, this professionalism leads to networks by which families and/or neighbors create communities that reflect certain levels of food security, food justice, or forms of food sovereignty without eliminating food's cultural significance. While a number of articles directly speak to these aspects of Latin@s' food professionalism, others stress how issues of gentrification and cultural appropriation through the food industry's process of commodifying edible products attempt to erase Latin@s' culinary knowledge as well as cultural (symbolic) representations.

In order to speak of Latin@s' labor within the food industry and of new discourses of professionalism that enable reflection on how micro levels of food systems are created, a definition of these two food entities—industry and system—is in order. In our effort to provide a definition that illustrates the "exact" difference between these two organizing food structures, we consulted recent scholarship on the subject matter only to discover that these components of food production—distribution and consumption—literally feed off each other.[12] The relationship of a food industry rooted in neoliberal economic policies (particularly NAFTA) to food systems, such as those that originate at a local, often sustainable and culturally viable level, tends to be one of appropriation and displacement.[13] The relationship of alternative food systems—organic, locally grown—to industrially produced and distributed foods is one of resistance. By exploring Latin@s' presence within different aspects of the food industry, including cultural representation through food advertising, we hope to problematize the binary construction of appropriation (global/fast foods) and resistance (local/slow foods). The chapters in this collection show the "rich texture of daily social [and cultural] interaction"[14] by focusing on the lives of individuals maneuvering the *contradictions and paradoxes* between the food industry and alternative food systems.

The US food industry tends to be defined as the global network responsible for mass industrial production and distribution.[15] The food industry embodies an economic and social infrastructure, which enables it to produce, transport, and deliver foodstuffs at a national and global level. It is technology and science that underwrite the productivity and efficiency of food production.[16] Corporate control and interest in capital gain ground all of the operations of the food industry.[17] Part of what sustains the standard mode of operation seems to be the argument that in order to feed a growing global population with limited land resources, new technologies and business paradigms need to replace traditional models of agriculture.[18] This argument becomes an excuse not to truly and fully address the structural vulnerabilities the US food industry creates, particularly for a large sector of its workers, the majority of whom historically have been undocumented immigrants often from Latin American and Caribbean countries.[19] Aspects of these vulnerabilities also extend to health-related issues often caused by cultural displacements. For example, Marion Rohrleitner's chapter in this volume examines anxieties experienced by those perceived as having "illegal" bodies due to their ethnic background.

Elizabeth Fitting, in her chapter included here, defines the concept of "food system" as one that "focuses our attention on policies and practices related to food—its production, [provision], and consumption. Food systems are embedded in larger social, economic, and ecological contexts and can include alternative or counter practices." Her definition captures the ways in which much of the literature conflates food systems as "one and the same" with food industry,[20] but it also shows one of the basic differences: resistance. An area in which there is a strong distinction between these two entities is within discussions of alternative food practices. The Slow Food Movement has led to a proliferation of food activism that speaks about different localized food systems that stress a return to agriculture rather than agribusiness and a renewed ethical concern for viability and food justice.[21]

In her study of Seattle's food activism, Teresa M. Mares explores how this movement does not actively engage, either as consumers or contributors, displaced *campesinos* from the Global South living as undocumented immigrants in Seattle. Mares sees this lack of engagement as a missed opportunity "to democratize contemporary efforts in food activism" as "displaced farmers from the Global South often hold tremendous knowledge about local food systems."[22] While it is important to explore ways of integrating Latin@s into existing food movements that address food justice, it is equally important to recognize how some Latin@s strive for food justice by other means. For example, two chapters included here challenge the idea that food justice is accomplished only through a form of resistance to the food industry. Lidia Marte's and Norma Cárdenas's chapters, 6 and 7 respectively, show how two working-class women, one in San Juan, Puerto Rico, and the other in San Antonio, Texas, create forms of food justice and security within their communities using the networks already put in place by the global food industry. Cárdenas and Marte show what Sydney Mintz calls "*food of moderate speeds*" to address the practical and beneficial ways in which the food industry and "alternative" food systems do in fact feed off each other.[23]

Our focus is to show not only the links of these two aspects of feeding a global or local community, but also to argue that intersections of these organizing entities can lead us to discover new ways of how people navigate the maze of food production and distribution to create food practices relevant to their lives. We call this overlapping a circumstantial or situational food system. These culinary practices are informed, influenced, and complicated by people's locations, age, gender, ethnic, class, and sexual subjectivities. To make sense of all of these factors, a multifaceted and multilayered analytical method that simultaneously addresses an array of concerns is needed. In an article on the symbolic and metaphorical use of food in Latina/o literature, I, Meredith, suggest a "holistic culinary approach" as the method to underscore the integral connection of nature, food, and people. This approach shows that these connections are never static, but are constantly changing. Holistic defines "the simultaneous practices of preserving and evolving, remembering and re-creating, discovering, and inventing. A holistic culinary approach is one that honors traditions with relevance and vitality."[24]

This same approach is applicable to the study of Latin@s' presence in the food industry on at least three fronts. First, a holistic culinary approach to studying the food industry cannot be reduced to issues of efficiency, consistency, or mass production of food commodities. What prevents this reduction is that people's subjectivities are deeply rooted in food's cultural significance. Second, this approach reinforces what Psyche Williams-Forson defines as the "intersectionality" of food studies that demands to see food and people as integrally connected. She writes,

> When we move from thinking of food as unraced, unclassed and unfettered by the binds of sexuality and physicality and therefore socially equal, to discussions of food as an inherent part of the social inequality of our lives, then the "real" complicated nature of our field [Food Studies] begins to unfold. When we branch out from the food as object [as commodities] to consider thinking in more integrated ways, then the intersections are exposed, the obstacles are made clear, and opportunities [are] revealed that force us to confront the complexities that inhere and surround the study of multiple peoples, cultures, and behaviors.[25]

Finally, a holistic culinary approach applies to the very interdisciplinary nature of food studies as suggested in the above quote. In order to understand people's complex relationships to food, in terms of food's practical and material realities as well as its symbolic and metaphorical implications, we must approach this study through the multiple facets it affects and effects by engaging in a conversation across scholarly disciplinary fields.

A holistic culinary approach frames *Latin@s' Presence in the Food Industry* to reveal the multiple and complex meaning people place on food both as commodity and symbol. We show the personal and affective meanings of food with the opening chapter, which is a personal narrative, as a reminder that food is integrally connected to people's daily lives and acts of agency. We conclude with a rhetorical analysis of images used to sell food as an affirmation of food's communicative power that is also expressed in visual and symbolic forms. Furthermore, rather than grouping chapters based on disciplines—history, anthropology, cultural, literary, and rhetorical studies—we have placed them in sections where authors are in conversation with one another on similar aspects of food, but address them through different disciplinary lenses, periods, and geographical locations. Our notion of holistic in this context includes addressing food narratives that speak to different aspects of the food industry: forms of building community, food preparation and consumption, and the use of visual images to portray complex and problematic symbolic and cultural representations. The stories about people's food practices presented in this collection are glimpses of how Latin@s create and demand spaces for themselves in at least three ways: first, through informal economies; second, by asserting their labor as a profession and not as cogs in a machine; and, third, by affirming new constructions of foods as an expansion of their culinary traditions. All four sections in this book show ways in which the food industry seeks to turn food into a commodity, but they also show how the very presence of Latin@s as producers, distributors, and consumers "constantly find ways to decommodify food, to make it personal, meaningful, cultural and social."[26]

Part 1, "A Mother's Food: The Production of Place and Knowledge," as mentioned above, includes a single personal narrative. Josie Méndez-Negrete's "*Desde el corazón*: Nurturing Bodies, Feeding Souls" makes food personal and intimate. This narrative discusses a migrant's life rife with different vulnerabilities, particularly those stemming from a violent and abusive father/husband. She speaks of how "Cooking and food preparation serve as ways of teaching and nurturing those who are the recipients of this gift and as a way to contest and resist the difficulties of patriarchy." The gift is revealed through her mother's creative agency and culinary knowledge, which become a shield against these vulnerabilities. Faced with the necessity to feed her children "in the meantime,"[27] Méndez-Negrete's "Amá" approaches industrialized processed foods in creative ways to maintain a "home" wherever they are. While depending on industrialized foods, "Amá" enhances her cultural repertoire of Mexican foods by relying on her agricultural knowledge, which allows her to identify edible plants that otherwise might be dismissed as "weeds." Her mother's gift of food is what eventually allows Méndez-Negrete to approach the global food industry as a venue by which to honor a Mexican culinary heritage. Purchasing food via the Internet has made it possible for her to "reclaim fruits, products, spices, and ingredients" from her childhood. Through a global market, Méndez-Negrete reclaims an "*inalienable wealth.*"[28] Her chapter illustrates how the private and daily food practices of a working-class mother express social, cultural, and economic concerns that other chapters present through more historical, analytical, and theoretical discourses.

Part 2, "Displacement and Re-Creation: Food and Place," offers four chapters stressing the fact that displacement of Latin@s' formal and informal food-based economies and appropriation or replacement of their culinary knowledge does not strip them of their ability to recreate their cultural (culinary) subjectivities. In terms of time span, over one hundred years, beginning in the 1880s and ending in the early 2000s, are covered in this section. In terms of geography, two chapters situate their analysis in the US Southwest: El Paso, Texas, and New Mexico. The other two are based in Mexico: one in the city of Puebla, Puebla, and one in the Tehuacán Valley of San José, Miahuatlán. Collectively, they illustrate the economic, political, and cultural ideologies embedded within the US food industry's entrance into the terrain of Mexican foodscapes to either appropriate or replace Mexican's food practices. As a group, the chapters also show how such attempts engender acts of recreating culinary subjectivities.[29]

In the opening chapter, Juan Manuel Mendoza Guerrero addresses the complex and contradictory history of Mexican food in El Paso, Texas, from 1880 to 1940. This complexity, he argues, results from consumers' changing palates. Changes in the social and economic environment of the region as well as new patterns of immigration and new food industries resulted in modifications of Mexican food. These factors not only "enriched" Mexican food, but also gave it a "plasticity" that allowed it never to lose "*lo mexicano*" even when its production had been appropriated by non-Mexican food businesses in order to serve a non-Mexican palate. With the theory of "plasticity," Mendoza Guerrero invites us to question whether Mexican food created in Texas, especially in regions that share a border with Mexico like Ciudad Juárez–El Paso, should always be understood as Tex-Mex. For him, this relationship is one of kinship that reflects "a mosaic of colors without losing its essence." Mendoza Guerrero teases out how the US food industry takes ownership of Mexican food via its marketing and advertising practices; this theme becomes a central concern in the last two chapters of the book where the focus is the appropriation of cultural and historical knowledge.

Monica Perales focuses her analysis on a brief moment mentioned in Mendoza Guerrero's study. She brings our attention to New Mexico by addressing a government-funded project created and implemented from the 1910s to the 1960s with the intention to change the food practices of rural New Mexican women. Perales explores the "unintentional" results of the New Mexico Agricultural Extension Service (NMAES). This program, which she argues was "rooted" in attitudes "of cultural imperialism and racial superiority," had as its intended goal the Americanization of ethnic families' eating habits and culture. Through an exploration of Fabiola Cabeza de Baca Gilbert's participation in NMAES, Perales demonstrates how "what emerges from the NMAES circulars is a regional cuisine that reflects a history of conflict and assimilation, but also compromise and adaptability, and that, by virtue of being published by a government agency, had its stamp of approval." While not explicitly stated by the mission of the NMAES or by Perales's study, a benefactor of this Americanization process was the food industry. The program advocated the implementation of a modern kitchen and cooking technologies and the publication of cookbooks, all of which are linked to the food industry.

Sandra C. Mendiola García underscores the irony embedded in the gentrification process that converted Puebla, Mexico's historical downtown into a "world heritage site." Gentrification "assisted" in this conversion by eliminating the social fabric that served a working-class community through networks of food producers, distributors, and consumers. This working-class network created by street-food vendors has been replaced by American fast food franchises; in the process, street vendors' reliance on seasonal fruits and vegetables has been replaced by industrialized process and imported foods. While Mendiola García agrees with Francisco Toledo, who sees this process of replacement as a "*comercialización salvaje*" (savage commercialization) that exhibits a "reckless disregard for the unique and irreplaceable," she does not fully agree with the irreplaceability. Street food vendors have circumvented governmental regulations and permit requirements simply by moving a few blocks from the Puebla's designated historical sites and, thereby, continuing to sell their food.

In the last chapter in this section, Elizabeth Fitting continues the discussion of the displacement of deeply and culturally rooted ways of making a living experienced by rural indigenous Mexican *campesinos* (small farmers). She centers her argument around the effects neoliberal economic policies have had on the ability of rural campesinos in the southern Tehuacán Valley of San José, Miahuatlán, to sustain small *milpa* (cornfields), even for personal consumption. She addresses the paradoxes and contradictions inherent in practices of the US food industry (i.e., the "dumping" of US corn to Mexico) and food activist groups (i.e., fighting to restore and maintain a culturally "sustainable" way of living for Mexican campesinos) as creating a dichotomy that romanticizes rural life.[30] Fitting states, "Food activism and scholarship importantly criticizes how neoliberal capitalism and the modern food system contribute to rural displacement and 'accumulation and dispossession.' [But] food activists and scholars [...] need be careful not to romanticize rural life in a way that overlooks the desire among younger residents to escape the farming life of their elders." Careful attention not to romanticize the way things were "highlight[s] the agency of workers [to] ... make decisions on how to manage, get ahead, or even challenge and sometimes change the social and economic condition in which they find themselves."

All chapters in part 2 discuss the agency of food producers as inventors, campesinos, vendors, and home cooks to affirm their ever-changing cultural identity. Part 3, "Food Professionalism from the Ground Up," takes this affirmation one step further. The three chapters of this section demonstrate Latin@s' professionalism through their culinary knowledge and efforts to serve their community by way of their presence in cocinas públicas. The spatial site of public kitchens takes different forms: a private house converted into a site of home-cooked "take-out" meals, a reinvented food truck, and the socially complex dining rooms in restaurants. In these public/private sites, food, gender, race, class, and sexuality intersect, and thereby alter the constructions and perceptions such identity markers might hold. Part 3 offers new perspectives on how to think of Latin@s within the food servicing sector as agents of change, support, and community building who, subsequently, help create new forms of food justice.

"*Las Gallinitas de Doña Luz*: Dominican Women Public Kitchens and Trans-Ethnic Networks in San Juan," by Lidia Marte, is an ethnographic account of a Dominican migrant woman who makes a living selling stuffed hens in Puerto Rico. Marte uses "foodmaps" as a methodological and theoretical frame "to study food practices as they occur in-place and at specific historical times, and in response to particular grounded perspectives." Doña Luz's food routes document the "transformations" brought about by the intersections of cross-ethnic realities experienced by Dominican immigrants living in Puerto Rico. The global food market makes this transformation possible by providing the ingredients necessary for Doña Luz's transnational signature dish of Puerto Rican *gallinita* made with a Dominican sauce containing imported ingredients from the United States. Doña Luz's cocina pública becomes the nucleus for these connections, revealing her professionalism as a "cultural food broker" who transcends ethnic divisions by creating a community of similar shared palates.

Norma L. Cárdenas in "Queering the Chili Queens: Culinary Citizenship through Food Consciousness in the New Borderlands" introduces Ana Fernández and her food truck business, the Institute of Chili, that operates in San Antonio, Texas. While Marte calls Doña Luz a "cultural food broker," Cárdenas refers to Ana Fernández as a food cultural steward. Fernández's culinary performance embodies a challenge to the historical, economic, social, and cultural processes that have both marginalized the cultural significance of the original Chili Queens and appropriated the chili itself. Cárdenas demonstrates how Fernández's business "serves as a retribution agent in public spaces to vindicate the original Chili Queens." In addition, it provides meals to communities where food trucks normally do not operate, including a homeless shelter where she donates and serves food. Through social media, she navigates power structures to resist "multiculturalism and the politics of marginalization" palpable throughout the history of San Antonio, Texas. With her role as a food cultural steward in her own Institute of Chili, Fernández creates a space for herself as a new "Millennium Queer-y-ing Chili Queen."

Cristina Herrera's chapter analyzes Chicanas' work as waitresses in order to argue that waitresses are in fact more than invisible bodies that place food on the table and refill water glasses without "'disturbing' [the] dining experience." People interested in the food industry should not dismiss literature as a site to read food narratives and to hear perspectives that scholarly works in other fields, such as sociology, history, or anthropology, for example, do not always address. Herrera's chapter examines three Chicana novels to reveal the protagonists' "critical reflections on life, community, social justice, and art that occur while working in restaurants." Herrera makes visible the Chicana waitress's experience to stress how these protagonists fuse "activism, art, and waitressing into a working-class Chicana feminist sensibility embodied in their waitress occupation." Through the analysis of *Face of an Angel*, Herrera frames waitressing as a profession of service. This frame challenges a "single story" that represents, through visual images, the labor of waitresses as nothing more than racialized and sexualized "servants"—a point that Karen Cruz broaches in her study of Judith Ortiz Cofer's writing included in this book.

Two of the three chapters in part 4, "Producing and Reproducing Identities," continue to anchor their examination of Latin@s' presence in the food industry through literary analyses. All three chapters look at food not only as a commodity of calorie exchange value, but also as a commodity of subjugation and objectification exchange value. Collectively, they address issues of culture, gender, class, and sexual representation as they are either reflected through people's food consumption or embedded in visual representations of food images.

Marion C. Rohrleitner's chapter, "Conspicuous Consumption? Eating Disorders as Nervous Immigrant Conditions in Contemporary Latina Fiction," argues that literary representations of Latina eating disorders reflect complex cultural, social, and economic structures inherent in the United States' attitudes toward immigrants. While an immediate response to Latinas' eating disorders could be framed as a result of "unhealthy eating practices" or lack of access to healthy foods, Rohrleitner argues that the cause is much more tenuous. She explores what kinds of food certain ethnic and socioeconomic communities have access to and examines what cultural, health-related, and environmental implications are suggested by the available food choices. She juxtaposes two novels to underscore two sides of the same coin. With one of the novels, she shows how some Latinas who experience "nervous conditions" are manifesting signs of their anxieties about their ever-questioned presence in the United States. With the second novel, she examines similar forms of anxieties that result from the inherent structural vulnerabilities experienced by farmworkers who are limited to consume processed foods and produce past their prime. Both novels reveal how "food production, preparation, and consumption . . . marginaliz[e] Latina immigrants from successful integration into the US body politic."

Karen Cruz examines what she calls the "aesthetic of objectification" through an analysis of visual food narratives as presented in advertisements. Cruz shows how the food industry uses language to conflate food and women's bodies as one and the same thing. She juxtaposes this correlation with her interpretation of Puerto Rican writer Judith Ortiz Cofer's cross-genre book *Latin Deli: Telling the Lives of Barrio Women* to show the association between food and women—particularly Latina women. For Cruz, Ortiz Cofer's narrative challenges this limited association by effectively describing the use of culinary knowledge and practices to mediate power relations between the sexes. Food as an item of consumption, as well as a symbol of culture and economics, is represented in Ortiz Cofer's writing. Cruz argues that Ortiz Cofer's works not only dismantle the "aesthetics of objectification," but they also function to articulate and explore cultural perspectives and sexual desires that directly challenge the food industry's correlation between food and women's bodies.

In the final chapter in this section, "Food Marketing Industry: Cultural Attitudes Made Visible," we offer a rhetorical analysis that focuses on how Mexican food has been represented in the public domain to entice its consumption. We analyze three images often used to define Mexican food, Mexicans, and their labor in order to interrogate the "single story" that remains when images are presented through a historically, socially, and culturally based racist and classist stereotype. The focus of our investigation is food images because they are the most visible "node" within the "web of meanings" created at the intersections of food production, distribution, and consumption. Ironically, the very visibilities of food images render people's cultural knowledge and labor realities invisible. It is this invisibility that allows marketers to create and offer commodified perceptions of culture. By de-commodifying such perceptions, we can explore the possible histories and knowledge that are hidden behind the "single story" presented by the food industry.

Latin@s negotiate their presence within the food industry to (re)define and (re)present their relationship within the practices, attitudes, and ideologies embedded in the food industry. One way in which Latin@s negotiate and survive the tensions, contradictions, and paradoxes that mark their participation *in* and representation *by* different networks of the food industry is through creative niches in which their culinary knowledge affirms their ever-changing subjectivities. The culinary professionalism explored in the first three sections resonates with Doña Margie's action of serving those in need of nourishment. Doña Margie's food narrative is an affirmation that there is much to be gained by examining small-scale circumstantial or situational food systems that do not *explicitly* speak back, against, or resist the global food industry.

Latin@s' Presence in the Food Industry highlights the negotiation and acceptance of change due to systemic power structures reflected in geopolitical conflicts, gentrification, technological modernization, mass and global production, and distribution of food and images. We invite readers to explore these moments by observing the overlap and crisscrossing that occurs within each section and also across the chapters. We also invite readers to pay attention to how Latin@s' particular location, gender, class, ethnicity, and sexuality shape and affect similar overarching aspects of the food industry.

Through the holistic culinary approach presented here, we hope that we might begin to change how we think about food. It is through seeing Latin@s' presence in the food industry that a food consciousness can be fostered so that new notions of professionalism and cultural self-representation emerge. Food consciousness expresses a critical awareness that demands an analysis that strives to simultaneously examine the material conditions surrounding food as a commodity of production, distribution, and consumption, as well as a commodity vested with symbolic and metaphorical substance. Changing how we think about food allows for, at least, three things to happen: see the acts of agency and kindness from those who cook in their personal kitchens to serve a public audience; recognize the multiple food narratives of how Latin@s mark their presence within the webs of the food industry; and understand how the history of Latin@s and their foods are often obscured through visual images. Because the food industry has historically made Latin@s an "invisible" presence and yet a necessary labor force, we hope that readers leave this book thinking of how Latin@s' food narratives within different aspects of the food industry affect the readers' own food consciousness.

PART 1 ▪ A Mother's Food

The Production of Place and Knowledge

CHAPTER 1

Desde el Corazón
Nourishing Bodies, Feeding Souls

JOSIE MÉNDEZ-NEGRETE

Cocinar era algo muy especial . . . me sentaba a mirar a Chenda . . . ella cocinaba con mucha autoridad—todo tenia su ritmo, las brasas, el tiempo, la comida, y el orden del sazón. Cocinar, para mi, era el modo de enseñarles que los quería . . . lo hacia con mucho cariño y amor—el cocinar me daba fuerza—al darles sustento, yo me animaba.

(Cooking has always been something special . . . I would sit to look at Chenda . . . she cooked with much authority— everything had its rhythm, the embers, the timing, the food, and the sequences in her use of spices. Cooking, for me, was a way to show you that I loved you . . . I did it with much care and love— cooking gave me strength—nourishing you, enlivened me.)

—AMÁ

Daily Life and Its Complexities

Framed inside the emotions of everyday life is the love of making food. The cooking practices and philosophies I learned from women ancestors still guide my cooking, as well as the ways in which I express love.

Their voices and sage advice still resonate deep inside me, beginning with the warning of the power of emotions: "Don't cook when you're mad because anger disconnects you from the portions and taints your ability to salt the food"; and, "Be careful, rage does not allow you to detect the fire in the chile pods and your salsa will be too hot to enjoy." Other voices spoke to the process of preparation: "Distractions distort timing. When making tortillas, pay attention, otherwise when you cook them they will come out raw or burnt and won't even be good enough for the *chuchos*"—what we called dogs. Still, others' messages of food as nurturance come through in connection to love. "It's through the belly that you find love," Doña Cata, our neighbor, would often chime in when talking about the value of food preparation.

Founded in the collectivity of women's practices of the everyday, our oral cooking tradition relied on storytelling, or *pláticas*, where *comadres*, blood related or social kinswomen, traded recipes in conversation with each other. Their talk about food and cooking framed the *recetarios* of our lives—where they detailed *recetas* (recipes) and cooking technique but also focused on the travails of the daily lives with which we contended. Patience and the willingness to share what was produced became central to our understanding that *cocineras* who made the food had the authority. As such, I honored their admonitions: "No se meta en mi cocina. . . . Si menea el mole se hara ralo, ¡dejelo!" (Do not enter my kitchen. . . . If your stir the pot, the mole will thin out; leave it be!)

It was from these women that I learned one finds love through the belly and not the heart because the passage to the heart is through the stomach, the source of our emotional core. "The best way to snare a loved one," they would say, "is to pay attention and imagine the best meal you could prepare for the intended." From these women, Mague, Fela, my sisters, and I learned life lessons that defied expectations of authority assigned by the rigid gender rules that see women only in reproductive roles: reproducing workers and the food to maintain them.

My mother imparted lessons through her cooking. From her we learned to navigate our everyday lives in a home where contradictions —physical, psychological, emotional, and sexual violence—were perpetrated by Juan, our father, who was later diagnosed as a sociopath and serial pedophile. In the context of intense and varied types of pains, we found sentient connections to the delectable dishes prepared by our mother. The nourishing practices that mended our wounded hearts and bodies emerged in the special dishes Amá created. The dishes consoled us from the violent perpetrations no one within the house spoke about or those outside the house dared to imagine taking place in our so-called sacred space of the privacy of our home.[1] More often than not, her cooking was the only consolation we received from the physical, psychological, emotional, and spiritual pain we confronted in our domestic lives. The food Amá prepared for us was always the bridge to our hearts as Amá made every effort to convey her unspoken actions of protection through her food.

Amá's Reimagined *Cocina*:
Cooking Lessons in the Practices of the Everyday

Whether it be *con el casí nada*—just a few wild greens—*quelites, verdolagas u otras yerbas comestibles*—tossed, cooked, or blanched, ordinary edible weeds in a salad, or broth made into a *caldo* or soup, Amá often reminded us to share what we had. *Con una estufa de brazas o madera, o un fogón*—with a fire stove fueled by coals or twigs, or with a gas burner, Amá's delectable dishes took care of us. In food preparation she taught us to read the world. The connections she made through food deepened relationships with *comadres*, relatives, and neighbors. Literate in the ways in which food can strengthen connections, Amá recognized that allies are critical in contesting the boundaries of domestic containment.

Food, emotions, and nurturance are expressive aspects of reproductive responsibilities generally assigned to women. Meredith E. Abarca examines women's work in the kitchen as an act of agency that transforms that site from the "women's *place* into her *space*."[2] Through the voices of *mujeres* with whom she talked, we learn that not all women perceive their work as "socially mandated" labor but as a "celebration and affirmation of [their] talent, knowledge, and affection."[3] Abarca argues that it is women's labor in the kitchen that "sustains [their] sense of self by validating emotions and claiming the right to [their] own *sazón*, culinary knowledge and talent based on the epistemology of the senses."[4] Moreover, Abarca posits that women take charge of and transform their everyday cooking practices in their "culinary creations inspired by an array of emotions."[5] Such cultural practices can be witnessed in narrative films such as *Like Water for Chocolate* directed by Alfonso Arau.[6]

Emotions are central to women's work in the domestic sphere, including cooking and food preparation, and these acts are not limited to the socialization of emotions and feelings as gendered ways of interaction. I offer that culinary creations are possible because of women's abilities to listen, see, smell, and taste, as they "theorize about the aesthetic value" of their cooking.[7] Cooking and food preparation serve as ways of teaching and nurturing those who are the recipients of this gift and as a way to contest and resist the difficulties of patriarchy. Patriarchy is a rationalization under notions of the privacy of home where gender power distortions are enacted, especially when serving the so-called master of the house. The place and space of the kitchen provides a site for a consciousness of being that frames the experiences of those who cook as they learn to deal with distortions of power. Pérez and Abarca argue that "[f]ood is fundamental to the workings of identity and belonging, power, and social change."[8] As was the case for *Las hijas de Juan*,[9] we, the daughters, were carving out an identity in the context of oppositional and oppressive experiences— on the one hand, the silent love of Amá, and on the other, the vicious and depraved ways of Juan. It was in this space that I learned to use all of my senses to give meaning to my environment. I understood the value of food for us, as well as in the lives of those who lacked resources of every type. I amassed ways of negotiating the emotions and feelings of others, as well as my own.

When cooking occurs in the private realm of volatile homes, a mother's food can act as a revolutionary gesture that fights to soothe the consequences of trauma. Her cooking can convey the multidimensional, subtle, and not-so-subtle power food has to appease pain. In our home, while the brute physical force and authority might have been the venue of the patriarch, and the relegation to kitchen duty was construed as submission to patriarchy, Amá's food often served to counter, neutralize, and even equalize Juan's power. Amá turned her "submissive" role to one of strategic power by pacifying the beast with any one of his favorite dishes, thus taming him while freeing us from the abuse at least for one day. Because it is inside the domestic sphere that sociocultural messages and expectations are gendered, Amá used the kitchen as a powerful site to teach us how to reclaim our humanity through food practices that we now reproduce in our own kitchens.

Food as Voice against Cultural and Social Violence

Feminist food scholars present methodologies to explore the relationship between violence and food within the domestic sphere.[10] Carole M. Counihan displays "differential consciousness" through her methodology of food-centered life histories that reveals "women's voice, identity, and world view."[11] Similarly, in her *charlas culinarias*, Abarca theorizes on issues of agency and power of Mexican and Mexican American working-class women. She enacts a type of *testimoniando* to narrate the witnessing of the ways in which women engage in the everyday practices of preparing and eating the food they cook.[12] For Amá, it was her singing and whistling while cooking that let us know that she was connected to her self—an act of defiance to the messages we received about our gendered status through Juan's authority. The delectable morsels Amá so lovingly created for us became the unspoken signal to let us know that Juan's moments of violence would pass and that she would take care of us in the only way she could.

The common assumption about food is that its preparation is often associated with oppression rather than power and creativity. Counihan, relying on Chela Sandoval for the theoretical framing, argues for a differential consciousness through which "women can challenge subordination and strive for agency through food-centered life histories."[13] Furthermore, this method "is a key strategy used by dominated peoples to survive demeaning and disempowering structures and ideologies but at the same time to generate alternative beliefs and tactics that resist domination."[14] In the kitchen, Amá taught us about food practices as a way to resist, challenge, and contest the patriarchal imperative.[15] In a similar vein, Counihan speaks about spaces of reciprocity and mutuality, and Abarca examines "issues of subjectivity and acts of agency" to document women as "critical thinkers in their own rights who use the language of food to formulate their theories."[16]

Abarca suggests that her research "offers the women ... public recognition, acknowledgment, admiration, and respect for their lives, their struggles, their knowledge, and above all their *coraje* (courage) grounded in the mundane activities of everyday cooking."[17] Because it was in her kitchen that Amá dispensed her love for us, she taught us to see the kitchen as a space of power rather than a place designed to serve the man whom society perceives as the master of the home. In her everyday domestic practices, Amá contested power through the creation of nourishment. She showed us that even at the individual level of resistance love shapes an oppositional consciousness that carves the path to emancipation.

Reflexive autoethnography, a process of self-interrogation and the study of relationship in the context of shared memories, allowed me to query Amá, brothers and sisters, and others who lived within the vicinity of our lives about the recollections of memories we carried regarding the violence we survived. However, it was never my intention to document the foodstuff or culinary practices of those who loved me and protected me. Intertwined with the everyday experiences of what we lived, contended with, and survived, these narratives surfaced to the forefront in the telling of our story. We shared special meals and memories of food that marked our creative and resilient spirit as *las hijas de Juan*.

Abarca's analysis of my book[18] inspired my return to Amá's kitchens to reflect on the culinary cartography she carved as we moved as (im)migrants from place to place: from Mexico to the United States and from rural to urban spaces. It was in Amá's kitchen where I learned that cooking takes place inside dialectics of nurturing, contestation, and resistance, a lesson marked with significant importance when there is active violence in the home. In Amá's kitchen we learn viscerally the meaning of "food consciousness." As Abarca and Pascual Soler argue, "food consciousness" allows us to "not only turn food into a means of thought but also align consciousness with a sense of taste."[19] My "food consciousness" helped me to enable my sense of taste as I was able simultaneously to recognize Juan's abuses so well that I could taste them, and just as powerfully, to savor the spiritual and emotional resistance to such abuse in Amá's cooking. In this essay, I speak about food memories and recollections that allow me to discuss the ways in which Amá enacted agency despite the confines of a domineering husband. I also focus on the ways in which she expressed subjectivity by modeling for us a revolutionary spirit that keeps food as the central source of love and nourishment.

De allá 'Pa Acá: Learning about Foodways

For Amá, love and nourishment were a part of the many recipes she still carries in her *recetario*, which contains recipes filed in her memory, not written on lined paper. In her hands, common greens and other foodstuffs became gifts of the goddesses. With her special *sazón*, she kept her *escuincles* (children) salivating as we awaited her gifts. In her kitchen, foodstuff became food and medicine that would nourish our bodies and heal our soul and spirit. Amá cooked with produce and herbs that have a long ancestral history. Our food history and legacy long taught us that the *avocado* was not just about *guacamole*, a word that comes from the Nahuatl *ahuacamolli*, a sauce (molli), and avocado (*ahuaca*). Avocados have curative properties that placed the fruit in high esteem. Amá had many uses for this curative fruit: she took the leaves to spice up special dishes, especially *caldos* and *moles*; she used the bark to fight *torzones*, or stomach pains and diarrhea; and she used the outer skin to rid the children's stomachs of worms. She transmitted her knowledge not just of avocados but also other edible *yerbas*, wild greens, that we almost lost when we migrated north.[20]

Once in the United States, Amá crossed many culinary borders. For her, each new space provided cooking experiences to explore. She had no choice but to find new ways of doing old things, thus expanding her culinary repertoire. In Mexico and the United States, Amá adapted her cooking practices while gaining new ways of preparing food.[21] In the United States, she did not have to overcook the meat because there was refrigeration, a luxury that she had not always had. Refrigeration allowed us to keep goods that would normally spoil. However, it also took away the fresh taste of those meats and goods that were more delectable when freshly taken from the market or when fruits and vegetables were freshly picked. She learned to add more spices such as garlic, pepper, and salt. She adopted others such as cumin. Through her flexible and innovative ability to engage new spaces, Amá taught me to negotiate the locations and positionalities I encountered in unfamiliar and new environments. For example, once in the United States, I had to not only contend with gender discrimination, but also with race and class biases.

One of Amá's innovations was to use what was at her disposal to dress whatever she cooked. In Mexico, we dressed our tacos and tostadas with *pico de gallo de repoyo y queso* (freshly diced chile sauce with cabbage and cheese). In south Texas, although known as the Winter Garden, it was hard for Amá to find greens to feed us. Outside St. Patrick's Day when cabbage was harvested en masse, she had a hard time finding it for our tacos and tostadas. Since *Mexicano* products were no longer available to us, we learned to eat iceberg lettuce and yellow cheese, even though it was too greasy and rich for our bellies. We missed our *queso cotija, queso panela y queso de chiva*, especially *la rata de la familia*, Amá's nickname for me because I love cheese.[22] Of course, I complained the most and had the most difficulty adjusting to the changes, but Amá's revolutionary spirit to find moments of strength and joy regardless of all oppressive and limiting factors served as a model of thriving adaptation.

Our tortillas reflected another adaptation. Despite the fact that corn is a staple for *Mexicanos del sur*, who cling to their Indian ways, she nonetheless learned to make *tortillas de harina* because corn was difficult to find. What was never difficult to create were metaphorical and symbolic associations with food. Even though we did not have much occasion to engage with "white" people, since we lived and shopped in areas that were predominantly Mexican, we created an imaginary, though racialized, relation with "whites" by calling flour tortillas *gringas* due to their white color. By the same token, the only time whites entered our personal spaces was through their own dispersion of racial food insults: "tío taco" and "taco bender" as a type of Mexican identity, to name but two. Food served as a way to teach us who we were in relationship to our cultural and social environments, in Mexico and the United States.

At times, Amá discovered Mexican culinary staples while working in the fields alongside her husband. Amá never got a penny for working *en el campo* because Juan kept the money; however, one day her "free" labor paid off. For the first time, she found those edible weeds she had long used as a part of our diet growing wild among the cotton bushes that she helped her husband tend to for *el patron*. It was just another ordinary workday when she found them. Double-checking and bending to see if the weed was really what she thought it was, her mind repeated a child's ditty to underscore her disbelief:

> *Verdolagas y quelites que deveras te creistes . . .*
> *(It'll be purslane and pigweed for you, if you believe that . . .)*
> *Verdolagas y quelites que deveras te creistes . . .*
> *(It'll be purslane and pigweed for you, if you believe that . . .)*

Swiftly, Amá snipped a handful of new growth and placed its leaves in her mouth to taste them. Her eyes had not deceived her. She was right. It was the precious weed she had savored in her village. It was the *verdolagas* (purslane) we longed to eat. That day she delighted in knowing that she would provide special food for us. She picked enough greens to add them raw to the *ensalada* (salad) and to fold them into those mouth-watering *carne de puerco* (pork dishes) that she so lovingly prepared for her children. In those fields she spied verdolagas, the magical weedy herb with bright yellow flowers, to make her special *guisos* (stews) and soups that protected our kidneys. Finally, something good had come out of working in the fields.

While working in the fields, she continued her search for edibles on her path. In time she found *quelites* (weeds) that she cooked with pork meat and nopales, or that she sautéed with onions, tomatoes, chiles, and other spices to add to the pot of beans. In Nahuatl, quilitl or quelites were vegetables or edible greenery. I had long learned from the elders in my family to identify weeds called *xihuitl*, distinguishing the edible ones from those used for grazing or as feed, *tzacatl*, now known as *zacate* (grass).

The vegetables she had the most difficulty finding were nopales, the emerald of vegetables, known for their healing properties. In those days in south Texas, these pads were not even available in Doña María cans or jars as we find them today. However, Amá learned from the locals of south Texas about *nopales de castilla* or wild cactus, and she soon incorporated the cacti baby leaves into our diet. At first, we did not like them that much, longing for the varieties we left behind in Zacatecas. Not having other options, we decided these slimy nopales were better than none at all. Soon, Texan nopales became part of our diet despite their almost invisible bristles that no one wanted to tangle with. Those near-see-through *espinas* or thorns on its pads were enough to keep people away from the staple, but Amá found a way. She built a broom with twigs from the Texas *ceniso* (sagebrush) to dust the pads off, ridding them of those pernicious thorns. That is the way nopales became a seasonal staple at our table for the duration of their harvest, especially during Lent.

As a result of Amá's culinary creativity, we became very happy with our nopales. It was almost like being back in Tabasco, Mexico, our hometown from where the family originates. Yet, our love for nopales was often a reason for others to deride us. We proudly wore our nopal, not just on our *frente* or forehead as they branded those of us who came from Mexico, but we also carried it snuggly inside our bellies. Still, there were those who thought us weird because for them nopales were feed for cattle and livestock roaming the ranges of south Texas and were not for human consumption. Later, I would appreciate these culinary practices through the work of Gloria E. Anzaldúa, who relied on nopales as metaphors for self-identity and protection. In her poem, "Nopales," they are both a lifeline and a threat because Anzaldúa has to "defang the cactus" to eat it.[23]

Food was not the only weapon Amá used to create a semblance of home, notwithstanding living in a place of violence. She dressed up the environments of our poor dwellings with plants of spices and flowers she grew and tended to. Her hand-embroidered tablecloths and napkins, *manteles y servilletas*, adorned our table. She made those manteles from cloth discards, *trocitos de material*, or cotton sacks of flour. Sometimes they had tiny flowers. Other times the cloth was lined in radiant greens, passionate purples, or ravishing reds, or in small plaids of pastel yellows or blues. She matched their lines just so, joining six or eight *bolsas de harina* to make the most elaborate tablecloths. With her sewing skills, one could not detect where a bag began and the other ended. When she pulled out a near-border design of threads, she reinforced it with hand stitches and fringed them with a crochet border or *deshilado*, making them look prettier than the ones sold at the store. Her décor helped buffer the fear and violence Juan's abusive authority created. Her décor gave us the feeling of home.

And . . . We Were not Dirty Mexicans

Home was sacrosanct to Amá. As an agricultural worker, she was fastidious about the way we looked. She often reminded us that we were *"pobrecitas, pobrecitas, pero siempre lavaditas, planchaditas y limpiecitas,"* really poor, but always washed, ironed, and very clean. Her effort was as if to reinscribe pride in our brown and Indian bodies when someone tried to imply otherwise. We were clean Mexicans. She did not want anybody to think we were any less worthy because we came from Mexico. For that reason, she always told us to mind our manners. Amá affirmed that we knew how to act and that we came from a proud people. Just because she came from a *rancho* did not mean she lacked the *cultura* to know how to act. Amá would tell us this as she gave us our lessons on proper behavior: "Pick up the cup with your thumb and the two nearest fingers. Lift out your pinkies just so, to show that you know how to act like the best mannered people in town."

Her recetarios of culinary knowledge were not just about cooking. They included lessons about social graces and ways to tend to home and children. Her life's recetarios reflected a "food consciousness" that guided our everyday interactions around and with food. Growing up, the social graces she taught us seemed paradoxical to me. They reflected contradictions to the violence, gender, and sexuality standards we navigated living inside a house of horrors and the racism and classism we often confronted outside the house. Growing up, it never made sense to me how etiquette of social graces would help, but I learned it anyway. In retrospect, what she taught me has given me the skills to negotiate identity and power in multisited spaces.

En Mexico: As If We Did not Leave

Amá traveled back and forth from Mexico to the United States, but in every space she would soon get into the local routine of life. In Mexico, Amá went to the garden to gather whatever greens were in season for our food. She walked over to the neighbors' *milpa*[24] to see what she could buy. She sent us to the corral to collect eggs or to milk the cows or goats that would yield the milk for our cream of oats or make the *atole* for our breakfast. What we did not gather from the garden, the field, or the barn, we got at the *mercado*, the food market, to complete the needed staples for the day. Our bread did not come from bakeries or grocery stores, but out of the open-air wood-fueled oven.

Amá always knew how to make use of leftovers, but nothing could compete with the corn tortillas she made while we were in Mexico. To make tortillas for the day, she began from scratch by grinding the *nixtamal* on the *metate*. When she grinded the corn, her movement was a divine act; she became one with the *masa* as she put her entire self into making the dough. The work that she put into making her tortillas was so replete with soul that her perfectly shaped tortillas became a slice of love in our belly. I could feel my heart doing a jig with the clap, clap, clapping of her hands; it was music to my ears and nourishment for my *panza*. Her *tortilleo* made my stomach sing and dance with anticipation. Amá's tortillas, a few *frijoles*, and her best *chile salsa* became the perfect meal, especially when crowned with sprinkles of homemade cheese.

She often set aside some of the masa to use for our morning atole and as a condiment to other meals. Like other foods, atole is an ancestral gift from the Nahuas. It derives from the words *tlaolli*, for ground corn, and *atl*, for water. Amá knew how to make all kinds of atoles from many substances; *maizena* (cornstarch) and oats were but a few. Our favorites were *atole de avena*, *arroz*, and the chocolaty-rich *champurrado* she made for special occasions or when we wore her down with our requests. If we got sick, we did not even have to ask, as some atoles were medicine to her.

As the granddaughter of a *curandera*, Amá believed food was medicine and had many ways to cure. She used oats to stop loose bowels, or what we called *corridas*, a take off from the word *runs* in English. I remember she would soak a cup of oats in a pitcher with two cups of water, sometimes overnight, to use as needed for our stomachs. Before she gave it to us to drink, though, she separated the oats from the water, making sure that not a speck of the product filtered into the liquid. It only took one day for us to be okay. With her cures and her cooking, on this side of the border or *en el otro lado*, Amá forged heaven on earth with her creations. Her belief in the curative power of food, and the reality of the abusive environment affecting our lives, converted her cooking into a revolutionary act that aimed to heal bodies and souls.

A MOTHER'S FOOD

Manjares del Pueblo

Recollections of Amá's culinary knowledge and the lessons imparted with it are not complete without mentioning the fruits and edible flowers of my childhood. Second only to Amá's food was the fruit of our childhood that was disappearing from our diet in el norte. While plentiful in our hometown of Tabasco, fruits were not easily accessible in the patrón's store.[25] My palate's memory, however, could easily help me imagine and taste the *xoconochtli*, a round and somewhat unappealing verdant fruit that hid inside its heart a pulpy sweet delight with the taste of *pitaya*, prickly pear, and *guayaba*, all in one. It made me dream. My palate's memory could also help me savor *piñas*, mangos, papayas, and *guayabas* that had the sweetest taste. Even though their cousins in the United States came from Mexico like us, they were no competition in terms of flavor. But then again, I imagine my palate not being as receptive to fruits' natural sweetness while living under Juan's authority.

The *zapote* fruit taught us patience, as we contemplated the ripening of its deep green ovoid fruit as it turned to yellow, a sign that it was ready. We left it alone because it tasted best when it fell from the tree. Its white mushy pulp inside, with one single deep brown seed, was heaven sent. The *chirimoya*, a green round fruit with snakeskin designs on its outer layer, had a pulpy off-white inside with round black seeds that perfected our target practice as we ate the fruit and spit out the seeds to see who could send them the farthest. *Chia*, small seeds used for *agua fresca*, along with *arroz, jamaica*, and other fruits that were a bit *pasadas*, or a tad too mature to eat, became *aguas frescas* fit for kings. Quenching our thirst, we did not even think to complain about overripeness and overlooked the presence of those rice grains that would sometimes end up trapped between our teeth.

Flower petals were also food for us. We used them for *aguas frescas*, as cooking ingredients, and as medicinal cures. Hibiscus, or jamaica, and *flores de calabaza* were the two I most loved. The deep magenta of the hibiscus got my mouth watering just thinking about its agua fresca taste, and Amá's *guiso* of pumpkin flowers sautéed with vegetables and spices, topped with my favorite cheese, was a meal to celebrate. We loved the pumpkin flowers when she melted them into our *quesadillas* with the just-off-the-*metate* corn she made into a turn-over, which we later learned to call *tlacoyos*.

Transiciones de Amor

Counihan argues that food is a source of contesting gender power relations.[26] Certainly, this was the case in our home. It was through food and cooking that Amá aimed to protect us and create a home for us. But it was through food that Juan tried to diminish Amá's power as he tried to dictate what she could or should cook. For example, we found ourselves having to eat the heart of mature nopal pads that I detested because it was Juan's favorite dish. I managed to avoid liver because its taste and texture were too weird for my palate. She tried to protect me from that awful liver by not cooking it or feeding me only arroz or *fideos* in a bowl with beans in its juice, flavored by chile salsa, and sprinkled with cheese. Thanks to our migration that availed goods previously unavailable, Amá gained the empowerment of selecting and experimenting with food items that resisted Juan's domination, as they were not part of his culinary demands; nevertheless, we could enjoy eating them. Amá knew how to reward and soothe us to make our lives emotionally bearable.

Once Amá was free of Juan,[27] who had believed he controlled her kitchen, she could prepare whatever dish she desired without having to use food as the balm to tend to our broken hearts. While cooking still felt like a responsibility, there was no hierarchy or authority to control her love in the kitchen. Juan's absence did not change the con-nection she had carved into that language of food that gave her a voice when she had no tongue to speak. In her body and mind, she knew the kitchen was her dispensary of love where only she had control over its space. Still now, at the age of eighty-four, Amá continues to pre-pare *chilaquiles*, her famous enchiladas made with Salsa Las Palmas, the canned sauce that substituted the *chiles cascabel*, *puya*, and *ancho*. Even with this canned product, her enchiladas are like no other. And her *picadillo de carne desebrada* and her *nopales con carne* and *chile colorado* are among those dishes often requested by visiting relatives.

Mague, Fela, and I treasure Amá and the ways in which she made a hostile home tolerable through cooking, as well as the ways in which she cared for and supported us through the food she prepared. Because of her and the care she exercised to impart silent messages of love, we have created our own sazón in the kitchen and have learned to identify emotions in others with an intuition bar none. In addition to learning to become creative with what was available to us, we learned to create community through food. During an adolescence that was framed in the poverty of being a charge on public assistance, *en la mesa de* Amá we ate what was available. We also opened up our home to others to create community in a culture of breaking bread, where there was always food to share—*donde come uno, comen todos.*

Amá's philosophy of food, inscribed in the words she uttered, gave us the freedom to open our home as a site for sharing love. She taught us to survive as we took in the environment and conditions under which we had to participate in the creation of the everyday. Regardless of what was happening around us, Amá never failed to nurture us with the love she could quietly give us as she prepared and placed our food on the table. Identifying each of the special meals we enjoyed, she doled out her love to the one she perceived was most in need of it, while continuing to create ways to let us know we mattered in her and one anothers' lives. Throughout our later upbringing with her alone, the anger, pain, and violence dissipated in the comfort of knowing that she would be there to love us in the best way she could. In her own way, she did what she could to nurture and take care of us, to the point of having taken abuses and mistreatment in our place.

Agency, Love, and Empowerment in Amá's Kitchen

I love to cook. Food making and preparation is an act of creation. I make art with my food because it is the glue that binds our communities, and I share my appreciation for others by cooking for them. The palette of colors, the flavors, and the aromas that merge when I practice the legacy I have inherited from the cooking *curanderas* with whom I grew up inspire me. Like Amá in the early years, because my options have expanded with the global market I have at my disposal, I have made my own modifications. I add things I never would have imagined. I have also made changes for health reasons. Because I like to invent tastes, I mix ingredients or create new dishes. Moreover, I make conscious choices about the food I use by often avoiding the purchase of goods that rely on pesticides that harm workers and consumers alike, even when costs are higher.

New options, new ingredients, and adventurous taste buds have pushed for modification and improvement of the dishes I love. Adding new spices and changing ingredients to the panoply of dishes I have inherited, I make new creations while still honoring those that have a special place in my life. Unlike Amá, I do not grind corn in the *metate*. The masa I use has been packaged as a dry good or I buy it at the *tortilleria* already prepared; although, I exercise care to stay away from genetically modified corn. Depending on need, I could use a coarse *masa harina* for *tamales* and fine masa for tortillas, *atoles,* or as a thickening agent. *Masa seca* has become part of my cooking repertoire; my labor and my taste buds have adjusted yet again. Virgin and classic olive oils are central and main ingredients in my cooking. One dresses the salads I make, and the other is an integral part of the dough for my tamales. Classico is the oil with which I make sautés, and the oil signifies my commitment to preparing Mexican dishes that are already healthy and good. Regardless of cost, olive oil has long substituted the lard or Mazola in those dishes I learned from Amá.

Still, as it was for Amá, love is the main ingredient with which I cook. Love is the energy that guides the choice of dishes and the tastes I mix. Because I believe that our stomach is truly the heart of our emotions, my senses and my love for self and others serves me to tend to those for whom I care and who have become my social family. The division of labor in the kitchen also has changed. Children and men participate in the work that precedes and follows a meal; men and boys now do work they had not done in the past.

With few exceptions, I have reclaimed those fruits, products, spices, and ingredients that I ate in the Mexico of my childhood. The global market has erased inaccessibility to the products with which I grew up. These products are now at my disposal because I can order nopales and other foodstuff through the Internet. With these global linkages, the art of cooking acquires infinitesimal possibilities. Past practices I continue to use include the sprinkling of lemon and chile pepper in my cooking. My husband, who has been known to comment that Mexicans put *limón* and chile on everything, makes lip-smacking sounds to celebrate the condiments I use in my *picos de fruta*. He continues to delight in the food I prepare for us. If he comments as I prepare one or another of the foods with which I grew up, I retort with a word of caution, telling him to be careful or I will spice him up. My *picos* have become *nuevo-Chicano* dishes that now incorporate ingredients not previously available to Amá. In my kitchen, kiwi now substitutes for that chameleon *tuna* or prickly pear of yesteryear. In the context of the United States, these dishes become new ethnic expressions of food bridging the Mexican and Chicano experiences in which I interact. *Salsa de mango, guayaba, piña, o tamarindo* are the Mexican chutneys that flavor the tortillas or spice the fish that I prepare for our meals.

As resilient women who survived the emotional and psychological traumas of violence, in addition to reproducing the dishes of our legacy, *las hijas de Juan* now create our own recetarios as we modify the spaces we occupy to degenderize the kitchen. We incorporate the food tastes, recipes, and labor of those with whom we have made family and community. With our cooking practices we have created an equal and revolutionary environment where the men in our family participate in the creation and production of the dishes that make our household a home. In our respective homes, we rely on a family culinary consciousness to create a space where we can reclaim ourselves, as we tend to our loved ones, and as our loved ones also become an integral part in the preparation of food.

I must add that my now more than thirty-seven-year relationship to my husband was the product of the culinary sensibilities I learned from ancestral women sages. My intuition and ability to read the environment, as well as my husband's predilection for food, was the *anzuelo* with which I *fished* him or *cooked* him—words my friends are prone to use whenever they hear the story about how I caught him, even though I was not looking. Without asking or providing him notice, the first meal I prepared for him consisted of all his favorite dishes: *carne de puerco con espinacas*, nopales, and a *guiso de chile verde*, arroz, frijoles, and flour tortillas, as well as an apple pan pie and a sweet tea that connected him to my sazón for life. Despite the years, he continues to appreciate and value the meals I prepare, with comments such as, "You haven't made this," as he smacks his lips with pleasure. My cooking is a testament of love to those who are dear to me. It is a form of self-love that inspires me to create from *lo que tengo* for those I love.

Amá only assumed domestic responsibilities when she married because when she was a young woman her older sisters protected her from these chores. Later, she learned to cook by memory through her creativity and imagination and, thus, has given us a legacy. She called back the food of our ancestors and gave us the gift of cooking as a dispensary of power. She taught us to see food as love. Instead of raising us to think of cooking as a burden, Amá showed us food was nurturance and art-in-the-making. Most of all, for her, food was central to the relationships among those we love and with whom we were making community, as she tried to protect us as best she could in an unsafe home. Through her culinary actions, we learned lessons to deal with the violence surrounding us. We learned to fight it through her efforts to diffuse the power of the patriarch.

Mague, the sister after me, who cooks with knowledge gained from a home economics high school curriculum and the enfolding of Pilipino foods she adopted from her first husband, has created alternative food practices from other ethnic food expressions. Her chicken adobo has been adopted by all of us, making our kitchen a multicultural expression of love. Through Amá, she learned that the kitchen was a place of expression and one where all whom we love are nurtured in a space of care and love.

Fela, our younger sister, learned how to cook to feed her first husband, and has also incorporated the Cuban dishes of her second husband's family recipes of *Havana Vieja*. She creates such delectable fares such as *moros y cristianos* (black beans with rice) and *ropa vieja* (a type of beef stew) like no other in the California Bay Area. Fela cooked to mediate the volatility of her first marriage, while in the second marriage she relied on a "food consciousness" to reclaim her own self from a failed and violent first marriage. Like Amá, Fela tended to the needs of her children and made the kitchen her space of expression and self-nurturance.

Amá's hijas carry legacies carved out of revolutionary options of everyday life in the midst of turmoil and violence.

PART 2 ▪ Displacement and Re-Creation

Food and Place

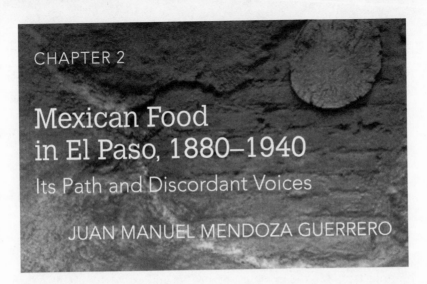

CHAPTER 2

Mexican Food in El Paso, 1880–1940

Its Path and Discordant Voices

JUAN MANUEL MENDOZA GUERRERO

The history of Mexican food in El Paso, Texas, has been complex and contradictory. Its construction has been very plastic, which means that the food and its meaning has changed over time. This plasticity has expanded to include various culinary manifestations under the name "Mexican food," taking materials from here and there. The creation of "Mexcian food" involved members of the Mexican community (immigrants and descendants of Mexicans born in the United States), small non-Mexican businessmen, and industrial processing companies. The main characteristic that defined the history of Mexican food between 1880 and 1940 was a continued appropriation and redefinition of Mexican culinary capital by packaging companies, changing restaurant ownerships, and recipe modifications. These changes came from inside and outside the Mexican community and from Mexican and non-Mexican people in El Paso, creating a necessary culinary adjustment to the flavors, aromas, and textures of a Mexican food re-determined by the dominant culture. The appropriation and redefinition enacted by non-Mexicans made them the major beneficiaries of economic profit and the main authors designing and manufacturing "Mexican food."[1] In so doing, these non-Mexicans who owned companies and restaurants were largely responsible for building a new meaning of "Mexican food" based on establishing the settings for the consumption of food, as well as the locations for buying the raw materials for the production of these foods.

Beginning in the 1930s, it was very common to see restaurants and shops announcing the sale of *comida Mexicana para gustos Americanos* (Mexican food to the liking of American palates).[2] However, the cultural affiliation of the food in all its varieties was always constructed as Mexican. Despite the undeniable influence of non-Mexican people and companies in the design and production of the so-called "Mexican food," *lo mexicano* in food was not eliminated. Regardless of who produced or consumed Mexican food, the cultural affiliation of Mexican food became so popular that, with time, it became one of the most important markers for the construction of Mexican culture on the border. The conflict to define how something could or could not be considered Mexican food was not only a recurring topic, but also a topic consubstantial to the existence of a Mexican border culture. Despite the increased industrialization of Mexican food production companies that redefined the presentation and content of Mexican food, the cultural affiliation of the food, its Mexicanness or Mexican origin, was rarely disputed. Thus, the cultural presence of lo mexicano grew thanks to modified and industrialized Mexican food.

The appropriation of Mexican food businesses by Anglos in El Paso took several fronts. First, Mexican food was an asset that could be marketed at a scale beyond the place and the social group where it was being produced and sold. This meant that in order to make it profitable it was necessary to produce it in larger quantities with low cost and high profits. The result was an industrialized food, which meant changes to the content and the presentation not only to make it more manageable and transportable, but also better to suit tastes of non-Mexican consumers. Second, even with small changes, the industrial producers kept the Spanish names of foods. Translation into English could have happened, but it did not because businesses could capitalize on the cultural traditions embedded in the foods' Spanish names. Third, recipes became intellectual property of non-Mexicans as they were the first to publish Mexican food recipes. Fourth, all of this established the large industrialized food producers as the major economic beneficiaries of the business and provided them an undeniable influence as people began to understand what Mexican food was through these producers' products, images, and discourses.

Mexican Food in El Paso, 1836–1926: Its Origins

For much of the second half of the nineteenth century, El Paso, Texas, remained economically and culturally isolated. By 1870 the town had a few hundred inhabitants and was not considered a city. El Paso's culture at this time, says Oscar J. Mártinez, remained Mexican since the presence of Anglos never exceeded three hundred persons: "The native way of life remained a long time without change in the ancient Mexican communities who had a combined population of perhaps 13,000 people on both sides of the river in the early 1870s."[3] It was not until the last quarter of the century when El Paso's demographics began to change. The projects of economic expansion in the American Southwest led to the development of large irrigation works in the Rio Grande Valley, which allowed the expansion of cotton and the growing of vegetables and citruses in the area. Such activities required the import of nonqualified labor, and Mexican immigrants, who came from different places across Mexico, met this demand.[4] Immigrants who arrived to El Paso came mainly from Chihuahua. Thus, neighborhoods such as Chihuahuita (little Chihuahua) began to fill with immigrants fleeing the agricultural crisis in Mexico and seeking new employment opportunities.[5]

This economic and agricultural expansion was accompanied by improved transportation systems. By 1880 El Paso had a population of 736 inhabitants (mostly Mexican), and the border region was then connected to the rest of the nation by railways. It was then that the movement of goods and people grew. With the railroads came technological novelties, businesses, migrants, and cultural practices from diverse backgrounds. Mexican food trade grew with the arrival of new immigrants, which led to the development of an ethnic food economy. The cultural contrast was most evident as El Paso was flooded with goods from many parts of the world during this time.[6] It was in this context that the *Mexicanidad* broke ground as never before, aided by the very fact that general popular consciousness and publicity took care of emphasizing the differences between Mexican and non-Mexican food.

Although some saw with regret that El Paso was gradually being filled with "Yankee's customs," the geographical and cultural isolation El Paso had been in for many years allowed Mexicans to have an emergent and significant presence in manufacturing and in the sale of food products in the late nineteenth and early twentieth centuries.[7] El Paso business people like Juan Alvarado, Cristobal Aguirre, Apolonia Duran, Juana Hernández, Benito Lucero, Esteban Sambrano, the Escageda brothers, and José Aviña, among others, became respected food merchants in the town. The number of *fondas* (inns) and Mexican food restaurants increased as more Mexicans came into town. Between 1891 and 1904, the *Restaurante Mexicano*, located at 220 Overland and Oregon, opened. It had a series of owners: first Eulogio Provencio and then Angela Guzmán. Later, once Josefa O. López took over, she renamed it *Fonda Mejicana*. During this period other Mexican food businesses also opened such as Mrs. B. M. Lerman's *menudo* (beef tripe) eatery, and three other restaurants, all with the same name, *Gran Restaurante Mexicano*, owned by Apolonia Duran, Lázaro Hernández, and Juana Leal. In the 1890s Evarista García's *La Tamaulipeca* Restaurant and Josefa Brunier's *Las Dos Repúblicas* began their operations.[8] This boom of Mexican restaurants was the preamble to an unprecedented growth in the number of Mexican grocery stores. These male and female restaurant owners, along with grocery retailers and the consumer community, pioneered the construction of an ethnic economy based on the material and semantic definition of food. Additionally, these business owners invented a niche market where Spanish was the language of business and the construction of a lo mexicano presence in food was an umbrella that included the diversity of immigrants' regional backgrounds and, thus, the El Paso Mexican border identity was defined by such diversity. Since the very beginning, Mexican food was, and still is, a plastic concept that includes all culinary manifestations related to production and consumption of food associated with people of Mexican origin.

Social Boundaries and Food

It is commonplace to say that Mexican food is a historical artifact. Newspaper advertisements and personal testimonies are good sources to help determine when each Mexican dish reached popularity. Dishes such as *burritos* and *quesadillas* are recent cultural inventions. In the late nineteenth century, newspapers such as *El Defensor, El Paso del*

Norte, and *El Ciudadano*, among others, realized the popularity of *fideo* (pasta), ranchero cheese, *piloncillo*, *chorizo*, tamales, enchiladas, *mole*, *menudo*, and *chalupas*. Although immigrants began to introduce new foods like *queso de tuna* (prickly pear cheese) and prickly pear itself, some culinary and beverage traditions were trapped at the border crossing. This was the case of *pulque* (alcoholic beverage that is then distilled to make tequila) and *nopal* (cactus).[9] Meals such as *atole* (a hot corn-based drink), *cecina* (beef jerky), *eslabón* (a kind of dessert), *quelite* (pigweed), and purslane also entered a border-crossing predicament because the industrial society saw them as primitive and unsafe foods.[10] The *chalupitas* (small tortillas served with hot sauce and cheese) that were later remembered as a popular dish of the nineteenth century disappeared from the commercial scene during this time.[11] Corn tortilla, a key part of the narratives of travelers who visited El Paso during the mid-nineteenth century, was also soon taken over by the use of wheat flour.[12] Mexicans in El Paso discovered foods like *galletas de animalitos* (animal crackers), *chiles en vinagre* (brine chiles), and *maicena* (cornstarch). Items such as these became part of the Mexican food repertoire and, years later, became part of El Paso's Mexican immigrants' culinary nostalgia.

According to historian David Montejano, during this time two separate societies, one Mexican and one Anglo, were constructed throughout Texas as well as in El Paso.[13] This separation also included food sites. The semantic and material separation of food was materialized through the construction of social boundaries that took the form of the exclusion of certain foods and ingredients, the regulation of the sale and production of food, and the spread of discourses that pointed out what "correct" eating habits should be. Foods like menudo (beef tripe) and pork feet began to receive strong criticism.[14] Other products such as the prickly pear and pulque, whose historical records are full of mysteries, simply never reached the category of commercial products. With the exception of beef tripe, these products were not part of the commercial advertising of El Paso in the early decades of the twentieth century as they were in the nineteenth century.[15] According to the newspaper *The Lone Star*, Ciudad Juárez's peddlers, who crossed the international bridge daily to sell different kinds of food, began undergoing a rigorous inspection that often led to the confiscation of their goods. The news of this hardening of the border spread out among other newspapers. Mexican merchants in El Paso, mostly composed of food businessmen, were also long excluded from the local chamber of commerce to such an extent that they had to form their own organizations.[16] Mexicans were often the recipients of constant criticism and pressure to "modernize" and change their diet. They were encouraged to replace their old culinary instruments with modern technologies such as stoves and refrigerators.[17] While Mexicans were pushed to modernization and Americanization, many non-Mexican food business owners began to sell meals and ingredients as "Mexican" by referring to them with Spanish names. This maelstrom included classifying Asian spices as Mexican, which angered some members of the Mexican community.[18] These simultaneously contradictory trends, the Americanization of Mexican cooking and the Mexicanization of non-Mexican foodstuffs, speak to the complexity of Mexican food history.

Recipes were also sites for the construction of social boundaries. The twentieth century began with the appearance of the first publications of recipes in Spanish.[19] These recipes, while in Spanish and published in local newspapers, had little or nothing to do with what the vast majority of Mexicans ate; instead, mainly European dishes were featured. For the most part, such recipes served to demonstrate to a non-Mexican audience the existence of a Spanish-speaking community cultured in culinary knowledge. Yet, most Mexicans in El Paso, due to their economic limitations, had a much different diet than what these printed recipes reflected. Implicitly, written recipes functioned to supposedly "elevate" the primitivism of orally transmitted recipes. They were meant to model a sophisticated cultural group with aspirations to have a good kitchen beyond the stereotypical triad of beans, tortilla, and chile.[20] Several authors, including historian Jeffrey M. Pilcher, point out that these three foods were understood as the basis of the Mexican diet, especially for the working class. However, this was not as true for Mexican communities in the United States where wheat flour was a crucial component in daily intake.

The first cookbook ever recorded and published in El Paso came out in 1909, and it included some Mexican recipes. Even though the text shows an intellectual appropriation, given that the signatories of the Mexican recipes were non-Mexican, this first cookbook recognizes the success of Mexican cuisine. The need for good neighborly relations between the border cities Juárez–El Paso and the historical presence of Mexicans in Texas were the reasons alluded to for the justification of publishing Mexican recipes. In the 1926 reissue of this cookbook, the editors included recipes for pork loin tacos, *tortas*, and pudding tamales, not to mention Mexican toast (a kind of corn chip), *gaznates* (dessert), *jamoncillo* (cured ham), Mexican ice cream, and a green chile sandwich.[21] As a pushback to the intellectual appropriation reflected in the 1909 and 1926 cookbooks, in 1927 for the first time a newspaper recognized Veracruz, Mexico, as the place of a recipe called *bacalao a la Veracruzana* (cod Veracruz style).[22] In the 1930s recognition of the existence of Mexican food via published recipes was accompanied by an unprecedented expansion of industrialized Mexican food. According to the *Business Directory of the City of El Paso*, the recognition of the success of Mexican food, as already stated, was accompanied by Mexican growth in the ownership of small businesses engaged in selling food.[23]

Canned Mexican Food and Criticism

El Paso's urban population growth and the industrial development of food helped augment the presence of packaged food. In the first decades of the twentieth century, these canned and packaged foods shared the shelves with fresh and bulk products in the shops of El Paso.[24] Industrialized foods influenced many Mexicans living in the United States in ways that compromised their palate for fresh food and, by the same token, led them to accept new foods as "authentically" Mexican. At first, people with Hispanic surnames were the ones who pushed a nascent industry of their own food in El Paso. The industries that stand out are the "Hidalgo" food factory, the Cuauhtémoc factory (inventor of the corn noodle), and the business owners Manuel Caballero, A. Suárez, the Cotera brothers, and A. de la Torres. Mexicans took part in the construction of the industrial market as either small industrialists or as inventors of new products, such as the taco shell, and in the ways of marketing Mexican food, such as the concept of fast food based on the taco. This was done through consumers or through trade by selling small amounts of products such as chile powder, gingerbread, and chipotle chile.[25] The fact that some Mexicans participated in the development of the industrialization of their own food, and their willingness to change its presentation, is indicative of their desire to succeed in the new food industry.

Due to the lack of funds and limited opportunities for business expansion, small firms that were engaged in the commerce of Mexican food could not compete with ambitious and innovative companies such as Ashley and Old El Paso. The non-Mexican owners of these companies, who had already been serving the Mexican market since the nineteenth century, took advantage of the evolving industrialization. With their economic resources and access to technology, these companies took ownership of much of the industrialization of Mexican food. Furthermore, their vast cultural resources (knowledge about consumer behavior, language, expectations, etc.) afforded them the ability to adjust Mexican foods to their own dominant, and non-Mexican, cultural palates. Unlike these larger food companies, Mexican business owners depended on the small-scale grocery shops in Mexican neighborhoods and did not have access to the same resources. Although the role of Ashley and Old El Paso was decisive in the 1930s, their predecessors such as Coca-Cola, Gold Medal, Uneeda Biscuit, HJ Heinz, Border Eagle, Procter and Gamble, and the small businesses mentioned above, paved the way within the Mexican market niche for the arrival of Ashley and other companies. Some of the companies entered into partnership with Spanish-speaking people to understand better how to target Mexicans as consumers and as cultural culinary sources for the commercialization of new Mexican food products. These companies bombarded this market niche with advertisements in Spanish. The economic success of the big companies catapulted the Mexican food market and created a formation of trade corridors, for example, Los Angeles–San Antonio–El Paso, where Mexican products were exchanged.

Early on, there were discordant voices that questioned the commercialization and industrialization of Mexican food. The industrialization of food created a polysemy. For example, dishes like *mole*, which for a long time were reserved as a Sunday family meal, ended up losing that identity of a particular time and occasion as they became available to be served in any location and on any occasion. Changes like this prompted the defense of a past that for some seemed to be fading. In this effort to defend Mexican food and its traditions, in an editorial printed in *El Paso del Norte*, Aurora Valle called on her countrymen to "return to [a] simple life," by which she meant to live as far as possible out of the consumerism of the time.[26] Additionally, in 1919, and due to the frequent criticism of Mexicans' bean consumption, a pamphlet whose title was "Praise Beans as a Food Base" was published. It states, "if beans are not in the everyday fare in the Anglo Saxon households it is unexplainable because it is proven that those are a food of the first order, superior even to many who are in good standing." The pamphlet not only recommends several ways to cook this legume, but it also seems to challenge the stereotypical term "beaner" applied to Mexicans in Texas.[27]

Apart from articles where the rationality of Mexican food is defended and contrasted with American food, as with the case of beans, the 1920s was a time to show a joy for food. For example, a verse composed for El Paso's *Restaurant Mexico* reflects great enthusiasm for Mexican food:

> *Que en él siempre se ha servido*
> *Lo mejor, lo delicado*
> *De ellos se muestran ufanos*
> *Siempre Sánchez y Castillo*
> *Y al restaurant le dan brillo*
> *Los platillos mexicanos*
> *Las muy sabrosas tostadas*
> *El mole, los pollos fritos*
> *Y los frijoles refritos*
> *Y las ricas enchiladas.*[28]

(The restaurant has always served
The best, the delicacies.
Of this they feel pride
Always Sánchez and Castillo
Make the restaurant shine [with]
The Mexican dishes
The tasty tostadas

The mole, fried chicken
And the refried beans
And the delicious enchiladas.)
(Translated by the author.)

The Mexican anthropologist Manuel Gamio also captures the importance of food for Mexicans in El Paso. He describes it as a blend of tradition and modernity:

> The food among Mexican residents in El Paso and Mexicans born here [within the United States] is what is usually called "Mexican." It is composed of many dishes where the chile is used in both: meat or vegetables. The chile is mostly bought canned. It is shipped from California and arrives clean and toasty, saving time for the cook. This chile is prepared with cheese, potatoes and other ways. It is called "Chile Santa Isabel." Green peppers stuffed with meat, is another dish. Other canned goods such as, sauces or Mexican dishes are sold in large quantities, in addition to tomatoes. Since vegetables are relatively cheap, they are eaten regularly. The meat sold in neighboring Ciudad Juarez is fresh and cheap, so they also eat it regularly, as well as eggs and ham. Fruits, salads and milk also are on the menu. Foods are generally cheaper in Mexican neighborhoods, an estimated twenty percent cheaper than in other parts of the city. Bread is consumed more than the corn tortilla, in French rolls or bolillos.[29]

Gamio was right when he described how Mexican food in El Paso was the result of many influences related not only to consumption decisions, but also to what was available in the existing environment and provided by the food industry. In this sense, Mexican food was being enriched with materials found in its path. This kind of cultural eclecticism, as is the case with almost every foodway in the world, began accumulating recognition in the third decade of the twentieth century.

Anglo Appropriation and Mexican Pain, 1927–1940

Notwithstanding what could be considered significant achievements in terms of recognizing Mexican food heritage, the cookbook of 1909 (reedited in 1926) placed Mexican food in a separate section of what is considered American, pointing to the idea that it was foreign for the American culture. However, the authorship of recipes for Mexican dishes remained non-Mexicans. It was not until 1947 that Spanish surnames appeared in cookbooks of El Paso; notably, these people were given credit as informants and not as authors. By the 1940s the famous Mexican food writer Josefina Velázquez began publishing food recipes in Spanish newspapers of El Paso. Nevertheless, this did not necessarily establish a local presence in the culinary discussion since Josefina was part of the Mexican government's efforts to construct a national food and, of course, did not represent the Mexican community in El Paso.[30]

The 1930s and 1940s were a time of profound changes in the material and symbolic culture of Mexican food. By this time there was already a large group of Mexicans whose identity was better defined as Mexican American. Moreover, much of the design and manufacturing of Mexican food was made on American soil, which made the adjective "Mexican" in the foods' labels sound ridiculous. However, the largest food company of Mexican products in El Paso, Ashley, never put the word "Mexican" on their cans or packages, as other companies had done in previous years. Instead, Ashley always used the slogan "Made in USA."[31] Identity redefinition along with the processes of industrialization and modernity changed what stores sold. On the one hand, foods such as aged cheese and brown sugar were questioned in terms of issues of hygiene; on the other hand, Mexican consumers stopped looking at labels that had once added important value to products such as "del Valle," "corn bread," or "homemade."

Companies like Old El Paso, the El Paso Chile Company, Casa Moneo, and Ashley, especially, became food producers and distributors at a national and global scale. Ashley operated the first US plants to sell tortillas, Mexican rice, and enchilada sauce in cans or packages. Later, in 1955, Ashley became number one in the country in sales of Mexican food products. This was soon after it developed a global presence that included Hong Kong, the Philippines, and Venezuela, among other countries.[32] Thus, companies such as Ashley were following a pattern of culinary appropriation of Mexican culinary capital that was first established after the United States' conquest of Mexico in the mid-nineteenth century. Some of the earlier culinary appropriations that resulted in mass production were the famous Tabasco sauce, chili,

chili con carne, chili powder, and tostados (renamed *fritos*).[33] All of these changes ultimately resulted in many Mexican trade and cultural institutions being supplanted by others. The small family factory was replaced by mass production. The disappearance of grocery stores, the economic bulwark of Mexican neighborhoods, implied the end of a place both for meeting and for building relationships and identity.

The *abonado* system was another one of the most important food-related sites for constructing social capital and maintaining a culinary Mexican identity. It began with Mexicans' nomadic and migrant status in the nineteenth century and continued until the late twentieth century. This system consisted of serving dinners at a restaurant or a *casa de asistencia* (a private home where food was sold) through a credit arrangement established by a verbal agreement for a weekly payment to the business owner. Usually the abonado (the customer) received twenty-one meals a week.[34] The abonado system was based on a *paisano* (countrymen) loan, which was crucial for the survival of a newcomer given the lack of money he arrived with. This system also allowed the abonado to have a meal more suitable to his taste, and allowed the supplier to perpetuate Mexican dishes according to the wishes of the abonado. Both restaurants and casas de asistencia were spaces where migrants knew and helped each other. However, these sites of community building disappeared over time.

Although the processes of appropriation and cultural redefinition of Mexican food was continuous, it was also true that Mexican immigrants never abandoned the idea of producing and sometimes selling food they found most original or more "Mexican." *El Continental* newspaper, the publisher of the *bacalao a la veracruzana* (Veracruz-style cod) recipe in 1927, continued to print recipes that were closer to the Mexican migrant taste like Guaymas-style tostadas and *tamales taquitos de nata* (similar to the English delicacy called "clotted cream"), Mexican roast, dry tortilla soup, and *enchiladas de jocoqui* (a thick cream).[35] In addition to these written recipes, and in an attempt to be more attuned to notions of modernity, the newspaper *El Continental* began to publish a section called "Good Manners" in which news and advice on the latest food trends and etiquette were given.[36] By the late 1950s, this section was reinforced with another one called "Fine Dining," which included recipes like *lomo poblano* (pork loin), oyster mushrooms, and *pescadillas a la duquesa*, Italian-style ground beef.[37] It is likely that both books and newspapers shared certain audiences; but given that many Mexicans in El Paso were poor and mostly illiterate, perhaps a newspaper was the most accessible source for those who could read since newspapers were cheaper and more readily available than books.

In the late 1920s and 1930s, feelings of nostalgia were enhanced by significant changes in Mexican food. By that time, as previously mentioned, industrialized Mexican food was popular. Additionally, there were cookbooks that did not recognize Mexicans as authors of their own recipes, and, increasingly, consumers purchased Mexican food produced by large factories, which influenced their notions of Mexican food. The messages in letters sent to Spanish newspapers indicated perceived changes in food as a blow to Mexican culture, traditions, and ways of family life. A writer for the *El Continental* mocked industrial food for creating a soulless food by "inventing" *pozole* pills and refried bean capsules, because any food without soul cracks the relationship between people.[38]

This feeling of nostalgia was also expressed in San Antonio, Texas, where a collaborator of the newspaper *La Prensa* said that the more famous Mexican food became in the United States, the more it moved away from its origins and originality. Mexican dishes in the United States were not only altered, but they also represented the less "sophisticated" Mexican culinary traditions. The real Mexican foods, according to this anonymous writer, were not enchiladas, refried beans, or turkey mole, but what Emperor Maximilian and his wife, Carlota, ate in Mexico in the nineteenth century. This writer lists items such as *sopa de huevo* (egg soup), *sopa de menudo* (tripe stew), *ensalada de calabacitas en adobillo* (squash salad), *criadillas de ternero* (calf testicles), *lengua* (cow's tongue), *albóndigas de pescado* (fish meatballs), *chuletas de carnero* (pork chops), *pichones en vino* (pigeons in wine sauce), *pichones rellenos* (stuffed pigeons), *gallinas de olor* (aromatic hens), and *barbacoa de cabeza de vaca* (barbecue made with cow's head). In respect to confectionaries, he mentions *pan de la vida* (bread of life), *bollito de almidón* (muffins made with cornstarch), *arequipa de coco* (coconut candy), *albóndigas fingidas* (fake meatballs), *tortillas de cuajada* (curd filled tortillas), *chicha de maíz o de limón* (sweet candy made with corn or lemon), *bigotes dulces* (sweet whiskers), and *cocada de almendra* (almond cocada). This same newspaper writer concludes his editorial by affirming what he sees as the superiority of Mexican food: "For breakfast I had the famous Mexican cuisine *huevos rancheros*; superior undoubtedly to the *ham and eggs*" of an American breakfast.[39] The strongest voices that opposed the paths of the industrialization of Mexican food were mostly middle- or upper-class Mexican immigrants who came to Texas during the Mexican Revolution. Considering that the writer of the San Antonio newspaper expresses the "essence" of true Mexican food based on what the aristocrats ate, one can assume that he probably identified with such socioeconomic classes. Due to a social status that was reduced when they emigrated, this group tried to raise their social worth by generating a discourse anchored in cultural retention of an aristocratic past that distanced them from their working-class countrymen.

Gender and Mexican Food

These nostalgic feelings also covered the area of gender relations because the changes in eating patterns were linked to both family structure and female roles. Mexican women suffered systematic attacks by American newspapers and magazine writers, which characterized them as quiet and suffering bodies. There were many attempts to educate and civilize Mexican women on issues of domestic economy and the use of modern cooking utensils. Yet, members of the Mexican community made them a scapegoat by blaming them for the changes in Mexican food that had led to a breakdown of the traditional family model. An anonymous writer in 1927 wrote:

> The former female education especially intended to get single women to become excellent housewives and to do this, it was imperative that they knew how to cook perfectly, keep the house clean and do [the cooking]. The pace of modern life has other requirements [for women. They] must know how to recognize a typewriter, [speak] foreign languages, [know about] accounting or possess a university degree.[40]

The problem expressed by men was that women had multiple demands put on them with this new rhythm, and this prevented them from learning to cook. According to this newspaper article, women cooked fried eggs or grilled pork chops, "things that can be made by the dullest of men." Journalist Uunez Dominguez had the idea that these changes had created a "disastrous woman," resulting from foreign influence that had made them lose their customs. The result, Dominguez said, was the depravity of taste and loss of femininity and Mexicanness.[41] Women's presumed lack of culinary skill was a source of friction in marriage as it was said that a good dish reconciles any problem and is the main factor of marital harmony.[42]

Some newspapers, however, framed this debate as a female empowerment that was making gender roles more parallel rather than as a catastrophe in the Mexican family and in food production. Angelina Valdéz, an advertising figure for SY Green Sauce Products in El Paso, who made presentations at Piggly Wiggly shops, saw the Americanization of Mexican food and Mexican women as a modern way of life and coexistence.[43] In this same vein, Rita Weaver Darden, from the *Odessa American* collaborator, said that industrialized Mexican food eliminated time-consuming and difficult preparation, thus allowing more time for women's other demands as well as allowing Mexican food to be accepted more widely by non-Mexicans.[44]

In addition to the changes in women's roles and their use of manufactured food, another element that distressed those who missed the notion of a traditional Mexican woman was that she was no longer completely dedicated to working in the kitchen. Furthermore, issues of class also added to this change. For example, the fact that many employers in El Paso required their (Mexican) maids to utilize the latest in home technologies and to learn how to cook American dishes may have influenced these women's cooking practices in their own homes. Pamphlets and books were published in order to achieve these expectations, which catapulted those nostalgic views that saw this as a form of acculturation and a challenge to established traditional Mexican gender roles.

Women were also a factor in the construction and survival of Mexican food in El Paso. In the construction and retention of Mexican food, the role of Mexican women was crucial because many continued taking charge of the kitchen and the domestic space despite a relative women's liberation based on paid labor outside the home. Through their work in the kitchen, women fought back against power relations and greatly contributed to their Mexican food culinary traditions remaining alive.

Conclusions

The trajectory of the commercial propagation of Mexican food in El Paso did not mean a distancing from its Mexican cultural affiliation. Although there were discussions on notions of originality and authenticity and, certainly, the food processing companies changed the content and presentation of the food, its "Mexicanness" remained. Moreover, the version of Mexican food that spread in El Paso and the rest of the United States was not the food of the upper-class immigrants announced in the first El Pasoans' recipes published in newspapers, but was a food associated with working-class people. This is an oddity in light of the experience of what happened in Mexico and many other countries such as France, where the model of the country's "good food" was the food eaten by the upper classes. Pilcher is right when he notes that the kind of Mexican food that flourished in the United States was that coming from the working class. This remains true regardless of the changes this food experienced when it was produced on an industrial scale. Finally, the history of Mexican food within the context of El Paso, and the rest of the United States, is a good example to understand how cultural affiliation, in this case Mexican, may include a mosaic of colors without losing its essence. As Gustavo Arellano asserts, "We must consider the infinite variety of Mexican Food in the United States as part of the Mexican family—not a fraud, not a lesser sibling, but an equal."[45] However, it is important not to exclude debates on notions of originality and authenticity because social groups can hide behind agendas that drive toward imperialist domination of one culture over another. The fact that El Paso shared the construction of Mexican identities with Ciudad Juárez complicates this mosaic of many colors more so than in places were there are no territorial boundaries. Mexicans in El Paso constructed their identities in such a way that they tried to be different from other cultural groups in the United States as well as from Mexicans of Ciudad Juárez.

This chapter helps make clear how important Mexican food in

the region of El Paso, Texas, was in producing identity markers that helped to define a community and a culture. It also helps to understand how diffuse but also rigid are the boundaries that define people's ethnicities. This situation of uncertainty created a unique scenario of understanding and disputing the definitions of Mexicanidad. From 1880 to 1940 Mexican food was part of the politics of Mexican cultural adjustment into American society. The proliferation of canned Mexican food after the 1920s should be understood not only as a result of the growth of urban spaces where people demanded diversity, comfort, and modernity, but also as the influence of a Mexican "second generation" that formed an active force in identity politics, thereby displacing or sharing the power with the immigrant generation called "Mexico Lindo."[46]

While this study focuses on the period of 1880–1940, in other time periods there are similar patterns of the industrialization and modernization of Mexican food. In World War II, Mexican food received a new impetus, not only for the war economy that implied a requirement to diversify food for the soldiers who traveled overseas and the families who stayed at home, but also for a greater acceptance of Mexican food in the context of an international military alliance. Provisions of "Mexican" food were integral to the massive incorporation of Mexican Americans in the war effort, which too found pockets of resistance. What we must remember, however, is that the distinctions between industrialized and modernized Mexican food and challenges to resist such changes by different sectors of the Mexican and Mexican American community only continue to reinforce the plasticity integral to Mexican cuisine and, in fairness, to all cuisines.

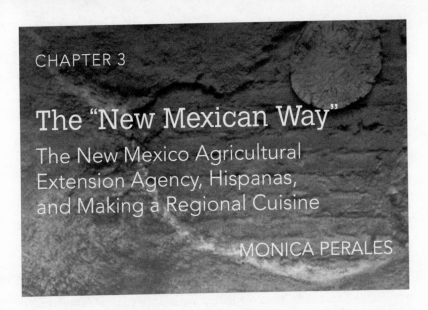

CHAPTER 3

The "New Mexican Way"
The New Mexico Agricultural Extension Agency, Hispanas, and Making a Regional Cuisine

MONICA PERALES

In the 1950s, Edith M. Lantz, a home economist with the New Mexico Agricultural Extension Service (NMAES), detailed the research she conducted to "improve" the nutritional value of the *tortilla*, one of New Mexico's staple food products. With the assistance of Marjorie Paiz, a sophomore studying home economics at New Mexico A&M College who was "familiar with the foods used by the Spanish-American people of New Mexico," Lantz tried to increase milk consumption by adding nonfat dry milk to a range of foods. Dry milk was an inexpensive source of calcium and protein already used in commercial bakeries to "improve texture, flavor, and nutritive value," and Lantz reasoned that adding it to tortillas could be an easy way to increase milk intake among New Mexican families.[1] Given her stated interest in Hispano dietary deficiencies, Lantz turned to the classic recipes found in Fabiola Cabeza de Baca Gilbert's wildly popular *Historic Cookery* (originally produced as a circular distributed by the NMAES in the 1930s) as the basis for her experiments, adding reconstituted milk to everyday foods like *atole* (cornmeal gruel), *queso fresco* (fresh cheese), and pinto beans.[2] But Hispanos may not have been the only targets of her work. Women who made tortillas every day did not need recipes. However, instructions for different types of tortillas—white flour, whole wheat, *harinilla* (a prepared meal made of lime-treated corn), and *masa*—would be necessary for a non-Hispano audience new to making tortillas and growing accustomed to seeing them at the dinner table. Thus, Lantz, Paiz, and the NMAES were not just teaching Hispanas about nutrition, but also informing a broader audience about Hispanic New Mexican foods—not only how to make them nutritionally "better," but how to make them in the first place.

Lantz's report, which wove together the NMAES's scientific methods with the classic recipes carefully documented by the state's first Hispana home demonstrator, is an example of the NMAES's adaptability to the realities of the people it aimed to reach. Using NMAES publications from the 1910s to the 1960s, this essay argues that NMAES workers helped to define a regional cuisine grounded in Hispanic New Mexican foodways and highlights the distinct—if brief—moments of collaboration and Hispana voice found in these publications.[3] Home economics programs like those promoted through NMAES are often viewed as embracing an assimilating mission meant to Americanize ethnic families' diets, eating habits, and culture that was rooted in a sense of cultural imperialism and racial superiority.[4] Yet, the agency necessarily adapted itself to the historic particularities of the state and, in so doing, unwittingly privileged Hispana food knowledge and reinforced the nutritional and cultural value of New Mexican regional foods. NMAES employees adapted recipes, taught readers about native ingredients and foodways, and circulated those lessons under the official cover of the agency. In this way, NMAES publications highlight a more nuanced story of the making of a regional cuisine, one that is neither totally about cultural appropriation nor cultural preservation, but rather a convergence of needs and desires of the agency, rural women, and everyday eaters.

Acknowledging the power wielded by agencies like the NMAES, this essay examines how these publications reinforced rather than eradicated regional Hispano cuisine, albeit one adapted and mediated by the agency's vision. Despite a lack of sources documenting the voices of everyday Hispanas involved in NMAES programs, this essay also shows how focusing on spaces for negotiation and exchange in the circulars offers important evidence of how Hispanas were active participants in the process. Furthermore, highlighting moments of exchange—however limited—illuminates the varied ways that *nuevomexicanas* articulated their own interests, concerns, and struggles in the face of historical change, and offers clues to the power and self expression that exist in women's kitchens and the foods they grow, make, and share.[5]

In this essay I consider circulars from three periods. First, as early as the 1910s, circulars prioritized modern techniques and "American" recipes, but also included regionally specific foods, recognizing their durability and the influence of local food customs on everyday eating. The presence of local New Mexican products, recipes, and food-preservation technologies offer glimpses into Hispanas' influence on agency practices and suggest the cultivation of an Anglo audience increasingly accustomed to Hispanic fare. Second, in the 1930s, Fabiola Cabeza de Baca Gilbert's circulars made a more forceful case for the centrality of "traditional" recipes to New Mexico's cuisine. In Spanish and English texts, she preserved Hispano recipes with an eye toward modern tools and techniques, elevated Hispanas' food knowledge and labor, and persuaded a non-Mexican audience that these foods represented the state's rich cultural heritage as shaped by native and Hispano influences. Third, the essay concludes with a brief look at the 1950s and 1960s, when publications asserted the nutritional significance of native New Mexico staples, including chile, as part of the state's cultural heritage and identity. Ultimately, the NMAES may have failed to transform rural life, alter rural foodways, and incorporate rural Hispanos into the national body on equal terms, but its publications are critical documents that reveal that the unintended results of programming are as important as the intent.

Adaptation in New Mexico: A Brief Overview of the NMAES

Long before the arrival of the NMAES, adaptation was central to women's efforts to sustain their families and communities. Multiple waves of Native American, Spanish Mexican, and Anglo migration and conquest brought new products and technologies to the region, which also required the incorporation of local knowledge of native items. According to the historian Maria E. Montoya, "new cultural identities" were forged through conflict and accommodation.[6] Women played a primary role in every aspect of food cultivation and production. They planted gardens, raised chickens and goats, and made cheese that not only supported their own families, but also forged and maintained community bonds. In Hispano communities, food preparation and exchange symbolized "female virtue" and "[w]omen's production of food, like women's creation of neighborhood, was thus both imbued with the communalism of the village, and vital to it."[7]

Migration and territorial expansion presented moments of tension around food as well. In the nineteenth century, disparaging descriptions of Spanish Mexicans—including their food and perceived propensity toward alcoholic beverages—served to mark American "superiority." Historian Deena González shows that American travel accounts often represented Hispanic New Mexicans as lazy and cast especially unflattering views of Hispanas who "simply 'grind corn on a rock, make tortillas, and dance.'"[8] Nineteenth-century Anglo visitors to the Southwest described Mexican fare as unappealing and unappetizing even as they described the contexts in which they were served as exotic. Susan Shelby Magoffin famously catalogued her initial distaste for the food she encountered in her 1840s travels through New Mexico on the Santa Fe Trail, commenting on the hard bread, "tough, mean looking and . . . unpalitable [sic]" cheese, and the strong "chilly [sic] verde."[9] Such descriptions, combined with structural changes in the political and economic life of the region, served to enforce American rule and Hispano and Native Americans' place in the social hierarchy. As the historian Pablo Mitchell contends, bodily comportment (including what and how people ate and drank) became an important social marker linked to racial power, whiteness, and ultimately, civic belonging.[10] The NMAES, with its lessons on "modern" food preservation and cooking, was simply another chapter in a much longer history.

Yet, it is important to note the brief moments of cultural exchange. For as much as American popular culture denigrated all things Mexican, food could also represent a common ground. Over time, Susan Magoffin came to appreciate Mexican cooking, and as the historian Katherine Massoth argues, New Mexican women's hospitality toward visitors and food sharing taught newcomers about Mexican and New Mexican dishes, allowing Hispanas to confront conquest on their own terms.[11] Much like the twentieth-century rural women who allowed extension service agents into their homes, this earlier generation of women was able to exert a small measure of control over the terms of cultural exchange within their kitchens. An examination of the NMAES and its influence on New Mexican foodways requires an understanding of both the history of conquest as well as an appreciation for adaptation.

The NMAES carried specific goals and imperatives that connected food cultivation, production, and consumption to a set of ideas rooted in American identity and promoted by the state and federal government. Established by Congress through the Smith Lever Act, the NMAES consisted of 119 state and county workers coordinating the programs of the state agricultural college located in southern New Mexico and those of the federal government.[12] The agency was a product of the Progressive Era reform movement, which attempted to bring order to the myriad social problems wrought by late-nineteenth-century urbanization and industrialization. For some, this meant encouraging the move out of the cities and onto farms as a means of solving urban problems.[13] Unfortunately, life was equally hard for the nearly half of the American population who resided in rural areas and who remained isolated and impoverished.[14] The NMAES sought to improve the quality of life for rural residents through a wide range of programs including a Farm Bureau, county fairs, courses, 4-H Clubs, and county councils. Through these efforts, the agency worked to raise farmers' standard of living by teaching scientific management and marketing, encouraging the more efficient use of credit and capital, and promoting the cultural, spiritual, and educational life of rural communities.[15]

Home economics curricula were critical to these efforts. Home demonstration agents sought to create the wholesome American rural family through food, making "good" eaters one scientifically crafted meal at a time.[16] Early home economics work consisted of organizing boys and girls' gardening and canning clubs and conducting visits to ranches and family homes. During World War I, home economics work expanded substantially as food preservation took on added importance. The Women's Auxiliary of the New Mexico Council of Defense contributed influence and resources to expand the home demonstration program to "preach the gospel of 'Food Conservation'" as a matter of patriotic duty.[17] Wartime emergency led to the addition of six demonstration agents and two statewide workers dedicated to home economics.[18] From this point of view, the agency's work focused on elevating a specific identity linked to "American" foods, preservation methods, and technologies.

A closer look suggests that while the goal may have been to assert an American identity, day-to-day agricultural extension and home demonstration required accommodation. According to the historian Joan M. Jensen, the Extension Service was a "crossroads" where local conditions intersected with national- and state-level policies.[19] At the time of NMAES's inception, approximately 60 percent of rural women were Hispanas, most of whom only read and spoke Spanish. Thus, the agency was forced to address the needs of the bilingual state if it hoped to be effective.[20] From its earliest years, the agency employed a small number of Hispano staff; by July 1918, Hispano agricultural agents served six counties, and Gertrude Espinosa was hired with wartime funds as the assistant in club work.[21] The president of the New Mexico College of Agriculture and Mechanical Arts, Austin Crile, recognized the need for the extension service to be able to communicate with Hispanos, explaining that the service must "appoint from the native people . . . who can work among the women and children of the Spanish American population."[22] While this recognition of New Mexico's bilingual needs does not diminish the agency's assimilative approach, it does suggest that the NMAES contended with the particularities of the state in which it operated and placed agents and clients in positions for direct conversation.

Results were mixed. Some Hispanas initially resisted NMAES efforts. Hispanas' own voices are scarce, but home demonstrators complained that Hispanas were skeptical of the agency's work stating that they were "retiring" by nature and unwilling to attend meetings with Anglos, even if they were conducted in Spanish.[23] Limited bilingual skills and agents' perceptions of them as uncooperative resulted in far fewer demonstrations for Hispanas; only 162 of nearly 800 demonstrations in 1918 were held in Spanish.[24] Still, the NMAES did reach Hispanas, and some welcomed the NMAES on their terms. In late 1917 in Guadalupe and San Miguel counties, state demonstrations held in Spanish were "evidently decidedly successful," according to demonstrator reports.[25] Edna Wagner, assistant state demonstrator, reported on an especially well-attended demonstration in Las Cruces in 1917, where fifteen Hispana housewives participated in fruit and vegetable canning. Based on the enthusiastic response, the agent prepared a Spanish-language circular for the women.[26] Such reports illuminate the complex ways Hispanas negotiated the presence of the NMAES in their lives. Some rejected NMAES agents' intrusion into their homes and its efforts to reorganize their households and tables, while others were open to technologies that would allow them to provide for their families and lessen their workload. In both cases, Hispana actions speak clearly to their personal interests. These moments of negotiation created spaces in which agents collaborated with the Spanish-speaking women they hoped to reach.

The expansion of New Deal policies in the 1930s that were increasingly attuned to the needs of Native Americans and Hispanos changed the focus of extension work.[27] The NMAES hired Fabiola Cabeza de Baca Gilbert in 1929, whose ethnicity may have persuaded more women to open their homes to NMAES. Raised in a prominent New Mexico ranching family, Cabeza de Baca Gilbert possessed a strong awareness of socioeconomic class and pride in her Spanish lineage, and what one biographer termed a sense of "noblesse oblige."[28] Still, having a representative who shared cultural traditions made a difference. Her experience as a rural schoolteacher working among Hispano, Native American, and Anglo children, and her love of her own history and culture, provided her a unique platform from which to work.[29] "The public worker must be sympathetic with the people she works with regardless of their background or extraction," she wrote in a 1942 article.[30] Initially, she too encountered resistance in her extension work. Cabeza de Baca Gilbert reassured women that she did not intend to force them to expend limited resources, but instead simply wanted to use their homes to teach them new techniques. She said, "And after they knew me, they would come to me to tell them this and that."[31] Over time, she gained their trust and respect, and by the 1940s she reported that more Hispano families owned pressure cookers and tin-can sealers and were incorporating them with the classic, healthful recipes from the past.[32]

Early Circulars: Blending Old and New

This history of accommodating multiple interests—of both agents and Hispanas—is evident in NMAES circulars. Even as they contained elements of Americanization, the circulars simultaneously reinforced the significance of certain local products and foods to the region's culinary repertoire. For instance, patriotic wartime food conservation efforts led to the elevation of the pinto bean, a staple of Hispano diets. The July 1918 circular, *Pinto Bean*, extolled the virtues of the pinto bean in the effort to curb meat consumption to support the war effort.[33] Consuming pinto beans tapped into present wartime needs, a growing market for a major agricultural product of the state, as well as a long regional history. In the circular, the New Mexico pinto bean was not denigrated as a "Mexican" ingredient, but praised for its many nutritional qualities. It appeared that the primary goal of the circular was to teach Anglo readers unaccustomed to eating pinto beans how to incorporate them into their family meals in ways that were familiar. It included recipes for several preparations: baked beans, soups, soufflés, croquettes, muffins, and "bean tamale" (actually, more of a custard).[34] A circular devoted exclusively to pinto beans suggests that the NMAES was not unwilling to incorporate local ingredients when needed, even if not in Hispano recipes. In teaching rural families to prepare dishes including the Mexican "frijole" as a means of supporting wartime rationing and in the name of nutrition, the NMAES made the "Mexican" pinto bean into a small symbol of "American" patriotism.

While some agents viewed rural women's food preparation skills (or lack thereof) with condescension, NMAES circulars sometimes acknowledged Hispana and Native American preservation methods. For years, New Mexican women had adapted and used technologies for drying and curing meat, roasting and grinding corn, and drying fruits and chile.[35] Circulars deemed sun drying a practical and effective method for preserving food, even when they advocated bringing labor- and time-saving devices into the kitchen. A 1919 circular on preserving foods suggested that small peppers "may be spread in the sun" and whole peppers could be "strung out on a thread," much in the manner New Mexican women had done for generations.[36] In 1935 a circular on drying fruits and vegetables explained that "[s]un dry-ing is one of the oldest known methods of food preservation in New Mexico" and that it was a "simple, convenient, and economical method of saving the surplus fruits and vegetables." Although the circular went on to detail additional requirements and instructions for construct-ing a homemade dryer and evaporator, it is important to note that it recognized both the state's environment as well as Hispana knowl-edge about food preservation.[37] Though absent from the text, Hispana expertise influenced NMAES recommendations as the agency offi-cially endorsed the local way of doing things.

Recipes for dishes like "Mexican-style" *chili con carne* likewise established the place of Hispano foods in the state's repertoire and highlighted the work of the women producing them. By the early 1930s, the circular on home canning included recipes for a basic chili and a distinct "Mexican-style" chili con carne.[38] While the first chili recipe simply provided cooking directions (suggesting familiarity among the English-language readership), the chili con carne recipe included a longer list of ingredients. "Mexican-style" chili con carne was made with beef cut into cubes (as opposed to ground beef and suet) and contained "Mexican" (pinto) beans, chili pepper and dried pepper pods, cloves (garlic), and bay leaves. By the early twentieth century, chili con carne had gained popularity among Anglos, and the expansion of commercially produced Hispanic foods and prolif-eration of Mexican restaurants geared toward an Anglo audience may have contributed to the inclusion of these different varieties in the NMAES circulars.[39] However, chili con carne represented more than just an Anglo desire to consume difference. Given the long history of negotiation between the agency and Hispana home cooks, it is equally likely that demand from Hispanas for familiar dishes that could easily be canned and saved for later consumption resulted in their presence in the circulars. Hispanas, like those at the canning demonstration in Las Cruces, embraced canning as a labor-saving activity. However, they also wanted to add their own flavors and express their creativ-ity through their meals, incorporating what food studies scholar Meredith E. Abarca calls their "sazón" and "chiste."[40] The presence of these recipes in a government document suggests how the work of the NMAES reinforced an idea of New Mexican food—one that included *both* basic chili and chili con carne, as well as Hispanas' unique flavors and touches.

Boletín de Conservar, Los Alimentos, and Historic Cookery

Cabeza de Baca Gilbert's circulars most clearly represent how multiple interests converged to define New Mexican foodways in the NMAES. Circular 106, *Boletín de Conservar* (Bulletin on Preserving), and Circular 129, *Los Alimentos y su Preparación* (Food and its Preparation), reflected Cabeza de Baca Gilbert's and the agency's faith in scientific values as they applied them to cooking, canning, and preserving.[41] In addition to detailed information on "modern" methods for canning, preparing jams, jellies, and butters, drying fruits and vegetables, and preserving meat, photographs of pressure cookers, pots, strainers, and other canning implements encouraged participation in the consumer economy by providing visual examples of the kinds of items modern homes should have on hand.[42] Cabeza de Baca Gilbert also stressed the importance of selecting the right kinds and combinations of foods for healthy meals and included sample daily menus and photographs from the US Bureau of Home Economics of baskets of fresh produce, meats, and breads, asserting that healthy eating was a compelling state interest. Embracing the goals of the NMAES, Cabeza de Baca Gilbert viewed her work as serving an important purpose as it helped people who "still had some good food habits" after many years of economic and social dislocation, but who had "tended to change to the poorer urban diets."[43] In large credit to her work, Hispana clients adopted pressure cookers and canning, and regarding *Boletín* and *Alimentos*, she declared, "Next to her prayer book, the rural Spanish-speaking woman treasures these two booklets."[44]

Although the emphasis on modern tools, technologies, and methods could be interpreted as evidence of Cabeza de Baca Gilbert's internalization of the NMAES's Americanization efforts (not to mention her own class bias), the recipe sections also suggest adaptation and Hispana agency.[45] For all her praise of modernity, Cabeza de Baca Gilbert believed in the value of so-called traditional foods. "In every menu in the Spanish bulletin on food preparation, the native foods are featured with only such other foods added as are needed for a balanced diet," she wrote in 1942.[46] Moreover, as an official government document, the Spanish circulars placed New Mexican dishes on the same level as the other recipes. Among the recipes for roast beef, "Parker House" rolls, fried chicken, and pancakes—recipes that suggest an overarching desire to define "American" eating in a specific way—were recipes for a wide range of familiar dishes including rice, *posole, chile con carne, enchiladas,* and *chiles rellenos.* Hispanos embraced change in their lives too, in both the kinds of foods they consumed and the methods and tools they used to prepare them; but they also hungered for the familiar meals that linked them to community and culture. As one biographer notes, Cabeza de Baca Gilbert "offered rural New Mexicans a way to assert their tradition even as they also sought change."[47]

Perhaps more than any other circular, Cabeza de Baca Gilbert's *Historic Cookery* advocated for New Mexican cuisine, persuading an audience unfamiliar with Hispano New Mexican food to try it and convincing them of its flavor and nutritional value. Published as Circular 161 in 1931, and revised and reissued in multiple editions, *Historic Cookery* documented "traditional" New Mexican recipes through a distinctly Hispana voice, albeit one mediated by the NMAES. It would have a life beyond its original function as a circular, with more than 80,000 copies distributed well beyond the state's boundaries by mid-century, enticing tourists to New Mexico.[48] However, focusing on *Historic Cookery's* origins as a NMAES circular underscores how the agency, Cabeza de Baca Gilbert, and Hispana home cooks participated in defining New Mexican cuisine.[49] Devoted to Hispanic New Mexican cooking and privileging local flavors, ingredients, and methods of preparation, Cabeza de Baca Gilbert asserted "[t]he menu in New Mexico is *incomplete* without the real old time dishes including chile and other dishes *so beloved by the people of New Mexico.*"[50] There was no doubt as to the ethnic heritage of the "people of New Mexico" of which Cabeza de Baca Gilbert wrote. Emphasizing the geographic specificity of ingredients, she also prioritized the knowledge of the women who prepared these recipes; if a novice wanted to experience New Mexican food, "one should really taste the food as prepared by good Spanish cooks to know what is just right."[51]

As an author and NMAES agent, Cabeza de Baca Gilbert asserted an authoritative voice as an expert in New Mexican cooking, but *Historic Cookery* also relied upon the depth of knowledge that generations of Hispana home cooks possessed. In teaching nonnative readers (and eaters) about every aspect of Hispano fare, *Historic Cookery* offered insight into "*the New Mexican way*" (read, *nuevomexicano* way) of combining ingredients into tasty, nutritious dishes, as well as cooking techniques employed by Hispana home cooks. Descriptive English translations for common dishes like *albondigas* (meatballs), *calabacitas con chile verde* (summer squash in green chile), and *capirotada* (bread pudding) made the staples of Hispana cooks accessible for the uninitiated. Attention to their tools—a small coffee canister for molding cheese and earthenware pots for cooking frijoles—likewise acknowledged Hispana ingenuity in repurposing household items as well as their historic foodways.[52] Recipes for multiple chile sauces required careful attention and manipulation by hand, and lengthy instructions on roasting, peeling, and hand massaging—"the meat (of the roasted chile) should be . . . worked between the fingers, a little water being added from time to time to keep the pulp at a creamy consistency"—showed that this was painstaking, skillful work that was not to be rushed. Making chile sauce relied on Hispanas' tactile knowledge.[53] This kind of expertise extended beyond the mechanics of making chile sauce. According to Cabeza de Baca Gilbert, Hispanas also brought an indefinable finesse to their cooking. "*Guisar*, which has no exact English equivalent, is the most popular word in the native homemaker's vocabulary," she explained. "Roughly translated it means to dress up food, perhaps only by adding a little onion or a pinch of oregano; good food always deserves a finishing touch. Food must never taste flat, but it will—if its not *guisado*."[54]

For as much as *Historic Cookery* enshrined New Mexican traditions, ingredients, and recipes, it also reflected the kinds of adaptations Hispanas had engaged in for generations and which were emblematic of their interactions with NMAES agents. *Historic Cookery* incorporated the technologies and practices that the NMAES had been trying to inculcate for years and which made for successful replication of New Mexican recipes in any kitchen. For instance, it included standard abbreviations and all recipes included carefully measured ingredients lists. Recipes in different editions also incorporated the use of pressure cookers, food choppers, eggbeaters, sieves, fruit presses, glass jars, cake pans, and wax paper—all items recommended by the NMAES, which were becoming regular features in home kitchens. By 1939 quality ground chili powder had become an acceptable substitute for fresh chili, and the 1942 edition included instructions for using prepared meal *harinilla* that only required the addition of boiling water to produce the required masa for corn tortillas.[55] Such modifications were not solely intended for the benefit of the novice, but also may have offered convenience for Hispanas familiar with the dishes, but who—as Cabeza de Baca Gilbert noted in her other writings—were also becoming detached from the context in which food knowledge was handed down.

Historic Cookery centered the adaptability of New Mexican foods—and by extension, that of the women who made it—within the state's culinary heritage. "Many of the recipes which have been handed down were brought by the colonists from Spain. Others have come from Mexico and some have grown out of a need to use the products native to New Mexico," she wrote in the 1939 edition.[56] For Cabeza de Baca Gilbert and, arguably, Hispanas across the state, "tradition" and "change" equally shaped New Mexican food. In the 1951 printing, she explained, "New Mexico is a land of changes. . . . There have been changes in its people, in its customs and culture, and naturally in its food habits. The recipes in *Historic Cookery* are a product of the past and present—an amalgamation of Indian, Spanish, Mexican, and American. *They are typically New Mexican*."[57] What had also changed by this edition was the degree to which Mexican food and New Mexican food, specifically, had gained acceptance among a wider audience. "In recent years, New Mexican foods have become increasingly popular," she explained. "That's why you may have to stand in line when you eat in restaurants that specialize in New Mexican dishes." In part, it was the fact that "the food is good," but she also credited "recent research [that] has proved that many of our basic foods—chile, beans, purslane, lamb's quarters, goat's cheese and whole grain cereal, for example—are highly nutritious."[58] Indeed, it was the very research conducted by the NMAES, and Cabeza de Baca Gilbert's own work as its agent in elevating and honoring the work of Hispana cooks that helped to convince a wider dining public of that fact.

"Chile View": The 1950s and 1960s

By the 1950s and 1960s, NMAES publications readily accepted the nutritional value of New Mexican foods; this was the result of years of scientific research and of the years of negotiation between extension agents and Hispanas. Unlike *Historic Cookery*, the 1953 bulletin, "Nutritive Values of Some New Mexico Foods," seemed less concerned with persuasion than with stating the food value of certain staples and their importance to the collective well-being of the state's eaters. The authors noted that native foods like beans, corn, wild greens, rosehips, dried sprouted wheat, and chile were among the ingredients *nuevomexicanas* had long turned to in order to feed their families. In perhaps the strongest assertion of the nutritional value of native New Mexican ingredients, authors noted that the Hispano process of treating corn with lime to make *nixtamal* increased niacin, which may have accounted for the low incidence of pellagra in New Mexico, a condition prevalent in the South among the poor.[59] The bulletin also explained how these foods represented the state's long and complex history and regional distinctiveness. "The early settlers of what is now New Mexico had to depend on foods which could be obtained locally . . . the early Spanish colonizers adopted and modified Indian foods," it explained. "As a result they built up a dietary pattern which is quite unlike that found in other parts of the United States."[60] The authors highlighted the kind of adaptability forged through necessity and exposure to new foods when they explained that many of the Spanish-speaking residents of smaller, still-isolated villages continued to consume the old foods and "newcomers to the state learn to like some of them."[61]

Anglo newcomers were not the only ones changing their food habits. Younger *nuevomexicano* families, and those making their way to larger, less-isolated communities, were beginning to "[substitute] easy-to-prepare, ready-to-cook, or already-cooked foods from the store for the old foods which require much presentation."[62] As a sign of the changing times, the bulletin referenced the growing presence of processed and manufactured foods. Accordingly, whole foods were not the only subject of NMAES researchers' nutrition experiments. They also conducted experiments on commercially produced tortillas and chile, and on foods prepared in local restaurants, items sold frozen and canned in markets, and, not surprisingly, made in the lab according to recipes found in *Historic Cookery* and Cabeza de Baca Gilbert's novel *The Good Life* (1949).[63] Although some of the foods were no longer eaten as a regular part of Hispano diets and some were reserved for special occasions like religious holidays, "their use in early days is a good illustration of the way the early settlers met their nutritional needs from the foods at hand."[64] In this rendering, not only are Hispana cooks present as the preparers of such healthy dishes, but their families also appear dynamic and adaptive to the changing world around them—a perspective that challenged the model of static, tradition-bound New Mexico Hispanos in literature and tourism brochures.

Originally published in 1960 (and reissued in 1964 and 1966), Circular 309, *Chile*, further entrenched an ingredient commonly used in Hispano homes into New Mexico cuisine and culture writ large.[65] As evidenced in the circular, by 1960, there appeared to be no question about the significance of chile to New Mexican foodways. Ruth Sneed, NMAES extension specialist in food marketing, recounted a history of chile that stretched back to the days of Spanish exploration and of which the agency played a significant part. For Sneed, the role of the NMAES was critical to making chile a popular commodity: "The new varieties developed didn't 'just happen' but were the result of careful planning and selection" under the direction of Dr. Fabian García, the Mexican-born horticulturalist and state Agricultural Experiment Station director.[66] Developed to vary in pungency, heat, and flavor and to fit different tastes, the chile became a symbol of the kind of negotiations and adaptations that shaped the NMAES for half a century: a local ingredient "improved" through the scientific methods embraced by the NMAES (at the hands of a Mexican horticulturalist, no less) was finding a place on the national table.

According to Sneed, no food was more representative of New Mexico than chile. In describing its centrality to New Mexico culture, she tapped into well-worn visual imagery found in tourism literature and, notably, in the 1951 glossy edition of *Historic Cookery*. Blurring agency priorities and boosterism, this edition of *Historic Cookery* featured photographs of New Mexico domestic scenes from the New Mexico Tourism Bureau and the US Soil Conservation Service, as well as Cabeza de Baca Gilbert's poetic reminiscences of "New Mexico's golden days, of red chile drying in the sun, of clean-swept yards, outdoor ovens, and adobe houses in the landscape."[67] This food-centered imagery inspired Sneed too. According to Sneed, the "landscape accented by the brilliant red of chile drying in the sun is a picture long remembered by natives and visitors alike. *No other scene is more typically New Mexican*, whether the ripe pods are hanging in ristras from the eaves of the home, spread in huge sheets on the ground, or on drying sheds."[68] Although nuevomexicanas' food work often remains either frozen in time and anonymous (as in the photographs) or completely unspoken in the text, it is present. After all, who is drying and hanging all of those chiles? Hispana labor and knowledge are necessary components of this nostalgic view.

Yet, for Sneed, chile was not just the stuff of nostalgia; it was a thoroughly modern staple. By 1960 buyers of all persuasions could find fresh, canned, frozen, and dried whole chiles and sauces, as well as powdered chili in grocery stores, restaurants, and roadside stands. In just a few years the popularity of chile precipitated the expansion of commercially produced chile products, and technological advancements in dehydration made New Mexico chile a more uniform and durable food product available for sale across the nation.[69] Consumers looking for premade foods could choose from a wide array of items: from sauces to combination meals, Mexican TV dinners, cocktail tacos, and burritos.[70] Though these items may have only marginally approximated more traditional New Mexican dishes, chile clearly was seen as a product worth consuming.

As a true product of New Mexico, chile itself was at once traditional and versatile, and its adaptability encouraged both traditional preparations and experimentation. This was reflected in the recipes included in *Chile*. Unlike previous circulars, the recipes did not come from the experiment station lab, but "from the kitchens of homemakers who thoroughly enjoy chile and wish to share their enjoyment with you," some of whom, based on contributors' names, were Hispanas.[71] The recipes asserted Hispanas' food knowledge and labor, as did the circular's illustrations. Quaint hand sketches of women hanging chiles, storing jars in the cupboard, and kneading masa may have enshrined a static vision of Hispano families, but their presence here also marks their contributions to the state's foodways nonetheless. In the section "Chile is easy to peel," photographs of hands (perhaps belonging to an Hispana cook) illustrated the process of roasting and peeling fresh chiles. Though chiles may be conveniently roasted on an electric stovetop or in a broiler on a baking sheet covered in foil, the tip of covering roasted chiles with a tea towel to steam off the skins represents the kind of local knowledge passed down from woman to woman in the kitchen.[72] It is clear that chile had found its place as a "typical" New Mexican food in the eyes of the NMAES. Hispanas played a significant part in making it so.

Conclusion

A focus on negotiation and collaboration on the pages of NMAES circulars in no way mitigates the real presence of power in the relationship between the agency and its intended audience. In many ways, the NMAES and its employees condescended to Hispano and native populations and their diets, pushing a socially constructed vision of nutritional science.[73] Budgetary priorities often left Native and Hispano populations with few resources and limited access to extension programming designed to give rural families a helping hand. Home demonstrators and circular authors sometimes presumed that their way was the best way, and their efforts were informed by the Anglo middle-class nature of reform in the early twentieth century. Most important, the legacy of conquest had firmly shaped the contours of life in New Mexico. As one NMAES report on nutrition in the state bleakly noted:

> The landholdings of many of these people [Hispanos] have dwindled in size and decreased in productivity until they can no longer support the people who live on them. Whenever possible, their owners supplement their incomes by working as laborers or migrant farm workers in New Mexico and neighboring states, especially Colorado and Utah. The younger members of the families are breaking away from the old homes to seek employment elsewhere. Once accustomed to producing most of their food at home, they now depend on the local store.[74]

For an agency that could be accused of being shortsighted, this was a clear recognition of the deeply systemic problems facing New Mexico's Spanish-speaking population. A recipe for enchiladas or chile con carne, or Edith Lantz's idea of adding dry milk to tortillas, could hardly solve the many problems facing Hispano families.

Still, a closer examination of agency circulars reveals that even if government agencies like the NMAES intended to completely alter the foodways of their rural clients, the result of their activities was decidely mixed. Lantz's tortilla experiment proved that Hispano foods were not going anywhere, and if the NMAES intended to spread its gospel of nutrition, it would have to meet its audience at a common table. The story of New Mexico cuisine as seen in NMAES publications opens up a conversation about how governmental agencies, designed to promote a strong sense of national identity through food production and consumption, actually came to reinforce an American ethnic regional cuisine. This was certainly the case in New Mexico, where NMAES publications allowed foods and recipes to cross ethnic borders, for, as anthropologist Arjun Appadurai explains, "[R]ecipes sometimes move where people may not."[75]

Home demonstration agents may have initially intended to bring modern technologies of cooking and food conservation to the homes of rural New Mexican families to make them more "American," but Hispana homemakers had their own ways of doing things—technologies, customs, and foods that had evolved across many generations, as well as their own sazón to add to the mix. While Hispana voices are often hidden, reading between the lines of the NMAES publications enables their interests to come into sharper relief. Agents may have carried with them negative views of the native and Mexican women they were to serve, but they could not ignore the demands and desires of their clients, and perhaps they learned something from them in the process. In the end, what emerges from the NMAES circulars is a regional cuisine that reflects a history of conflict and assimilation, but also compromise and adaptability, and that, by virtue of being published by a government agency, had its stamp of approval. The exchange found in the circulars was as much a part of the history of New Mexico as its chile and native legumes. It was truly the "New Mexican way."

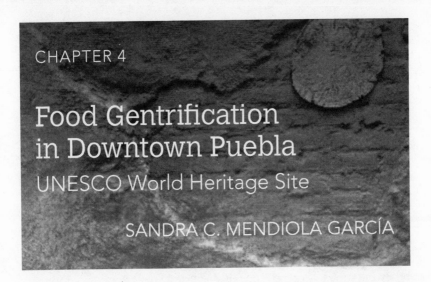

CHAPTER 4

Food Gentrification in Downtown Puebla
UNESCO World Heritage Site

SANDRA C. MENDIOLA GARCÍA

In September 2013, the travel section of the *New York Times* featured an article by Francine Prose entitled "Savoring the Pleasures of Puebla, Mexico" that described how visitors to the city enjoy the "best street food in Mexico."[1] Prose's favorite place is the Amparo Museum's coffee shop situated at the museum's rooftop where she can sip excellent coffee while working on her laptop. From this rooftop, customers can enjoy the magnificent view of downtown Puebla, which the United Nations Educational, Scientific and Cultural Organization (UNESCO) designated as a World Heritage Site in 1987. After describing some of Puebla's most visited places, Prose reminds readers that the reason why Mexicans go to Puebla is to eat. Indeed, she prefers "the city's street food ... But [she's] even more fond of the dishes served in the sorts of places that serve only one thing, places that you have to hunt down, or know someone who lives there, places that seem, like so much in Puebla, like the best sort of open secret." Except for a group of female vendors who sell *molotes* (deep fried tortillas stuffed with potatoes and other ingredients) in an alley, the author is not really talking about food sold literally on the streets. She is mainly referring to local food chains such as La Oriental that sells *tacos árabes* (Middle-Eastern-style tacos) and to a market of *cemitas* (large Pueblan sandwiches) located some blocks away from the *zócalo*, the main plaza at the heart of the city.[2]

The *New York Times* author captures how Puebla's downtown looks today to a tourist: some local food has to be hunted down. But there was a time when street food was not hidden, when no visitor had to ask anyone where to eat or buy it. Ironically, this was before the city's downtown became a UNESCO World Heritage Site in 1987. Dozens of street vendors, established market sellers, and mom-and-pop restaurant owners offered a wide variety of prepared and unprepared food. Puebla's downtown also housed the largest food market in the city, La Victoria, where a mostly lower- and working-class clientele could purchase fruits, meats, legumes, vegetables, and prepared food, such as *mole poblano* (the famous chocolate and chile-based sauce served over chicken, turkey, or tortillas) and cemitas, at affordable prices and in a casual setting.

The gentrification of downtown began taking place when, among other measures, local authorities displaced street vendors to municipal-built markets on the outskirts of the city and closed down La Victoria in the summer and fall of 1986, respectively.[3] Along with these policies, authorities gradually allowed the entrance of large national and international restaurant chains that, for the most part, had little to do with Mexican street food. These retailers, located in prime spaces in the city center, sell hamburgers, sandwiches, pizzas, ice cream, coffee beverages à la Starbucks, and some select, up-scale Mexican food. Since the mid-1980s, Puebla has experienced the homogenization of food choices that target a middle- and upper-class clientele. This change has resulted in a decrease in the number of local mom-and-pop restaurants and the disappearance of street vendors and market vendors from the heart of the city. Prices of food in downtown have also increased exponentially, making it as expensive as fashionable cities in the First World. In December 2013, one scoop of ice cream in Santa Clara, a shop some feet away from the Cathedral, was valued at 45 pesos (3.44 USD), and a 12-ounce regular coffee at 22 pesos (1.68 USD). These prices are extremely expensive in a region whose daily minimum wage is 61.38 pesos (4.70 USD). Without a doubt, these eateries are completely out of reach to working-class people who, before the mid-1980s, had access to a less expensive and wider variety of local food.

This process in Puebla, and in other cities in Mexico, seems paradoxical, especially as Mexican street food and peasant ingredients (i.e., *jícamas*, blue corn, grasshoppers) have become fashionable in cities of the Global North. Food trucks, taco stands, as well as high-end Mexican eateries have reached public spaces and trendy neighborhoods in cities like London, Portland, and New York City. In London, for instance, at a chain of restaurants named "Wahaca Mexican Market Eating," people can find "real Mexican food."[4] Its British owners claim, "[W]e're taking street food back to the streets in our mobile restaurants. We currently have two Mexican Street Kitchen's [sic] serving up a selection of delicious burritos, tacos, and salads to satisfy more people's Mexican craving on-the-go."[5] Other places like Portland, Oregon, praise themselves for having food carts in parks, parking lots, and sidewalks. Featuring food from all over the world, more than seventy food carts and trucks sell Mexican food, from *tortas* to *tlayudas* (large tortillas topped with beans, cheese, meat, and vegetables). According to street food enthusiasts, "[C]arts help create a vibrant downtown and central city by bringing what planning geeks call a 'social fabric on the street' which is great in cultural terms, but in economic terms also attract other spenders, retail outlets, and restaurants and cafes."[6] While many cities are creating and recreating a "social fabric on the street," Puebla's downtown has witnessed a different phenomenon: from the mid-1980s on, the heart of the city substituted popular prepared and unprepared street foods for globalized chains of international and local foods that targeted a middle- and upper-class clientele.

Focusing on downtown Puebla, this chapter examines the changes in food availability after 1987, when Puebla's so-called historic downtown became inscribed on the UNESCO World Heritage Site list. It seeks to explain why these changes took place and how the gentrification of downtown affected the food that *poblanos* and tourists ate when consuming in the city center. This chapter also demonstrates the effects that gentrification has upon the availability of food and the negative economic consequences for street vendors and working-class consumers. This chapter argues that there is an intrinsic paradox in the aftermath of Puebla's downtown inclusion on the UNESCO World Heritage Site list in 1987. As part of the process of obtaining this title, local authorities and elites committed to protect and preserve the so-called historic downtown.[7] In order to "safeguard" what constituted the historical aspects of downtown, the municipal government decided to close down the largest food market and to relocate all street vendors to the outskirts of the city. As a result of this removal and subsequent policies to gentrify downtown, the wide variety of foods that these mostly working-class people sold was increasingly replaced by food offered by chains of restaurants linked to the global economy, which in turn occupied prime locations at the heart of the city.

Downtown Puebla and Food Availability before 1987

The landlocked city of Puebla is Mexico's fourth-largest metropolis, situated only eighty miles southeast of the country's capital. Besides its centuries-old production of textiles, colorful ceramics (*talavera*), and the twentieth-century manufacturing of the old Volkswagen Beetle, Puebla is known nationally and internationally for its local cuisine. Puebla's cooks delight people with *mole poblano, chiles en nogada* (stuffed poblano peppers topped with a walnut-based sauce and sprinkled with pomegranate seeds and parsley leaves), and *pipián verde* (pumpkin and sesame seed-based sauce). Puebla's *dulces típicos*, especially *camotes* (yam-based candy), have also attracted thousands of people.[8] Most of these dishes are highly labor intensive to prepare. They require dozens of ingredients and many hours of preparation and care. Some, like chiles en nogada, are seasonal; their irreplaceable ingredients are found only in the late summer. Other less elaborate foods such as *chalupas* (small tortillas covered with green or red pepper sauce and shredded meat), *molotes, chanclas* (a kind of Mexican sandwich in red sauce), *tacos al pastor*, and *tacos árabes* are also characteristic of Puebla's local offerings. Mexicans refer to these foods as *antojitos*, snacks that are very appealing to the appetite at all hours, especially at night. Cemitas, another local favorite, are large round bread filled with cheese, avocado, and a flavorful herb called *papaloquelite*. Customers select the meat filling: chicken, *milanesa* (breaded pork), or pata (vinegar-based pork feet). Cemitas constitute a full and satisfying meal.

Many of Puebla's most famous dishes and antojitos have been sold by mom-and-pop restaurateurs, by hundreds of street vendors, and by established marketers downtown. Many have hawked their products on the streets in pushcarts; others set up semi-fixed stalls in corners, parks, outside churches, doorways, or inside private patios. Camote vendors, for instance, sold their boiled yam with unrefined brown sugar (*piloncillo*) in pushcarts that produced a particular whistle that everyone recognized.

Street vendors of prepared and unprepared foods always tried to find the busiest public spaces to offer their merchandise. As a basic business strategy, downtown represented the best area to sell. Up to the mid-1980s, Puebla's city center housed most economic, educational, religious, and bureaucratic activity. Department stores, small-sized shops, public markets, banks, bus stations, the state university, churches, and municipal and state government offices were all located at the heart of the city. Some of the busiest streets were those surrounding the two major public markets, La Victoria and the Cinco de Mayo.

One of them, La Victoria, became the most important and busiest market in the city. It dated back to the nineteenth century as an open-air market (*tianguis*), and then it transformed into a rather impressive neoclassical two-story building during the Porfiriato (1876–1911).[9] Hundreds of established marketers with fixed stalls inside and street vendors outside sold as many products as the mind can imagine: handmade tortillas, beans, all sorts of chiles (*ancho, mulato, chipotle, verde*), cheese, fruits, vegetables, legumes, *chorizos*, chicken, beef, and seafood. La Victoria's fame attracted local customers and people from surrounding towns and states.

La Victoria's customers could reward themselves by eating prepared food after doing their shopping at the market. People could enjoy a plate of mole sauce with chicken and rice sold by the many female marketers who cooked this dish. Indeed, a visit to La Victoria was a must for any local or tourist. Customers also found *comidas corridas*, inexpensive menus that consisted of two kinds of soups, a main dish, a drink, and a dessert. People remember the market as a place where "everybody" could go eat and find Puebla's specialties, such as mole, cemitas, and home food (*comida casera*), at affordable prices.[10]

The hundreds of street vendors outside the market became a magnet to a mostly working-class clientele. Vendors sold a wide range of products in small quantities at cheap prices and during long hours in strategic locations. Oranges, bananas, limes, tomatoes, cheese, and fish were among the most common products available.[11] The so-called *vendedores propios* were sellers who came to downtown Puebla from the countryside to sell, for a limited period of time, products that were seasonal or only grown in specific locations and usually not available inside the market or in supermarkets. For instance, these vendors sold *aguacates criollos*, peaches, *nopales*, and figs. Depending on the time of the year, street vendors also had the flexibility to sell seasonal food (*comida de temporada*) and other products like sugar cane, peanuts, *tejocotes*, guavas, *romeritos* for Christmas, and *pan de muerto* for Day of the Dead (sweet bread flavored with anise seeds and orange flower water, and decorated with sesame seeds). The rest of the year the common foods were chalupas, cemitas, chanclas, *molotes*, and *tacos de canasta* (soft tacos usually sold by women carrying them in large baskets). The fact that vendors sold on the streets allowed customers to buy their merchandise as they walked to their bus stops or returned home from their workplaces.

Another favorite space for vendors was *los portales*, the colon-naded arches that surround the city's four-century-old main plaza, the zócalo. The portales are symbolic of the heart of downtown where both secular and religious authorities are well represented. The Municipal Palace and the Cathedral, for instance, are both situated around the zócalo. For decades, small- and medium-sized established businesses and street vendors sold food in this prime and highly contested space. Over time, owners of bakeries, restaurants, and *torterías* shared spaces with street vendors who had fixed, semi-fixed, and mobile stalls in the portales. Municipal records show that often times there were tensions between the more-affluent restaurant owners and their less-privileged counterparts, the street vendors.[12]

For decades, La Princesa, La Flor de Puebla, and the restaurant of the Hotel Royalty were some of the most famous restaurants in the portales. These mom-and-pop restaurants set out tables and chairs outside their locales where clients sat down in a rather European fashion. Different genres of Mexican musicians played their instruments and made their living off tips from the restaurant clientele and the many pedestrians who enjoyed their performances. Senior folks danced *danzón*, a genre of African influences that arrived via Veracruz from Cuba.[13] On weekends and a few other nights, some restaurants actually hired marimba. Customers of restaurants such as La Princesa requested musicians to play their favorite pieces. In short, the portales housed not only a wide variety of local foods, but also a number of cultural practices like dancing and listening to music, which by the twenty-first century are almost extinct in this particular space.

Products and Vendors

From municipal archival documents, we know the kinds of foods that street vendors sold and the gender composition of the trade. In petitions to authorities, vendors or vendors-to-be identified the particular products they sold or wanted to sell. Usually men specialized in selling prepared food that did not require much preparation in anticipation to its sale. For example, men sold ice cream (*nieves* and *helados*), *camotes*, corn on the cob (*elotes*) and *esquites*, *tortas* (Mexican-style sandwiches in a special bread called *torta*), and cut fruit with chile and lime.[14]

Adult women typically cooked and sold foods requiring more elaborate preparation, from the time-consuming mole to chalupas, enchiladas, molotes, tacos de canasta, and chanclas.[15] Mole, for instance, requires over a dozen ingredients, and its preparation takes a few days' work. Female vendors prepared most of these foods, such as the chalupas, gorditas, enchiladas, chanclas, cemitas, molotes, and tostadas, right in front of the customers who then enjoyed a freshly made meal.

Based on archival photographs taken in the 1960s and 1970s, we know that some of these vendors, especially those who sold fruits and vegetables, appeared to be rural women who had ventured to the city to sell their products.[16] Their hair braided in the fashion of rural women, these vendors wore *rebozos* to carry merchandise, to wrap their infants and toddlers around their backs, or to cover their bodies and protect themselves from the cold or from the sun's rays. They sat on the ground and placed their merchandise over open burlap or plastic bags that they used as mats. These vendors came from the countryside to the city for a couple of days to sell products that they grew in their communities. Due to the distance traveled or because of the cost, these women did not have semi-fixed stalls.

Other vendors set up empty wood cases of fruit and used them as tables to display their products.[17] Those with more capital, if modest, used *carritos* (carts), not only to display merchandise, but also to allow some mobility in case of police raids. In more recent years, some used supermarket carts to prepare and carry their foods. Yet, others had semi-fixed stalls. Archival photographs demonstrate that these stalls were quite simple and consisted of a table, an *anafre* (brazier), and a chair. The more successful vendors had a few more chairs and tables to entertain their customers.

Prepared food vendors needed their family members to help toward the success of their trade. The helper usually served as cashier, as the provider of sodas and napkins, and as the one who cleared the tables. In short, the *vendedoras* handling the food almost always preferred to keep their hands as clean as possible touching only the food. Facing health authorities' constant attacks from their alleged lack of hygiene, vendors tried to present themselves as very fastidious, with some of them wearing aprons and putting their hair up in a ponytail.

Benefits to a Working-Class Clientele

People of almost all socioeconomic backgrounds ran errands and shopped for products downtown. But it was a mostly low-income clientele that usually bought from street vendors because vendors offered cheap merchandise in small quantities. Furthermore, working-class consumers with tight schedules enjoyed street vendors extended hours of service. Consumers of street prepared foods were typically low- and mid-level state employees (janitors, police, secretaries), people in the service sector (store attendants), students, low-budget travelers, and those engaged in the informal economy such as maids, shoe-shine boys, prostitutes, and newspaper vendors.[18]

Street vendors played a significant economic role. In a march that a group of street vendors organized in the fall of 1973, one female vendor addressed fellow vendors, blue-collar workers, and students. She argued, "[S]treet vendors carry out an important function that benefits the *pueblo*. Facing economic crisis, street vendors' cheap products help reduce the cost of living, offering better prices than established businesses."[19] Certainly, she was not the only one who knew this to be the case.

Authorities also understood that street vendors fulfilled the centuries long, informal, and important role of providing cheap products to the lower classes. Precisely for this reason, authorities allowed vendors to set up their stalls in public spaces until the mid-1980s.[20] Indeed, several scholars have shown that municipal authorities tended to tolerate their presence. Historian Ingrid Bleynat originally used the term "compassion" to refer to authorities' Catholic moral obligation to allow street vendors to make a decent living during the second half of the nineteenth century.[21] The anthropologist Judith Marti noted in her study of Porfirian Mexico (1876–1911) that politicians understood the need to provide cheap products to the urban poor as a way to subsidize their meager or nonexistent incomes.[22] Municipal archival documents in Puebla also suggest the same trend. In 1923, for instance, Puebla's mayor responded to a letter written by members of the Cámara Nacional de Comercio (CANACO), a businessmen's association, who demanded the removal of street vendors. The mayor replied that if authorities under his command removed vendors, they would violate street vendors' freedom of commerce. Officials even claimed that vendors were *gente humilde* who did not pose a major threat to the economic interests of others.[23]

Not all showed tolerance. Some authorities had tried to ban street vending. Depending on the mayor in power, and the pressure he received from the established business community, street vendors faced temporary removals, threats, and police harassment. On occasions, authorities did not grant selling permits to vendors; at other times, municipal workers violently seized vendors' merchandise in an effort to discourage people from selling in public spaces. On at least one occasion, in October 1973, local police tried to remove vendors from downtown using excessive violence, resulting in the death of several people. Vendors resisted their removal by confronting police, organizing, and defiantly returning to their selling spots.[24]

Changes in the Mid-1980s: Expelling Street Vendors

In 1986, the relative tolerance of street vending came to an end when authorities officially announced the definite removal of vendors from downtown as well as the closure of La Victoria, the oldest and largest market in town. How does one explain this sudden change? By the mid-1980s, local authorities had been devising Puebla's inclusion on the UNESCO World Heritage Site list. In the application process, both local and national authorities promised to continue their efforts in "safeguarding" the historic and monumental downtown area.[25] Among others, these efforts consisted of the removal of street vendors from the city center.[26]

City boosters, authorities, and the upper classes used many of the street vendors' practices against them. Vendors' appearance, products, location, clientele, and supposed lack of modernity and hygiene did not make them the kinds of citizens who should populate a World Heritage Site. The socioeconomic status of female vendors and their male counterparts kept them from being modern urban people; they were traditional lower-class vendors, some of whom came from the countryside and who mostly attracted a lower-class clientele. Both vendors and consumers represented an eyesore to the heart of the city. Additionally, health authorities stated that food vendors and La Victoria market posed a public health threat. In their view, vendors violated the most basic hygienic rules. Puebla's chief of public health argued that street vendors did not have access to running water and could not wash their hands, which polluted the foods they sold.[27] Some of the vendors' products were not covered and were exposed to air pollution. Other sellers did not have refrigeration systems and their products decomposed quickly. The rhetoric of the time was one of rescue: authorities and city boosters needed to "rescue" downtown from the lower classes' unhygienic business practices and make it available to those who, in their view, really valued the monumental downtown.[28] Only middle- and upper-class people, who were supposedly modern and educated, were capable of appreciating and understanding the history and the architectonical worth of certain buildings in the historic downtown.[29] Analyzing Puebla's gentrification, urban geographers Gareth Jones and Ann Varley have argued that these middle-class groups also identified themselves as racially and morally superior to the vendors who most likely were of indigenous descent. For these reasons, the middle classes felt the need to complete the "reconquest" of the city center and substitute the people who used these spaces: from working class to middle and upper class.[30] But as we will see later, this substitution went beyond the people to include the replacement of their cultural practices.

At the end of the summer of 1986, the city government, headed by Mayor Jorge Murad Macluf, finally expelled all street vendors from downtown. Through a series of negotiations with street vendors' leaders, and with the promise of relocating them to newly built public markets on the outskirts of the city, all vendors, willingly or not, left the city center.[31] Their removal meant that these vendors became invisible to those who visited, inhabited, and worked in Puebla's so-called historic center. At the same time, lower-class consumers could no longer access local food and other products in the streets most convenient to their everyday travel to and from work.[32] Some of these customers had to wait until the markets on the outskirts were finished and until public transportation vehicles reached these markets.

Closing La Victoria

The street vendors' removal was followed by the closure of La Victoria market in mid-October 1986. Local politicians and health authorities claimed that La Victoria was in terrible shape and that it also posed a threat to public health. Despite marketers' efforts to engage in campaigns to kill rodents, which they called *campañas de desratización*,[33] La Victoria was infested with rats. When authorities submitted Puebla's downtown application to be included on the UNESCO World Heritage Site list, they pointed out with pride that they had been working to "safeguard La Victoria Market" since the early 1980s.[34] Without a doubt, safeguarding the market meant emptying it of the undesirable population: market vendors, their customers, and the rodents.

By October of 1986, in the midst of great controversy and resistance from market vendors, approximately 15,000 sellers, their employees, and family members left La Victoria.[35] After the last marketer left, municipal workers immediately began destroying stalls. Authorities' and city boosters' original plan consisted of renovating the market and allowing some marketers to return to it once it was finished. Arguing that La Victoria did not attract tourists in its existing form, authorities sought to transform it into a "folkloric market" (*un mercado típico*) that would house small-sized restaurants, ice-cream shops, sandal stores, and flower shops.[36]

Some six years later, in 1992, municipal authorities changed their minds and lent the almost-renovated building to a private philanthropic organization, the Fundación Amparo, for a span of ninety-nine years.[37] Arguing that the market was an "integral part of Puebla's historical center," authorities claimed that La Victoria "needed to be architecturally preserved."[38] And no entity, in their view, could preserve it as competently as the Amparo Foundation. At the time, Manuel Espinosa Yglesias (1909–2000) led the Amparo Foundation and was also the head of the William Jenkins Foundation. Both organizations, especially the Jenkins Foundation, had invested millions in renovating downtown Puebla. Espinosa Yglesias (former CEO of Bancomer) had other larger projects in mind that eventually brought economic benefits to a small group of entrepreneurs.[39] In 1994, the Amparo Foundation opened the doors of the building that once housed the market and was now transformed into a shopping center, Centro Comercial La Victoria.[40]

In what used to be La Victoria Market, two Walmart-owned retailers were launched, Suburbia, a department store, and Vips, a mid-level restaurant. Vips was just one of over two hundred restaurants, which included El Potrón, Ragazzi, and La Finca, and supermarkets (Aurrera and Superma), all of which were operated by the Mexican retail conglomerate CIFRA until 1991. In that year, Walmart purchased these restaurants together with other retails.[41] In short, Vips replaced the hundreds of food vendors at La Victoria.[42]

At Vips, which resembles a combination of an American diner and an International House of Pancakes (IHOP), middle-class customers can have breakfast, lunch, and dinner. Its rather extensive menu, which is the same in all of Mexico's Vips, features "traditional" Mexican food such as sopa de tortilla, enchiladas, and tostadas, as well as a wide range of American-style food such as burgers, fries, and pancakes. Certain "specials," such as Puebla's chiles en nogada, are available depending on the time of the year. The prices for menu items are considerably higher than what prepared food vendors used to charge at La Victoria.

Today, the former La Victoria market is a semi-open-spaced shopping center that also houses small-sized shops, and kiosks that sell clothes, leather bags, underwear, jewelry, Chinese-made trinkets, cell phones, and beauty products. Customers can also get a haircut in one of the two hair salons, and get a massage in one of the kiosks. There is an arcade in the middle of the plaza, and a train for children, which runs inside the building. Food at La Victoria includes a selection of hamburgers, fries, nachos, chips, and hotdogs sold in kiosks. An ice-cream shop is located at the center of the shopping plaza. The former market's second floor features a rather unpopular food court with seven small-sized food stands. Four of the seven sell Mexican food (*pozole, caldo tlalpeño, mole, carnitas*), and the other three sell pizzas, crepes, and hotdogs.

The Gentrification of los Portales

The highly contested nature of los portales, the set of colonnade arches that surround the main plaza, due to their location made it increasingly difficult for street vendors to sell their products. Even small-sized mom-and-pop restaurants had a hard time keeping their businesses open. Although these restaurants were very popular and well attended, municipal authorities managed these spaces (*locales*) at los portales. As Puebla gentrified and as municipal authorities continued renting public spaces to large-scale retailers, mom-and-pop restaurants were forced to close. Of course, authorities had a harder time expelling these restaurateurs than the street vendors. The first restaurant to go out of business was La Flor de Puebla. Others resisted for a longer period, such as La Princesa, which closed down in 2007 after fifty years in operation. The empty spaces were then rented to more profitable businesses of food and other products, such as Telcel, the mobile communications company owned by business magnate Carlos Slim Helú.[43]

Today, Puebla's famous portales houses a mixture of local and international food chains and a few new mom-and-pop restaurants that sell their food to mostly middle-class consumers. These eateries include places like Santa Clara (ice creams), La Antigua Churrería (*churros*), Mi Viejo Pueblito (Mexican food), and the Italian Coffee Company (beverages). Since the 1990s, an increasing number of franchises of

American foods, some of them owned by the Alsea group, have opened in the portales: Burger King, McDonald's, Subway, and Domino's Pizza. In fact, McDonald's, the first American food franchise to operate in this space, and which used to occupy a rather small area on the ground floor of the portales, has now expanded vertically to a second and a third floor some feet away from the Municipal Palace.[44] From the terrace, customers can observe the zócalo and one of the country's most impressive cathedrals while eating hamburgers and fries.

Transnational corporations or large food conglomerates own some of these eateries. One such example is Santa Clara, an ice cream and dairy products shop that started operations modestly in the 1920s.[45] It has constantly grown and expanded and was recently bought by Femsa, a large food and drink conglomerate that is partially owned by Coca-Cola. Femsa also owns OXXO, a chain of convenience stores that, for some time, had a presence in one of los portales, a few steps away from McDonald's. A similar phenomenon occurred with the Italian Coffee Company, the local coffee shop. Started by a *poblano* of Italian descent in 1996, the Italian Coffee Company grew exponentially with great success and soon became a local franchise with approximately 388 establishments all over Mexico. Puebla now has about sixty-four coffee shops, two of which are located at los portales where customers sip coffee of low quality, choosing from Americanos to pricey Frappuccinos.[46]

The gentrification process occurring in Puebla is what Oaxaca-based painter Francisco Toledo calls a "*comercialización salvaje*" (savage commercialization), the "reckless disregard for the unique and irreplaceable."[47] Authorities have justified the need to carry out this gentrification process to increase tourism. But much of the food that Puebla's downtown now offers to locals and tourists can be purchased at any strip mall in the United States.

The Transformation of the Downtown *Barrios*

What happened in and around La Victoria and in los portales is part of a larger trend that spread to another area of downtown that also witnessed its gentrification. In the eastern part of downtown, at what used to be old working-class neighborhoods, state and private capitals

McDonald's at Portal Hidalgo, downtown Puebla. March 2015. Courtesy of Dana Albicker Mendiola.

dramatically transformed the barrios of El Alto, La Luz, and Analco from 1993 to 1998. Forcefully expelling old-time residents of this area and demolishing the *vecindades* (tenements) that they inhabited, some without any financial compensation, state and private funds built a convention center, a shopping mall, movie theaters, and a three-story parking lot. In the new shopping mall, many restaurants opened featuring Italian, Japanese, French, and American food. As anthropologist Nancy Churchill points out, in order to eat *mole poblano*, one must skip the mall, and find the open-air restaurants.[48]

Indeed, some food vendors have managed to remain in certain areas of downtown, but their conditions are far from ideal. These vendors are almost invisible to nonlocals and must have the financial resources necessary to pay for permits. For instance, about a dozen chalupa vendors have found spaces next to a middle-class open-space market of handcrafts in the old neighborhood of Analco. They can only sell during the weekends and they must acquire permits from the municipality to do so. Other food vendors have survived the increasing gentrification of downtown because they are located away from the zócalo. Some mom-and-pop small-sized restaurants (*fondas*) and *torterias* (shops that sell Mexican-style sandwiches) continue to exist about five blocks north of the main plaza in what has remained a largely working-class section of downtown close to the Cinco de Mayo Market.

There are also "invisible vendors" who provide food for people who work downtown. These vendors do not have stalls. Instead, they sell food in the interior of the buildings where their customers labor.[49] Other food sellers are less invisible. Their relative invisibility has to do with the limited time when they can sell. For instance, the American Subway restaurant at the portales displaced a female taco seller from her decades-long spot in the *pasaje del ayuntamiento* (the hallway between two of the portales). She moved some twenty meters away from her old spot to a corner in the same *pasaje* outside of a shoe store. She and her helpers only stay there for about three hours a day at lunchtime to offer her big tacos de canasta. The vendor puts together two tortillas and fills them with a choice of over ten fillings that include potatoes and chorizo, nopales, rice, eggs, *milanesa*, and *lengua*. Each taco, which is rather sizable, is sold for 21 pesos (1.59 USD). Her customers continue to follow her even though her new spot is somewhat hidden and her hours of operation are limited. Indeed, street vendors' relative invisibility and informality are conditions that allow them to exist in Puebla's gentrified downtown.

Conclusions

This chapter has traced some of the major changes that have occurred in downtown Puebla since the mid-1980s. In 1987, Puebla's downtown became a UNESCO World Heritage Site. In preparation for this designation, local authorities and city boosters took certain measures to assure Puebla's inclusion on this list. Among them was the removal of street vendors from the heart of the city as well as the closure of the largest food market in the summer and early fall of 1986 respectively. After this date, many changes occurred in relation to the availability and choices of prepared and unprepared foods at the heart of the city. At a slow but constant pace, the city center began to gentrify, and, with it, a number of local and global chains of restaurants began popping up all over downtown. Today, downtown features Domino's Pizza, McDonald's, Burger King, and franchises of Mexican and international food such as Vips and Shirushi (Japanese food). The introduction of these eating establishments has led to the displacement of street vendors and mom-and-pop restaurants from prime spaces, which has made life even more difficult for them and for consumers with limited purchasing power. In short, today's working-class people have a hard time making a living and finding inexpensive street food and local specialties at the heart of the city.[50]

The forced departure of small-sized restaurateurs, marketers, and street vendors also resulted in the erasure of popular foodways. Their presence had given the city center a working-class identity that involved customers from modest socioeconomic backgrounds from both the city and the countryside. Since the mid-1980s, this working-class identity has changed with the entrance of food conglomerates that specifically target the upper and middle classes.

The changes that downtown Puebla has experienced in the last few decades show the potential risks that large-scale economic actors introduce at the expense of ordinary people. These transformations seem particularly ironic as Mexican food has reached many corners around the world where taco stands, Mexican eateries, and peasant ingredients, such as blue corn, *cuitlacoche*, chiles, cacti, *jícamas*, and grasshoppers, have become a major attraction in places such as London, Portland, and New York City. Yet, scholars must analyze how savage (and not-so-savage) commercialization has occurred across space and time. For instance, to what extent have large-scale investors displaced mom-and-pop Mexican food restaurateurs and street vendors in the United States? What kind of knowledge about Mexican food and its preparation have restaurant chains reproduced? Are upscale eateries dramatically changing popular and working-class foods brought by several generations of ordinary Mexicans? Is Mexican food somehow safer and more palatable when it is created by well-read and well-traveled Anglo and Mexican chefs and mixed with local ingredients? Are restaurants such as Frontera Grill only reserved for a selected few?

Certainly, not everyone in the Global North can afford a meal in trendy Mexican food restaurants. Food historian Jeffrey Pilcher was right when he warned us about the future of Mexican food: the gentrification will result in the appropriation "of peasant cooking for a sophisticated, international elite [and] factory-made tortillas or Taco Bell for the masses, both in Mexico and abroad."[51] Of course, one should be aware that in Mexico the masses cannot afford to dine in many American-based eateries, just like many people cannot afford a meal in hip Mexican food trucks in the USA or Europe.

A final irony in Puebla's case is the fact that in 2010 "[t]raditional Mexican cuisine-ancestral, ongoing community culture, the Michoacán paradigm," was inscribed on the Representative List of the UNESCO Intangible Cultural Heritage of Humanity. Accordingly, this list enhances "the visibility of intangible cultural heritage and promote[s] respect for cultural diversity and human creativity." The UNESCO committee identified that "traditional Mexican cuisine is central to the cultural identity of the communities that practice and transmit it from generation to generation." The 2010 nomination file clearly stated that "to salvage this culinary system as a unit, concentrated efforts must be made in communities in Michoacán and other hubs of culinary knowledge," such as Puebla, "in need of protective measures."[52] Yet, authorities in Puebla continue to support exactly the opposite: the removal of popular food and its vendors from important spaces, including the city center, declared a World Heritage Site by UNESCO.

CHAPTER 5

From Working the Farm to Fast Food and Back Again

Rural Mexicans in the Neoliberal Food System

ELIZABETH FITTING

You know there's a sick joke amongst older farmers here because the average age of a farmer in the United States is approaching sixty right now ... in ten years the average age of the American farmer is going to be dead. Nonetheless, this country is full of farmers! They are standing on street corners looking for work. They come from Mexico, Honduras, Nicaragua, Guatemala, Colombia, Panama. They've been displaced! They mow our lawns, they pump our gas, they cook our food in fancy restaurants, those are farmers. We're surrounded by farmers. They're out of work.

—ERIC HOLT-GIMÉNEZ, food scholar, activist, and executive director of Food First, speaking in Seattle, 1999[1]

Juan is a returned migrant of twenty-six. He left school when he was fourteen to find work in a neighboring town and help support his seven siblings. In the late 1990s, at the age of eighteen, Juan decided to head north to Oregon, where he had an aunt and a cousin who could help him get settled. He borrowed money from a local lender to pay the $1,600 fee to a guide (coyote) to cross the US-Mexico border. The first job he got was washing dishes at a fast food restaurant. Although he had originally planned to work for three years and return home, he decided to stay longer, in part to learn how to speak English. Juan explains that he spent the first four years in the United States working to help support his parents and siblings back in his hometown of San José. He sent $200 a month back to his family to help with their upkeep, his sister's education, a small *milpa* (cornfield), and the cost of building an addition to the house. At his next job, as a waiter, he was able to save for a car and the construction costs of his own house in San José. He also opened a small store that operates out of his house. After traveling back and forth over the years Juan decided to move back to San José in 2004. He now lives with his wife and two children in the house he saved to build. Since he does not grow corn or work in the fields, he purchases his grain from the market in a neighboring town, where it is slightly cheaper. Like other migrants his age, he lacks experience and interest in *maize* agriculture. He is unsure about whether he can support his family without returning to the United States for work in the future.[2]

Rural Mexicans play an integral role in the North American[3] food system. While some grow food for their own communities and even for export, others are im/migrant workers on farms, in fast food restaurants, in meat-packing and poultry plants, and staff in restaurants in the United States and, to a lesser extent, Canada. Capitalism, particularly in its neoliberal phase, pushes rural food producers into migrant streams; at home, they face increased usurpation of their resources and mounting environmental and economic hardships, and in response, seek out earnings in urban centers and across national borders. The above quote by Holt-Giménez importantly highlights this process of rural displacement and farmers' search for work abroad. What it does not touch on is what migrant workers desire. Would they rather be farming?

The answer to this question depends on who you talk to and when you talk to them. Based on research in the southern Tehuacán Valley agricultural town of San José Miahuatlán (Puebla) from 2000 to 2008 (for different durations, with some more recent follow-up interviews),[4] I found that migrants from their teens into their early thirties prefer work in the US food sector rather than in Mexican agriculture despite the considerable risks of undocumented status and employment in the United States. "There is no money in the *milpa*," I was told many times over the years. However, generations differ in their attitudes about, and their knowledge of, agriculture. Young migrants discuss corn agriculture as burdensome work, unprofitable, and even as a backward tradition, while older residents describe agriculture as a dignified livelihood, which is linked to their identities as *campesinos*.[5] Since older residents view the cultivation of maize as a social safety net, the question remains whether or not young migrants will take up agriculture as they age; however, the economic, social, and environmental conditions for them to do so are increasingly difficult.

In this chapter I look at how valley migrants and indigenous campesinos fare under the contemporary food system[6]—or the shift to neoliberal policies and processes related to food and agriculture—and it also attends to the agency of residents in navigating these processes. It illustrates how interconnected the food system is across national borders and across a range of jobs and social locations. In addition to ensuring a steady supply of inexpensive food in the United States,[7] rural Mexicans are integral to the Mexican food supply as peasants because they produce food, especially maize, for local and—depending on the farmer—national consumption, and they maintain native varieties (*criollos*)[8] of maize in their fields. Peasants and migrant workers typically come from the same rural households; in some cases, they are one and the same, working in different areas of the food system at different moments in their lives. In other cases, migrants are children of campesinos and their earnings help maintain their parents' households or establish their own homes in the valley.

This raises questions about the role of generational groups in social reproduction, or how residents of different age groups maintain and advance their households ("simple" or "expanded" reproduction), and at another level, how their livelihood strategies are a creative response to, and in turn contribute to, the current capitalist food system. Capitalism draws rural agriculturalists into the world of waged labor, but it simultaneously differentiates and segments: within the same communities some benefit more than others, and experiences are shaped by gender, class, ethnic, and generational locations. In the valley, indigenous campesinos, depending on their age, resources, and gender, reproduce their households and families through maize agriculture, unpaid labor in the home, work in the valley poultry industry and clothing *maquiladoras* (assembly plants), and migration to the United States (and sometimes Canada) for employment in the restaurant and food processing sectors.[9]

This case study helps to challenge the romantizication of rural life, particularly of indigenous and campesino communities, found in some food activism and scholarship.[10] When rural life is romanticized some important dynamics are missed. For example, not enough attention is paid to the pull of capitalism—access to consumer goods and the promise of waged employment or making a profit on agricultural goods, which is, most of the time, not fully realized. Similarly, instead of treating rural communities as homogenous and conflict-free, we should consider how social differences and inequality *within* communities, and even households, are engaged and negotiated as rural populations increasingly diversify their livelihoods, relying on the cash markets for goods and labor. Finally, romanticizing rural life can also attribute migrants' hard work to a cultural disposition, which naturalizes their exploitation and subordination.

Corn and Capitalism: Social Reproduction and Rural Life

> *In times of crisis, when social services collapse or cannot effectively carry out their functions, corn's importance becomes self-evident. Recourse to corn is the last line of defense for security, for hope, for the retreat of lesser units of society in order to defend their very existence.*
>
> —ARTURO WARMAN[11]

In his book *Corn & Capitalism*, Mexican anthropologist Arturo Warman traces the history of maize from Mesoamerica to its emergence as a global staple crop.[12] Corn, he argues, is a particularly important crop for looking at how peasants fared under modern capitalism, as well as its relationship of capital to labor and other resources. Not only was corn the quintessential peasant crop of the Americas, it also was the key crop in the development of the commercial seed industry[13] and remains pivotal to the reproduction of rural life in Mexico today.

Political economy in anthropology, like the work of Warman, approaches capitalism as an economic system that has social, cultural, environmental, and political characteristics that play out in particular ways, in particular places, or as a "history of diversity."[14] While anthropologists have studied food since the emergence of the discipline, the study of food as a commodity—as a good produced for exchange—began later. In the 1950s anthropologists working in Latin America became interested in what commodities tell us about power, particularly unequal social relations and state practices.[15] Commodities embody the labor that went into making them and the system under which they are made. Scholars turn to the work of Karl Marx, who wrote in the nineteenth century, for thinking about commodities. He argued that commodities are fetishized under capitalism: that we worship the goods we buy, placing value in them as discrete objects rather than valuing the labor that made them.[16] The market mediates our understanding of where goods come from and, in the process, obscures the unequal and exploitative social relations involved in their making. Commodity fetishism normalizes inequality and exploitative labor conditions, and an important part of this normalization is how commodities, and the system in which they are made, are represented and framed. In recent years, food activism has taken up aspects of this approach—with different degrees of success—asking us to consider where our food comes from and what we know about the lives of those who farm, process, and serve our foods. As part of this line of inquiry, though, we need to understand the broader system of inequality and exploitation in which food producers and workers are located, as well as consider how food workers and producers feed themselves and their families.

Today's food system has its origins in capitalism and colonialism,[17] and it has undergone changes at different historical moments. With the implementation of neoliberal policies in the 1980s, there was an increase in nontraditional food exports from the Global South (fruits, vegetables, and meat), the continued export of subsidized grain from the Global North, the expansion of supermarket chains, the consolidation of agribusiness, the financialization of markets, the liberalization of trade, and the increasing precariousness of rural livelihoods.[18] Today's food system is also characterized by the rise of genetic engineering as the main technology for capitalist agriculture and by changes in regulation at national and international levels, which accommodate this technology.[19]

Agricultural life is always vulnerable to conditions beyond the farmer's control to a degree, like the weather or crop pests. Under capitalism, rural life is precarious in additional ways. As Marx explained, the emergence and expansion of capitalism involved "primitive accumulation," or the expropriation of many farmers' means of production, notably their land.[20] David Harvey refers to this process as "accumulation by dispossession" because it is ongoing in the contemporary world: profit is made from the usurpation and privatization of resources that were previously in the public domain or held communally, such as land, water, and, today, seeds and genetic resources.[21] This process also involves the commodification of forms of labor that were previously uncommodified or outside the cash nexus. It creates a surplus labor population that is dependent on paid employment but often does not make a living wage. In the valley, such processes have a long history dating back to colonialism, which includes not just the usurpation of land but also the use and control of spring water.[22] This chapter focuses on the contemporary period in the valley, but agriculture and residents' livelihoods were by no means static in earlier moments.

Scholars of agrarian change argue that accumulation and rural precariousness have intensified with neoliberal capitalism.[23] In Mexico, neoliberal policies involved cuts to rural subsidies, the implementation of counter-agrarian reform policies (such as those which enable communal landholders to sell land), increased corn imports (rather than prioritizing national food self-sufficiency), and exports of fresh fruits and vegetables to Canada and the United States, including organic produce. The country's dependency on corn imports has increased. Mexico now imports its most consumed and most important crop, maize, while its most significant export is labor. Mexico has promoted rural development through modern, commercial agriculture, improved seeds, trade liberalization, and the displacement of what various offices of the state deem "inefficient" campesinos. In this sense, neoliberal policies have sought to transform peasants into new rural subjects: into either agricultural entrepreneurs who produce for export or an inexpensive (and surplus) labor force.[24]

In this neoliberal food system, how do food producers and workers feed themselves? In Mexico, maize remains an important part of the diet, especially in rural locales like the Tehuacán Valley. Women are responsible for cooking, and this includes the preparation of tortillas and other corn-based foods. Women remove the kernels and soak them in limestone,[25] which is then ground to make the *masa* (dough) for tortillas. This process was enormously time consuming until the first corn mill was set up in town in 1953, which shortened the time required to make masa.[26] Meals are considered incomplete without homemade tortillas or tortillas bought fresh from a neighbor. As feminist scholars have rightly pointed out, what is called "reproductive labor"—such as raising children, preparing food, and care work—is central to the functioning of capitalism, yet is largely devalued and un- or under-paid. This type of reproductive labor is naturalized as an expression of biological sex, based on ideas about what it means to be a woman, and an innate predisposition for such tasks.

However, daily life complicates conceptualizations of "reproductive" and "productive" labor. The lines between such categories shift and change. In recent years, male migrants from the valley have taken up cooking for themselves and their roommates while living abroad and have remarked to me about the amount of work that goes into food preparation. To a certain extent, these migrants reevaluate assumptions about gendered domestic tasks. Although returned migrants reconsider some expectations about gender, other gender expectations are reinforced. Young women who worked in valley factories continue to contribute to household earnings after having children by staying at home and opening a store, a food stand, or more frequently, taking on piecework for maquilas. Typically, these earnings are seen as supplemental to their husband's or father's wages.

Men and women, teens, and elders work to "reproduce" their households or to secure "the conditions of life and of future production from what is produced and earned now."[27] In the process, their labor—paid and unpaid—contributes to the social reproduction of capitalism, a system in which "daily life depends upon the production of commodities produced through a system of circulation of capital that has profit-seeking as its direct and socially accepted goal."[28] Campesinos in the valley grow maize for reasons other than, or in addition to, profit, but they do so within a wider context of a changing capitalist food system.

As mentioned above, the cultivation of maize is central to the reproduction of rural households because it provides a form of security to older residents who have few sources of income. Maize can either be consumed as tortillas (and other foods) for the household or sold when cash is needed. Warman referred to peasant reliance on the crop as the "recourse to corn."[29] He argues that maize becomes especially important in times of crisis or hardship, when households or communities cope with loss of income or state support, or decide to engage wider markets only selectively. Although historically maize has been an excellent source of economic security, in what ways have valley practices and meanings of maize changed, if at all?

Crisis in the Valley of Corn and Changing Livelihood Strategies

The Tehuacán Valley[30] is known as the "cradle of maize" largely due to Richard MacNeish's important archaeological study of the 1960s, which uncovered maize cobs dating back to 5000 BCE,[31] although other regions of Mexico are more likely sites of maize domestication. In addition to Spanish, different dialects of Nahuatl are spoken in the valley's towns.[32] Campesinos and indigenous peoples from the valley and surrounding sierras look to the regional capital of Tehuacán for employment. The most commonly grown crops in this semi-arid valley are maize and beans. Garlic, tomatoes, sugarcane, fruits, and flowers, among other crops, are also grown commercially.

When a national economic crisis hit in 1982, and the government began to implement austerity measures followed by neoliberal policies, San José was already suffering from a water drought. Following the escalation of a local conflict over irrigation water, an initial wave of residents left to work in the United States for the first time since the 1950s.[33] In the mid-1990s labor migration from the valley quickly expanded. This was in part due to the implementation of the North

American Free Trade Agreement (NAFTA), with its rise in inexpensive US corn imports (which are subsidized in the United States and often sold abroad below cost, or "dumped") and changes to rural subsidies. Local concerns about insufficient irrigation water were also a factor. Valley residents found it increasingly difficult to support their families through farming or selling their maize for income.[34] As one resident in his early forties explained, the earnings and food from agriculture alone were often insufficient. He said, "I work the fields, but five months after harvest, where will my food come from? You can't live off the countryside alone. After the corn runs out, then what?"[35]

In response, valley residents further diversified their livelihood strategies or the ways they maintain their households, generate income, and produce food for consumption. I use "strategy" intentionally here in order to highlight the agency of residents under discussion. Food producers and workers are not simply pushed and pulled about by larger forces (nor are we as readers, scholars, or activists); rather, they make decisions on how to manage, get ahead, or even challenge, and sometimes change the social and economic conditions in which they find themselves. This response to neoliberal capitalism, and the stresses this type of development places on the environment, especially with declining groundwater levels and soil erosion, is part of a long history of adaptation in the region.

The increased diversification of agricultural livelihoods and the expansion (or initiation) of labor migration, which characterized much of rural Mexico in the 1980s, 1990s, and into the new millennium,[36] is experienced in particular ways in particular places. There are also exceptions. For example, in northern Mexico, farmers have taken advantage of changes to policy and the market and have made a profit from converting to maize production.[37] In other regions, some communities have selectively engaged the market by selling peasant crafts and foods like tortillas, strengthening their communities,[38] or organizing oppositional political movements and social alternatives to neoliberal policies (the Zapatista or EZLN movement being a famous example).[39]

In the valley, maize production and off-farm employment constitute part of a local strategy between age groups or generations to maintain or advance the economic position of their families. It is a strategy that embodies tensions, not only between wives and their migrant husbands but also between generations, as children are raised with an absent parent and teen workers, at some stage, reduce their financial contributions to their parents' households.

In a sociological sense, "generation" refers both to one's age group (or stage in the life cycle) and to the sense of identity and meaning shared by an age group at a particular historical moment.[40] Philip Abrams's concept draws our attention to the wider social, political, and economic changes in society and asks whether the sense of being part of a particular age group is static—that is, continuous with the previous age group or groups—or whether it is undergoing change in connection to those wider changes. In the valley, as young people work in maquilas and migrate north to work in the neoliberal food system, are their ideas about rural life and sense of identity distinct from a previous generation?

"We are *Campesinos*"

> *Some of us grow corn because there is no other work. Not every-*
> *one can get a job or make it across the border.*
>
> —Maize farmer, male, June 21, 2006

Maize farmers in San José are generally men who are either (a) in their thirties or forties, have worked in the United States (for periods between months to several years), and often have a small business or income like bus driving in the valley, a corn mill, construction work, and so forth, or who are (b) full-time agriculturalists in their fifties and older who are less likely to find paid employment other than work as local agricultural day laborers.[41] As the interviewee quoted above said to me, "Some of us grow corn because there is no other work." Both men and women of these older generations work in the fields. Women are also food producers and preparers. They farm crops like tomatoes and are responsible for selecting maize seed to save for future replanting; however, agriculture, and maize cultivation in particular, are considered "men's work."

Farmers in the valley refer to themselves as campesinos, a term which has a complex history in a country that experienced a peasant

Milpa (maize field) in the southern Tehuacán Valley. Courtesy of author, Elizabeth Fitting, 2008.

Husking and sorting dry maize. Courtesy of author, Elizabeth Fitting, 2008.

revolution in the early twentieth century and numerous development interventions aimed at improving rural production. In the early to mid-twentieth century, revolutionary leadership and the new state portrayed campesinos as the rightful owners of the land and the heart and soul of Mexico.[42] Such representations were undergirded by redistributive land reform and agrarian policies. While this imagery and discourse was used to generate support for the state, it also resonated with many rural peoples, including indigenous farmers in the Tehuacán Valley.

The term campesino remains in use in the valley today, but the context in which it is used has significantly changed. In addition to some branches of the state portraying campesinos as inefficient and culturally backward producers, agrarian policies and supports have been dismantled or radically transformed. For older residents, the term campesino recalls a past when the state had a responsibility—at least officially—to small-scale farmers. They use the term to signal hard work and a dignified life, which is in contrast to some official state narratives about inefficient peasants. In this sense, campesino as a self-label is one of the ways that residents criticize and sometimes challenge official policy and discourse. They also have refused to sell their communal land to agribusiness and have a history of petitions and conflict with the state (and valley neighbors) over access to spring water.[43]

In addition to signaling a previous era of state obligation to rural folk and a sense of respectable hard work, the term campesino connotes a preference for local or regional criollo corn over yellow industrial corn (grown in the north or the United States). Residents of all ages prefer criollo maize for making tortillas, even though I found that imported or industrial grain was 30 percent cheaper at the local market. When yellow corn is received through government programs or purchased at the local store, it is either fed to farm animals or mixed with local corn to hide its taste and texture. The industrial corn flour, Maseca, and yellow imported corn are seen as "pig food" that is considered not very tasty and not consistent with a dignified rural life. A female storeowner, who also has a small milpa for her household's consumption, told me that people grow corn despite the cost because they prefer the taste of white corn and because it makes tortillas of better quality than those found in cities. As she explains, "We grow corn because we want to have good, soft, white tortillas. They don't turn out the same in the city. In Mexico City, a truck carrying masa comes round as if it were mud. It's even uncovered! They say we live like animals here in the countryside, but in the city, they eat like animals!"[44] Through her comparison between rural and urban tortillas, the storeowner counters urban stereotypes about rural Mexico as backward or uncivilized ("they say we live like animals"). Access to local corn of high quality is connected to the idea that campesinos are hard working and deserving of respect. Ironically, for young migrants from the valley working and living abroad, Maseca, the industrial corn flour, has become a taste of home.[45]

Although maize remains the most cultivated and important crop in San José,[46] agricultural production is on the decline overall. There are now a number of households that no longer grow maize at all. Agricultural fields are transformed into housing for returned migrants, irrigation and rain water levels are reportedly low, and the price of inputs has increased. Indeed, under NAFTA, the cultivation of criollo maize for food in the valley came to cost at least as much as purchasing imported corn.

While male and female residents in their forties and older often view the cultivation of maize as minimizing risk, migrants and maquiladora workers in their teens and twenties do not believe that maize agriculture provides advantages, particularly not for their generation. At this stage of migration and their lives, young migrants have few agricultural skills, prefer nonagricultural work, and view corn agriculture as an unprofitable tradition with few future prospects.

"No hay dinero en la milpa": US Bound Migration and Back Again

> "You can't make any money in the countryside! There is no money in the milpa!"
> —Teenage migrant workers discussing maize farming, November 30, 2001

The younger generation has joined wage labor circuits that take them farther afield than previous generations. Most young men now migrate to the United States for work, and this migration is often undocumented and transnational in the sense that residents generally come home to the valley for months and sometimes years at a time, build houses, marry partners from town, and then return to the United States for another stint.

In comparison, young women of the same age tend to travel much shorter distances to work in maquilas and poultry plants within the valley, but they now do so unaccompanied by male relatives. Unaccompanied female travel, at this scale, is fairly new, and it generates discussion and anxiety among some residents. Even though men also work in valley maquilas and, to a lesser extent, women become migrants bound for the United States, these are gendered labor circuits because they are underpinned by assumptions about what is appropriate work for each gender, and because the distances that men and women travel to work differ. These are also transnational circuits: migrants remit money home and live transborder lives, while workers in valley assembly plants generate profit for domestic and foreign consortiums. Participation in these circuits of labor and capital provides much-needed income for rural households, but it also puts stress and strain on families and on the workers involved. Maquila work, for example, is demanding; it involves keeping up with an output quota and working long hours (sometimes in hot factories) for low wages. If and when women marry and have kids, one of the few options for employment is to continue working in the maquila industry as pieceworkers from home.[47]

Residents of all ages agree that income from off-farm employment, particularly in the United States where the wages are higher, is key for household maintenance and socioeconomic advancement. The southern valley has become a migrant-sending region. Previously, there had been up to three dozen contracted agricultural workers from San José under the Bracero Program in the 1950s and 1960s, but most of these contract workers returned home, and migration did not expand significantly. Migration from San José to the United States started up again in the 1980s and increased rapidly in the 1990s. This reflects larger trends in Mexico and the needs of the low-end service economy in the United States. An estimated 1.8 million undocumented migrants arrived in the United States from Mexico in the 1980s. The following decade, this number jumped to 4.9 million, despite the increased militarization of the US-Mexico border and the passing of the most severe anti-immigrant legislation to date. In the five years that followed, from 2000 to 2005 alone, there were another 4.4 million undocumented migrants.[48]

In the wake of 9/11, there was a temporary drop in migrant trips across the border, due to heightened security. In 2008, there was also a decline in unauthorized entries. While the cause of this decline remains debatable, it could be due to the rapid drop in US employment (particularly in sectors like construction) or the delayed effects of heightened border enforcement and a decline in back-and-forth migration.[49] In the valley, migrants are indeed extending their stays on either side of the border, but many young residents either continue to journey across the border or are in the process of planning and preparing for such journeys.

Unlike their predecessors, who worked in Californian agriculture, young migrants from San José find work largely in the US food industry as dishwashers and bus boys in restaurants and fast food chains, in food processing and packing plants, and on fishing boats that leave from the northwest coast. Most of the young interviewees reported sending money home to help their parents. Generally, they earmark money for building their own cement block house or opening a small business, like a store. While some migrants were successful in saving for the completion of their houses, starting up a business, or purchasing agricultural inputs (a tractor, irrigation water, etc.) others were not. In other words, the economic benefits of migration are not uniform, which helps to widen class differences among residents.

Young migrants report little knowledge about agriculture: they cannot identify or describe the traits of local varieties, soil qualities, or other aspects of agriculture. This can be seen as a generational interruption in the transmission of agricultural knowledge. When I asked interviewees why they thought their older relatives or townspeople grew corn, I was told that maize was grown as a custom or tradition and to produce food, but that it was not a means to make money: "People grow corn here to eat, so they don't lose the custom, or to get out of the house. They don't grow corn to make money. It's not a business."[50] The value of growing maize is not only economic but also has to do with the flexibility of the crop's uses, the older generation's contribution to the household, the widespread preference for the taste of local varieties, and the sense of autonomy that such agriculture brings to farmers, at least in theory if not in practice.

In addition to wages, migrants and maquila workers bring home ideas about agriculture, how to earn a living, and even about indigeneity and gender. As in other regions, migrants and maquila workers enjoy new social status in their hometowns. The money that migrants earn abroad enables them to build and improve homes in Mexico, buy consumer goods, and participate in local celebrations.[51] Richard C. Jones suggests that migrant income and purchasing power translate into a new "migrant elite" whose prestige comes from "wage labor earnings rather than from land, commerce, social status, and political pull."[52] To an extent, this is also evident in San José, where younger returned migrants gain social prestige from their purchasing power and experience abroad rather than from their control of irrigation water, participation in ritual kinship and celebrations, or affiliation with political factions, as was true of older Sanjosepeños and even older migrants who are also farmers.

Young women see maquila work as an economic necessity, and residents often say they are glad to have it. It is repetitive and low-paid work, and some women endure harassment in the factories as well as face local disdain about their unaccompanied travel and interaction with nonrelated men at work. Yet, at the same time, the experience and income provides young women with a sense of independence and freedom from some of the social constraints that their mothers or grandmothers faced. Several young women mentioned to me that they felt their income gave them more respect in the home. Their journey to work challenges ideas about gender on the one hand, while the industry depends on normative ideas about gender on the other: the ideas that women are more subservient, have nimble fingers, and are supplemental earners who therefore can be paid less than men.[53]

In the United States, Mexican workers are inserted into the racial hierarchy as inexpensive, disposable, and deportable labor.[54] Despite harsh anti-immigration policies, there is tacit if not explicit acceptance of the employment of undocumented Mexicans, especially in the food system. Ruth Gomberg-Muñoz provides an excellent summary of the myths and realities of undocumented workers in the United States, pointing out that while hard work contributes to a sense of self-worth among migrants, it is also used as a cultural trope about Mexican workers. Undocumented Mexicans are particularly vulnerable because they are unable to complain or report unfair wages, dangerous working conditions, and abuse, or they might face enormous risks if they do so. Moreover, Mexicans, and other Latin Americans, are often assumed to be undocumented workers, regardless of their citizenship or immigration status. As Gomberg-Muñoz explains in her study of Mexican restaurant staff in Chicago, "[T]he desirability of low-end service workers is often evaluated on subjective criteria such as their 'work ethic' and 'good attitude,' conditions that are promoted by workers' powerlessness."[55]

Yet, migrants from San José also experience working abroad as an improvement in their social status and self-perception—in the United States they are seen as Mexicans and not *indígenas* (indigenous)—despite the exploitation and racism. Additionally, this experience, along with wages, work experience, consumer goods, and the ability to speak English, are steps toward assimilation—though not necessarily complete or successful—when back in Mexico. According to accounts by returned migrants, in the United States employers, customers, and residents tend to view Sanjosepeños as homogeneously Mexican. A group of teenage migrants told me that in the restaurant kitchen where they worked in Las Vegas, even though they often spoke Nahuatl to each other, their employers referred to them *as Mexicans.* Contrastingly, when they are in Tehuacán—historically known as the City of Indians—they avoid speaking Nahuatl because they do not want people to think that they are "indios" (Indians). It is just "too embarrassing," I was told.[56] Ironically, these young migrants felt more a part of a larger Mexican society based on their work experience in the United States.

Studies of migrants from other indigenous regions of Puebla have also found that their experience in the United States provides a path toward assimilation when back home,[57] but that assimilation often is not successful or complete. Ideas about, and experiences of, being campesino and indígena—not to mention male or female, young, middle-aged, or old—change over time and place, as well as in different social spaces and encounters.

Labor migration to the United States builds the confidence of some Sanjosepeños. But for those who do not learn English, their experiences abroad may confirm their insecurities about traveling and interacting with people outside the valley. Several migrants reported that if you do not speak English in the United States, your capacity to earn and save will be more difficult, as will be your overall experience. Not all male migrants preferred working in the United States over staying in San José, and many were not successful in saving part of their income. However, without other remunerative employment options, many are compelled to return to the United States regardless of whether or not they had a positive experience there.

Their income, travel experience, English-language ability, and greater access to consumer goods enable some migrants to cast off the negative associations of being indigenous or to redeploy them.[58] For others, their experience abroad as Mexicans and exposure to other, more positive ideas about Mesoamerican Indians contribute to their rethinking the meaning of being an indigenous. In contrast to their parents and grandparents, migrants and maquila workers have access to social prestige through their income and travel experience rather than via more traditional avenues such as patron-client relationships or ritual kinship. In this way the experience of working in the United States and in the valley maquilas is transforming some notions about rural life and identity, while simultaneously reproducing others.

I also found that in interviews with migrants who had worked in the US food sector, although they discussed low pay, the hardship of being away from family, and exploitative work conditions, they also reported feeling a certain amount of freedom from what they saw as the outdated agricultural livelihoods of their elders, as well as from parental and, in the case of women, gender expectations. A few migrants also mentioned that, back in the valley, they were "free" from the fear of la migra (US border and immigration enforcement agents) and from the exploitation of food service work in the United States.

Although a sense of freedom most often came up as a point of discussion among returned migrants, I interviewed one young mother in her early twenties who described living in San José as freedom. She sold lunch foods outside of a school in the valley when I first interviewed her. She lived with her campesino parents who grew maize for household consumption and sale. She told me that residents were "free [here in the valley], but there is almost no food or work."[59] She was referring to the freedom ("*somos libres*") of being able to go to one's own land to pick fruit or grow maize and, perhaps, as in her case, start a small business instead of working for someone else. Several years later, this young mother moved to the city of Tehuacán for work, telling me she hoped the move was temporary. Unlike the other residents and migrants I had interviewed in their teens and twenties, she had discussed rural life as a kind of freedom.

Accumulation by dispossession in the valley is a process that works over generations transforming increasing numbers of rural residents into disposable surplus labor. This also has paradoxical effects. Marx described "primitive accumulation" as the process that affected the European countryside starting in the sixteenth century, but that also characterizes capitalism in other places and times as "freedom."[60] Rural peoples were "freed" of their access, control, or ownership of resources (their means of production), and this "freed" them to search for work. The process generates an abundance of potential workers and consumers for market goods. However, this process cannot simply be reduced to a mechanism to generate inexpensive or reserve labor forces for capitalists. There are many instances when a living wage is beyond reach. Sometimes this process can also be experienced as a freedom from inherited social relations and cultural norms, as is certainly the case with a younger generation from the valley.

At this point, it appears that young migrants and maquila workers face conditions distinct from previous generations and also express new identities and ideas about agriculture. However, the question remains whether younger migrants will take up maize agriculture as they age. Older residents rely on maize agriculture as a social safety net. Yet, we have also seen that in a neoliberal food system, the processes that push young migrants off farms also undermine the next generation's ability to remain on the land, if they so choose, as agricultural producers. The ability to maintain an agricultural livelihood is undermined by increasing production costs, declining levels of spring water, changes to rural subsidies, counter-agrarian policies (which enable communal landholders to sell land), and other factors like home construction on arable land.[61]

Conclusion

I began this chapter with a quote about Latin American immigrants to the United States being out-of-work farmers, followed by my question about whether these rural migrants would prefer returning home in order to farm. My case study from the Tehuacán Valley complicates this further, compelling us to consider whether all of the im/migrants looking for work on street corners were in fact farmers back home or children and grandchildren of farmers. Juan's story about being a returned migrant with little knowledge or interest in agriculture, for instance, is typical among my interviewees in their teens, twenties, and early thirties. Older migrants in their thirties and forties were more likely to farm when in the valley or to send home remittances to be spent on agricultural inputs.

What does it mean for food activism when rural youth no longer want to farm food crops for their own communities or others? Food activism and scholarship importantly criticizes how neoliberal capitalism and the modern food system contribute to rural displacement and "accumulation by dispossession." Food sovereignty, advanced by Via Campesina, the international peasant rights group, promotes the ability of each community and nation to "maintain and develop its own capacity to produce its basic foods respecting cultural and productive diversity."[62] This concept and platform has gained considerable traction as a critique of, and alternative to, the current food system. My point is that in our support of alternatives to conventional farming and the idea that small-scale food producers should be self-sufficient, we—as food activists and scholars—need to be careful not to romanticize rural life in a way that overlooks the desire among younger residents to escape the farming life of their elders.

What larger lessons or questions for future research does this chapter raise? Learning from rural Mexicans about their livelihood strategies provides a window into the food system in North America, particularly the motivations, concerns, and cross-border familial and economic ties of workers and food producers. Such case studies are important because they can help challenge discourses about peasant inefficiency, romanticizations of rural life, and debunk culturalist arguments that justify the exploitation of food workers. They help us better understand how contemporary capitalism and the food system work "on the ground" in specific locales, while also portraying residents as agents who engage, negotiate, criticize, and may even help transform the system. The intergenerational livelihood strategy found in the valley—which combines migrant and maquila labor with small-scale maize production—has had paradoxical effects, particularly when we compare the experiences of residents of different resources, generations, and genders. This case study helps unsettle the idea of a homogenous rural community and illustrates the importance of taking the "intersectionality" of experience seriously, or how gender, age, class, and ethnicity shape an individual's experience.

Finally, does information about who produces and prepares our food help transform the food system? If consumers (and producers) translate such knowledge into political action, it certainly can make a difference. I think this is particularly the case if we examine the larger political economic context in which food producers live and work, the reasons rural peoples migrate, and how food producers and workers experience the food system, perhaps differently, over the course of their lives. At the same time, because nativism and racism against undocumented (or perceived to be undocumented) migrants is a powerful discourse in North America, and particularly against Mexicans and Central Americans in the United States, knowing *who* produces and prepares food, might not always generate change in and of itself. In our efforts to change the food system, we also need to strive to create policies that support those campesinos who want to stay home and work the land, improve food workers' rights, reform immigration policies, and challenge sexism and racism. Like all complex problems, real transformation of the food system requires multi-dimensional solutions at home and abroad.

PART 3 ▪ Food Professionalism from the Ground Up

CHAPTER 6

Las Gallinitas de Doña Luz

Dominican Women Public Kitchens and Trans-Ethnic Networks in San Juan

LIDIA MARTE

"*Within the context of food consciousness,
the mouth represents that boundary . . .*"

—MEREDITH E. ABARCA AND NIEVES PASCUAL SOLER[1]

In this chapter I propose an exploration of women's urban public kitchens in Puerto Rico as sites of place-making, food labor struggles, and alliances across ethnic boundaries. To ground these thematic frames, I offer a critical reading of Doña Luz's signature dish of *gallinitas rellenas* (stuffed hens), which can help us understand the role of food routes in social network formation in Puerto Rico (PR) as one instance of Latin@ active participation in the global food system. Doña Luz's public kitchen (home-cooking for sale) offers a space to document transformations of Dominican migrant women's food practices. Such an examination implicates global flows of food production through the ingredients available for their cooking, the labor they perform to support themselves, and the diasporic routes that brought them to their current localities.

Doña Luz shares with other Dominican working-class women similar economic challenges, and she contributes to the formation of new families and networks through her Dominico-Boricua children. The particular ways in which her food helps to form alliances (clients who have become friends) reveals wider strategies of community-making by Dominicans in PR, which has a sociohistorical context of discrimination as well as of hopeful solidarity. Many feminist political ecologists[2] have suggested an examination of community as a project, a contingent space of loss and reinvention, of partial alliances created in-place as well as an examination through labor. In the marginalized urban areas of San Juan, local residents face common predicaments; it is from these localities that Dominican gendered food labor becomes a site of network formation in particular neighborhoods. For diverse residents, their cuisine becomes a way to negotiate access to culturally appropriate and nutritious meals. Doña Luz's identities (immigrant from a nearby Caribbean nation and a dark Dominican working-class woman) destabilizes the Latino/Hispanic label she would otherwise receive on the US mainland.

This chapter is organized along three rest stops: (1) Doña Luz as a Dominican immigrant cook in PR; (2) her signature dish of gallinitas rellenas as a "visible" site of solidarity network formation and as a reinvention of Dominican and Puerto Rican cooking; and (3) the invisibility of Doña Luz's public kitchen in the food system in spite of her contribution to the local economy and to the global food import chains. I conclude with a few methodological and theoretical suggestions for furthering critical Food Studies projects, and as a way to further research place, race, and intra-Caribbean migration. Doña Luz's food routes and the trans-ethnic networks created through her public kitchen suggest the need for an umbrella of food justice and food sovereignty focusing less on ethnic or any other label groups, and more on place-making and local micro-histories.

An Ethnographic Vignette of Doña Luz: From *Barrio Obrero* to *Rio Piedras*

The images I have chosen to open this section—the gallinitas plate and Doña Luz's hand—point to the pleasures and challenges of representation as well as to the ethics of research that reside in our choices. I have taken many photographs of Doña Luz's surroundings and rare portraits of her face while documenting her cooking throughout the years. Do I pick the photo I love of her hands in the Placita del Mercado

Doña Luz's gallinita (stuffed hen) and hand, Rio Piedras, PR (2013).
Photos by author.

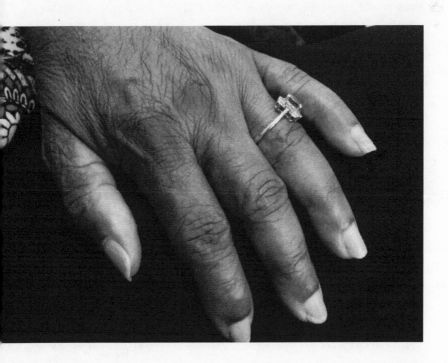

de Rio Piedras? Or do I choose a more informative and valid form of documentation, such as a likeness of the food? The diptych, as might have been suspected, is my way of trying to get away with being both poetic and useful, which are not necessarily in conflict. It is through the gallinitas plate that Doña Luz has found a way not only to make a living, but also to become appreciated and respected in her locality. The view of her beautiful, carefully painted nails and her blue ring, a gift from her mother, point to her humanity as well as her femininity. How she cares for her appearance, even at her eighty years, contrasts with the messy work of the kitchen by which she makes a living.

Doña Luz, a mother of four and a grandmother, was born and raised in El Tablaso, San Cristobal, Dominican Republic (DR). She shared some stories of the harsh working conditions and uncertainties of living in a rural area. Beginning in the 1940s, she worked in the fields with her parents in their small subsistence and cash crop farm. "*El trabajo del campo no 'e fácil, siempre se pasaba hambre, uno no puede comerse lo que se lleva al mercado*" ("The work in the fields is not easy, sometimes we would go hungry, you can't eat what you need to sell"). It seems that food insecurity and, from what I inferred, oppressive gender roles became reasons for her to migrate. Doña Luz went to Santo Domingo for the first time when she was twelve years old to join an older sister and help her with her job as a maid. Years later, after her first consensual union with a man, she became pregnant with her first child. Eventually, she married a Puerto Rican man with whom she had three more children, two of whom were born in PR. It seems that they migrated from DR to PR because "the situation was bad" economically and they wanted to give an education to their children, which they could not envision affording in the DR. It took years for her husband to get proper documents to bring her and her children legally into PR, but then, not long after they migrated in the 1980s, her husband died of a heart attack. She has remained a single widow ever since, supporting her children through her cooking.

The experience of raising her Dominico-Boricua children, the tragedy of losing her husband, and the pressures of being the sole head of household seem to have grounded her into developing a sense of local belonging. As a result, she traveled less and less to DR. Doña Luz's experience is unique, yet shared: private, in her migration choices and personal history, yet collective and public as she and other immigrants negotiate the global circumstances created by industrial food production. In particular, the land and labor economic restructuring since the 1970s[3] has pushed thousands of peasant women in DR to become urban workers, migrating to the capital Santo Domingo and eventually, like Doña Luz, transnationally. Unlike the usual portraits of Dominican women transnationalism, her routes are indeed diasporic, but more so between Boston (where one of her daughters resides) and PR than between the DR and PR. She appears comfortable in her locality; absent from her narratives was a nostalgia for a return to the homeland.

Doña Luz's cooking has become well known in working-class sectors between Hato Rey, Santurce, and the Rio Piedras districts of San Juan, PR. In her neighborhood in Barrio Obrero, she is well known for the sale of cooked foods and as a local resident. When I asked how she gets her clients, she responded, "*No me anuncio con tarjetita, la gente se entera*" ("I don't announce myself with business cards; people find me"). These people who find her are those she meets or clients who come to her as a result of friends' referrals. For a while, she worked in restaurants, and, after she quit, people who knew her cooking from those restaurants became her first clients. Puerto Ricans, Dominicans, and other customers have been made through a snow balling of sorts: *de boca a boca* (from mouth to mouth) recommendation. Her routes also extend to other neighborhoods for her food shopping, and to the marginalized urban neighborhoods in San Juan's "Dominican enclave," such as Barrio Obrero, Capetillo, and San José in Rio Piedras, where many of her clients live. These places have become a part of Doña Luz's food routes.

Doña Luz's life as a food vendor began as an occasional household business selling Dominican *pasteles*, which are similar to tamales. In PR she continued working in public cooking mostly at what is known as *cafeterias*, or modest home-cooking-style criollo restaurants. When I asked her why, even when close to eighty years old, she keeps cooking and selling foods, she replied: "*Yo siempre he cocinao, a mi me gusta cocinar . . . yo sigo cocinando, aunque ya toy vieja . . . porque lo necesito, y pa' uno entretenerse, asi me ditraigo*" ("I have always cooked, I like to cook . . . I keep cooking, even though I am old . . . I do it because I need the income and because it helps me distract myself. I enjoy it").

When I asked how she learned to cook the gallinitas, she said: "*Yo aprendí a sasonar mirando, en el campo . . . al ojo por ciento, luego una señora en la cafetería El Oasis me enseñó como cocinar la gallinita, pero yo inventé el secreto de la salsa*" ("I learned to season my foods in the rural area [of DR]. I learned by watching, eye-balling; later [in PR] an employee in the restaurant *Oasis* showed me how to make the gallinitas, but I invented a secret to the [*tamarindo*] sauce"). Doña Luz worked at many restaurants and cafeterias, including at a US naval base in Cataño, PR. She remembers that each restaurant she worked for had an unacceptable treatment toward workers; thus, she ended up quitting from many of them. One of her clients commented that "*ella se iba del trabajo por cualquier cosa*" ("she got offended easily and would quit her jobs"). This was the case until she found El Oasis, which served "*comida criolla*" (creole food). She worked there for ten years and learned to cook the gallinitas. Once her children grew up, married, and left for the US mainland, she left the poor working conditions of El Oasis, which had limited cooking options with its controlled menu. At such a point in her life, she desired to become her own boss by cooking from home and selling food made-to-order. Doña Luz said that she felt her health improved once she was away from the furnace heat of the cafeteria's kitchen.

In order to understand Doña Luz's food routes, it is important to travel them. This is why, whenever possible, I would not only document her cooking and the foodscapes of her neighborhood, but would also follow whatever routes she traveled in San Juan, especially the routes for her food shopping. One early morning in the summer of 2013, we went to the Placita del Mercado de Rio Piedras, a food market. We went by public bus, conversing along the way and complaining about the *pisicorre's* (bus) lack of air conditioning in ninety-degree weather. Once in Rio Piedras, we walked the narrow streets where the closed storefronts and "For Rent" or "For Sale" signs spelled urban decay.[4] Yet, the narrow streets had a surprising liveliness thanks to the small stores still open that kept the area from becoming a complete cultural desert. Rio Piedras has become a ghost town due to gentrification and urban renewal programs that evicted small food and clothing businesses, but never quite materialized into the development promised.[5]

Once in the plaza, we stopped at various produce kiosks and vendors, and we got *guandules* (green pigeon peas in their vines) and avocados; the butcher from whom she gets the hens did not have any available that day. She made comments about the freshness and quality of the produce. It was through these trips that I realized the time and effort required to maintain her business; I learned of the care she placed in choosing the best ingredients. Besides those of the plaza, the other resources Doña Luz uses for her cooking (and for her personal needs) are mostly in Barrio Obrero, her neighborhood, or they come to her via her networks of client-friends who deliver them to her door. The man who provides Doña Luz with her cooking gas lives nearby, and he and his wife are also clients. Construction workers, who are usually stationed at Borinquen Avenue, close to her residential street, have become clients through the Christmas celebration their contractor offers and which she caters every year. There are at least three regular clients who live at a distance and come to pick up food from her a few times a week, bringing in bulk containers needed to pack their food orders. Other clients, mostly women, drive Doña Luz to doctors' appointments since public transportation is quite unreliable in PR and she does not drive.

Most of the fragmented oral history and food narratives I gathered by shadowing Doña Luz around her food shopping and cooking preparation—listening, watching, tasting—has allowed me to bear witness to some of the cycles of her days as they are organized around food-related activities. Through piecing together direct and indirect passages of her narratives, I have developed the above rough outline of some aspects of her migrant routes. She does not seem to like sharing details of her life, as she did not freely volunteer information (unlike most of the Dominican women cooks I worked with in New York City). Her continued resistance to my attempts at representation, be it photos, recordings, or my endless questions about how she learned to cook, made her the kind of subject who feminist scholars hope and fear to find in ethnographic encounters.[6]

Auto-Ethnographic Food Locations and Labor Seasonings

Among feminist anthropologists, a choice of methodology is already a theoretical framing, which implicates the social location of the researcher and the kind of relation she has with the host communities.

Locating ourselves as scholars helps us take into account shared field-grounds and power differences, and such declarations add validity to qualitative research, as they also address issues of ethics and accountability, as is customary for feminist scholars.[7]

Doña Luz's foodmaps have intersected with my foodmaps through my sister's food routes in San Juan, for my sister has been one of her main clients and her friend for the last fifteen years. It is through their social network that I got to taste the gallinitas. After I met Doña Luz during one of my yearly visits to PR, while still a graduate student at the Universtiy of Texas at Austin (around 2003), I became interested in her food practices. In spite of these shared routes, there are significant differences between her social locations and mine, and even my sister's. Doña Luz and my sister appear darker in skin color and live in a marginalized neighborhood in San Juan. Our physical differences impact the level of access we have to negotiate our own terms of citizenship, education, and class mobility. These social locations create unequal visibility and invisibility in the ways we are "interpellated"[8] by the PR nation. It is because of these entanglements that I discuss methodology and my auto-ethnographic positioning in the same section. My food research—now from the Caribbean—is a direct result of these shared foodmaps. I am writing these notes during a return migration to PR, where I will reinhabit an old neighborhood, and reconsider how and why to continue doing my work. Hence, locating myself from Rio Piedras is significant, for it marks this as a return not simply to a field site, but also to a place that used to be my neighborhood. My family migrated to PR from the DR in 1979—as part of a wave of labor migration and due to food insecurity—and, later, we continued moving, then to the US mainland, except for one of my sisters who remained in PR.

This act of self-location serves as a good example of where to begin when tracing food routes. Labor is the first arch of food relations. It was a tenure job that caused my return to PR and to my alma mater Universidad de Puerto Rico. It was my "food consciousness"[9] and memory-history connections to PR and DR that motivated me to accept the position. My routes of migration and survival shape my views and explain, at least in some ways, why I produce the kind of academic narratives that I am sharing in this chapter. Thus, my connection with Doña Luz speaks of a type of encounter in the shared fields of the professional and personal lives of "native" (or insider) ethnographers who need to negotiate complex tensions of distance/ proximity through such intimacies.[10] I write this chapter, in part, to honor that kind of delicate complexity.

Alter-Native Ethnographies: Foodmaps, Field and Researching Locations

Where do these multilayered readings of food, place, and network formation come from? As a researcher using foodmaps, I pay attention to the particularly situated perspectives of food practices as individuals negotiate their life aspirations from concrete neighborhoods, cities, regions, and countries. One of the advantages of this approach is the diversity of media-centered data-gathering strategies that helps maintain the connection between narratives, place-making practices, and food material culture. Each route or food stop implicates a range of labor scales linking local consumption to global routes. This begins with the plate: from what a person eats, to how she/he produces such food, and from general food production and distribution, to actual shelters and kitchens where food is served. Food practices, communities, and places emerge and keep transforming in wider geopolitical contexts; hence, an ethno-historical layer of food mapping is necessary. Still we can use the immediacy of local foods to interrogate the contexts of their emergence, how such contexts have helped shape people's present food practices, and the conditions of the neighborhoods where they live. Finally, because food practices are necessarily situated, the present place is experienced via an embodied memory of other places someone has inhabited before, such as one's place of origin. Thus, a focus on cultural memory becomes a necessary counterpoint to understand the reinvention of foods and identities from the present grounds.

I cooked up this approach to food mapping as a methodological and theoretical framing, an ergonomic mixed method to study food practices as they occur in-place and at specific historical times, and in response to particular grounded perspectives.[11] When using this method, a rich diversity of primary sources are gathered during participatory fieldwork to help trace the trajectories of peoples' food routes and to compose a map of a particular person, social network, or community's food relations. Documenting at the micro-level the local routes individuals navigate to procure their meals helps to collect spontaneous narratives about how they experience and represent their relation to such routes. Because food mapping entails a configuration of sociocultural, political, and ecological contexts (macro-level), it serves to ground us in the materiality of food and its urgent global crisis. Furthermore, this micro-level helps us gather and document food narratives and oral histories that are otherwise left outside food-centered historical archives. This allows a way of sharing the fruit of our labor as gifts of reciprocity for the host community we are working with.

The hope with using food mapping is to contribute to more nuanced interdisciplinary food methods useful for understanding the food experiences of Afro-diasporic populations. Through the contributions of Psyche Williams-Forson, Carole M. Counihan, Syndey W. Mintz, Cruz Miguel Ortíz Cuadra, and David Sutton, among many others, I realized that a critical food justice framework for such studies is already a reality.[12] In looking at some coincidences in their writings, I garnered that the most inclusive, yet specific way of studying food is to focus on grounded practices and narratives, and through local relations as negotiated within wider global contexts. As Sutton has proposed, we need to taste, look, and listen to the sounds of food preparation since these carry embodied knowledge. We must also pay attention: to the micro-politics of cooks' everyday kitchens encountered in-place.[13]

Las Gallinitas de Doña Luz: Food Labor, Trans-Ethnic Solidarity, and Puerto Rico's Food Systems

The gallinitas rellenas that Doña Luz prepares consist of a small Cornish hen, cooked with her own sazón (condiments, seasonings), yet based on a recipe she learned from working at Puerto Rican restaurants. The bird is stuffed with mangú, a Dominican dish of mashed plantains,[14] or congrí, a Cuban version of rice cooked with black beans. The tamarind sauce with lots of garlic has Doña Luz's inventive touch, and she keeps it a secret. In this combination of food-to-order, there are at least three Caribbean national cuisines and nations implicated: Puerto Rico (gallinita), Dominican Republic (mangú), and Cuba (congrí). Furthermore, through the tamarind sauce, which is rarely used in Hispanic Caribbean cuisine, another global route is added: the Indian subcontinent. Other regular items in her repertoire further suggest this cross-national/cross-ethnic connection. These include desserts and dishes familiar to both Dominicans and Puerto Ricans, such as flan (cheesecakes), *mofongo* (her version of mashed plantain, usually with pork), rice and beans, *mondongo* (tripes), rice with green pigeon peas and coconut milk, pasteles (tamales) for Christmas, and Dominican *habichuelas con dulce* (sweet beans) for Easter. When I asked a regular customer why she purchases from Doña Luz, she said: "*Yo conoci a Lú porque ella le jugaba número a mi esposo . . . el le compraba patele, yo no conocia de comer pastele; ella me hacia de arroz, de yuca, de plátano pa' que yo probara, pastele en hoja, como se le dice en DR . . . y ahora de Lú e la unica persona de la que yo como patele . . . luego ella me regaló una gallinita y me envisié; encargo mi gallinita cada vez que puedo, desde hace 20 año.*" ("I met Luz through my husband who used to sell her phone cards . . . He would buy pastel from her; I did not know about them. Then she began giving me pasteles made with rice, yuca, and plantains, so that I could try them. In DR they call them *pastel de oja*. Now I only eat pastel from Luz. She taught me how to appreciate them. . . . One day she gave me a gallinita for my birthday. I got hooked instantly; I have been ordering them for 20 years.")

Tangentially, I wish to propose to think of Doña Luz's cooking as reinvention across ethnic boundaries of *la comida criolla puertorriqueña*. The changing narratives of "traditional" foods seems to be renegotiated and reimagined in many cases by the concrete labor of Dominican cooks, as fewer and fewer Puerto Ricans take on that kind of public kitchen work. This maintenance of comida criolla[15] is reinvented and nourished, pun intended, by the very foreignness of these Dominican cooks. Dominican immigrants in PR are helping to maintain the traditional Puerto Rican foodways in a number of ways. They do this through their small food businesses, such as bodegas, in which they sell produce in local neighborhoods to prepare staple foods, and through their work in businesses that sell cooked comida criolla, such as the food Doña Luz and other women sell from their homes.

Mapping the components of the gallinitas "inside the frame," as we have seen above in terms of the ingredients and their symbolic meanings that comprise the dish, allows us now to explore the wider contexts of readings "outside of the frame" that connect the food, people, and place to a global food industry. In order for the unforgettable taste of the gallinita to exist, Doña Luz navigates various food routes around San Juan: first, her neighborhood chain supermarket where the plantains are cheaper; next, the Placita del Mercado of Rio Piedras, where many kiosks sell imported produce and are owned or managed by Dominican vendors; and, lastly, she gets the hens from an older Puerto Rican man from Morovis, who has been a vendor in the Plasita del Mercado for almost thirty years.

Considering the work and marinating time needed to prepare the gallinitas, and the price of the birds (roughly $7 per pound), Doña Luz's prices for the hens served with rice and salad seem reasonable at $12. A plantain in PR could easily sell for 50 to 75 cents each; this starkly contrasts New York City, for example, where Dominican supermarket specials of ten plantains for $1.00 are frequent. According to Gustavo Setrini, close to 80 percent of PR food is imported; this includes basic staples that could be grown locally such as coffee, avocados, yuca, and mangos.[16] Despite the fact that the land in PR is fertile and could support local self-sufficiency, due to the US policy since the 1950s that governs PR as a territory,[17] PR does not produce food for local consumption, with a few regional exceptions such as coffee, plantains, and other local fruits.

Doña Luz's food routes intersect with the wider food system in PR implicating not only her and her clients, but also all local communities and the island as a whole. PR's economic dependence on the US food system has profound effects on food security for the whole island. Two factors have contributed to the lack of food sovereignty: first, the PR agricultural system was almost destroyed in the 1950s and 1960s, and then, what was left of it has been integrated into the industrial global food production. This has made it necessary for PR to rely on imports of tropical produce, such as avocados, guavas, and chickens that could easily be produced locally.[18] In PR, food insecurity is not as readily visible as in other Global South countries; yet, close to 40 percent of the population is receiving or has been a recipient of TANF (former food stamps), and, of these, an overwhelming 60 percent have been households headed by women.[19] Obesity, the other side of malnutrition, is epidemic, especially among urban, marginalized consumers of fast food.[20] The level of food insecurity among Dominicans is hard to measure, as there are no studies on this or any food-related matters about this community. Marginalized communities in PR are at a greater risk of malnutrition, hunger, and diet-related health conditions due to their dependence on supermarket imports, US subsidies, and social services (food assistance) that generally do not provide food that enables healthy calorie consumption. In some sectors of these marginalized communities, however, some people have responded to this dependency by creating a cultural resilience based on collective memory of vernacular and culturally meaningful food staples.[21]

The inside and outside framings of Doña Luz's gallinitas lead to questions such as: What do these gallinitas accomplish for her? What relationships do they make possible with the vendors she supports? Beyond providing food to consumers, what does this particular dish signify for them? Through Doña Luz's public kitchen, which serves clients in the neighborhoods of Santurce, Hato Rey, and Rio Piedras, a wider Dominico-Boricua, local, and trans-ethnic community of survival emerges. Her personal food routes as a Dominican immigrant have expanded into a trans-ethnic network. Her cooking functions as a site of encounters and as a space of gift exchanges. Some clients get her gallinitas and flans for birthdays or for other special occasions, and she also offers treats and free food to her regular clients, as they do favors for her on a regular basis.

Doña Luz's role as a cultural food broker is helping generate a hope of transcending prejudice through shared differences and similarities in taste. Her trans-ethnic networks of Dominicans and Puertorricans, who are regular clients, form a community of taste and sentiment. The customers' love of her gallinitas, flanes, and pasteles and the affection they have developed for her breaks boundaries and creates a space where they meet safe from each other's ethnocentric prejudice. These networks of "loyal palate,"[22] that mostly know of each other's existence through affection and support for Doña Luz, participate in networks of solidarity restricted to the informal food economy. Yet, they are also enmeshed via the imported produce she purchases from the US economy, and thereby establish links to the global food system.

Doña Luz's food labor has made it possible for her to transform and incorporate new skills to produce maps by which to navigate and reimagine a new sense of place, community, and home. It is through the flavor of her dishes that she has created a foundation of appreciation for her cooking skills and a respect for her humanity among her clients (hence the Doña, as a sign of respect), under otherwise unfavorable racial and ethnic prejudice against Dominican working-class immigrants. Her clients show an affection and respect for her that is created by extension of the shared love of her foods.[23] This sense of solidarity becomes a bridge for communication between working-class Dominican and Puerto Rican women and, in some cases, their husbands and families. Food labor, so common among Latin American working-class women, empowers the agency and independence of marginalized women who otherwise would unhappily be inserted into cycles of exploitation by becoming part of the vast and poorly paid tertiary sector of which Doña Luz opted out by leaving her previous restaurant jobs.

The historical, geopolitical, and sociocultural specificity of PR, and the urban space negotiations in San Juan where most of the Dominican immigrants reside, helps us situate wider implications of race, class, gender, and citizenship in the Caribbean and in the regional and global neoliberal contexts of new diasporas. For people who share the same neighborhood, it is easier to find ways to develop similar food tastes. These shared flavors could become conscious shared experiences. Many marginalized communities in PR, inhabited mostly by dark Puerto Ricans, are placed outside of the national agenda; thus, they remain economically at the margin of PR historical and current political representation through de facto segregation in housing, social services, and employment.[24] These communities, such as Doña Luz's Barrio Obrero or the barriada San José, the farthest point of food routes in San Juan where many of her clients live, might find racial solidarity with Dominican immigrants. In addition, and in contrast to the current state, they could feel more loyalty to a PR "cultural citizenship"[25] that offers them a minimal hegemonic advantage over the new "racialized" other. The kind of financial independence and solidarity networks Doña Luz has been able to create through her food work, in an atmosphere of prejudice, reveals the painful ruptures yet hopeful chances of Caribbean intra-migrations. Dominican migrants in PR are diverse. They find different ways of negotiating a living, creating a community, and eating what the Puerto Rican food system has to offer. They mostly participate in informal food economy niches, which are linked to global import foods and the island's colonial status. Nevertheless, from within these food realities they are reimagining the continuity of both Dominicans and Puerto Ricans through their recreation and consumption of comida criolla.

Within PR, Dominican immigrants and their descendants participate in the flow of the global food system. This participation takes place at the level of ownership: restaurants, street food vendors, and private/home commercial kitchens. At other levels of the food industry, they work as cooks and dishwashers, tend to market stalls where they distribute fresh produce, and/or serve as cheap labor for the few agricultural sectors remaining. In the formal and informal food economy, local Dominican migrant workers come to fill labor niches already abandoned by marginalized Puerto Ricans[26] who, due to the economy and endemic unemployment, have found other solutions to make a living such as migration to the US mainland, participating in the drug economy, and the reliance on social services. Dominicans and their descendants—as cooks, customers, and consumers in PR— are active agents who contribute to the economy and social life of their neighborhoods by way of their choices regarding where to purchase their food and from whom. Outside Dominicans' niches, however, their efforts to preserve traditional dishes remain invisible since such ethnic foods officially remain an unrecognized contribution. Nevertheless, this group is constantly reinventing their culinary practices that are necessary for place and memory making. Local food business networks play a major role as sites of Dominican integration into local communities, as they become sectors that generate employment and economic support for other immigrant families and help sustain and create new social networks of survival and solidarity.

Doña Luz's public kitchen is *visibly invisible*: known to her local food networks, but marginal to Puerto Rican society. As a Dominican immigrant to a neighboring Caribbean island, and due to her dark skin and working-class status, she is perceived eternally as a foreigner. Simultaneously, as an immigrant into PR, a colony or US territory, she belongs to one of many other marginalized "minority" groups. What this group shares in common is that their status as a marginal ethnic minority has to do with the direct and indirect effects of US imperialism. Despite their minority/marginal status, the roles of the Dominican immigrants in the local foodscapes of PR go as far back as to include Piñones, a beach area in Isla Verde. Piñones has a long corridor of sidewalk fry-food kiosks and dance halls that sell Puerto Rican fritters and beverages to both tourists and local consumers alike, thereby helping to fuel a sense of local "authenticity" for a Caribbean tropical vacation spot. There is an irony in having touristic *piñones* (pine nuts) with *empanadillas de chapin* (fish empanadas) and *alcapurrias* (fried bananas and manioc flour stuffed with meat) made by Dominican hands (both men and women), or vendors at Placita del Mercado de Rio Piedras selling avocados "*del pais*" (imported from DR), or selling *mofongo* (a typical PR dish) in Dominican kiosks. The irony resides in that it is Dominican immigrants who are preparing, selling, and continuing PR's food culture when PR national narratives state, and a good portion of Puerto Ricans consider, Dominicans un-assimilatable, or outside of proper US citizenship material.

Situated Seasonings: Doña Luz's Visible Kitchen and "Latin@" Food Routes in Puerto Rico

As migrants relocate to new societies, they try to reproduce the familiarity of their foods. In the process, however, accidental and unintentional changes occur due to people's income levels, the kinds of food they can buy, the choices and availability of ingredients, and the local access to food produce. For Doña Luz to earn her living and to indulge the taste of her clients, a global network of food production and distribution is already in place. This network is part of the same neoliberal forces responsible, in part, for the flow of food and people that brought women like her from the DR to PR, during the 1970s and 1980s. The migration of Dominican working-class women who are the head of the house increased especially after the 1980s.[27] Dominican immigrant women in PR, the majority of whom have barely completed an eighth-grade level of schooling (or less), and who are dark skinned and speak Afro-Dominican dialects, face a special kind of discrimination. Their presence and bodies are pathologized as a contagion due to their visible differences and to perceptions of uncontrolled sexuality and reproductive proclivities, not unlike the way African American and Latina women are represented in the mainland United States. And yet it is precisely from among these women that the taste of familiar public foods persists in PR.

The growth of Dominican migration to PR since the 1980s and the particular illegal labor migration that characterizes this flow[28] frames Doña Luz's migrant trajectory. This trajectory has become the main context for discriminatory practices and discourses in regard to first-generation Dominican immigrants and their descendants born on the island. The prejudices about this population are visible through media representation, daily interactions, police behavior, and at institutional offices.[29] Dominican women have become a particularly vulnerable group within this population.[30] The representation and treatment of these women's bodies positions them as marginalized urban subjects that try to both accommodate local models of assimilation and citizenship, as well as resist and affirm their cultural rights and human dignity.[31] It is impossible, for example, to ignore how Dominican women and men are, although differently, interpolated in PR in terms of race, class, immigrant status, and level of education, in that order. In terms of gender, there are specific structural forms of violence and discrimination, but there are also chances of creating a sense of place and belonging and of building local solidarity.

Doña Luz and other Dominican immigrants in PR are affected by the US institutions, under which an entire nation becomes a demographic minority. Puerto Ricans are considered a "Latino" minority under the US federal administration. It is hard to know how to locate Dominicans in PR: Are they US "Latinos" or foreigners within a nation? There is no separate "minority" classification in PR national institutions, yet through the use of the US legal framework and census, these categories do apply.[32] Unlike other immigrants, such as Colombians, Argentineans, Middle Easterners, and Cubans (post-1959 wealthy exiles), Dominicans are not bendable into the concept of *mestizaje*, or the perfect mixing of indigenous, white, and black, driven by the whitening aspiration of the PR national narratives.[33] At the same time, Dominicans are not exempt from expressing racist and ethnocentric attitudes toward others. Historically, for example, they have rejected Haitians who, in their immigrant status in PR, remain isolated from the affairs of PR as a nation; and, in addition, many assume no Puerto Rican is genuinely interested in developing friendships with this particular immigrant group.

Conclusions

Focusing on food, memory, and place-making could help us research wider angles in intra-Caribbean migration. What can we learn about food justice from Doña Luz's gallinitas? By having control over her food consumption and her financial sources, and while working a job that she loves but that is not easy, Doña Luz manages to create independent capital to support herself and to bring the joy of food to those who crave it. When my sister said that her best friend, a Puerto Rican woman, and herself fell in love with the gallinitas, it revealed a site of mutual appreciation and understanding that is possible because they are working-class women who have raised their children together and experienced similar marginalized edges from within their barrio in San José. As this shows, Doña Luz's trans-ethnic networks of Dominicans and Puerto Ricans form a community of taste and sentiment. The love of her gallinitas and the affection her customers have developed for Doña Luz breaks boundaries and creates a space where Dominicans and Puerto Ricans meet safe from each other's ethnocentric prejudices.

Examining how ordinary people find ways to survive meaningfully, a central issue in struggles for food justice, could be a refreshing and productive alternative to maintain a focus on social problems. By giving less "air time" to the horrors we do unto each other, and more attention to forms of solidarity, we could shift from a politics of reclamation and opposition to a research praxis and social action centered on instances when we can work together across differences. We might find that such moments are full of ruptures and conflicts, but it is precisely via the inclusion of differences by way of a hopeful solidarity that past social transformations might have been made possible. Part of this vision is perseverance with our workbenches, in spite of challenges, to continue producing our work from wherever we can, like Doña Luz. Using food as a portal to produce documents that are part of larger social justice archives, helps us contribute to the quality of life of our local neighborhoods and networks—those messy, beautiful, and dangerous zones of contact.

There are already diverse forms of collective "food consciousness" among and across Latinos. Yet these fragmented, partial, and sometimes intersecting, shared food routes could be more powerful than preexisting group boundaries. Food visibility, in both the concrete and figurative senses, could point us to food justice as a kind of bridge that shows the struggle among diverse groups, thereby helping to unveil otherwise taken-for-granted aspects of a profit-centered global food system, and, additionally, exposing the social inequalities and suffering it generates. Maybe the monolithic, monocroping mindset of the global industrial system that got us into situations of culinary displacement beginning in colonial times might not necessarily be a good model of aspiration for developing a single food logic. There is plenty of room for struggling together to find commonalities and to affirm the right to difference in the food system.

I am convinced—echoing Mintz and Sutton—of the power of food for the future of anthropology, as it helps us take into consideration the huge contexts of the global food industry, while also paying attention to the miniature and intimate details, such as how food tastes when remembered. Food and race are explosive subjects. When brought together, they could be a powerful way of understanding their intersections as spaces of both conflict and solidarity, of boundary policing, and of the desire to know the other. The similarities between Haitians' discrimination in DR, Dominicans' in PR, and Puerto Ricans' in the United States (in spite of their crucial role in the host country food system) should not escape us. The clearest link between the migration that brought slaves to the Caribbean, and brought labor migration after the 1960s from DR, is food, the search for food security, the loss of rural land in DR, and/or issues of employment in urban areas. The colonial legacies and common history of neocolonial relations with the United States have conditioned the histories of the

DR and PR and Doña Luz's migration journey, within more ancient diasporic routes from even before 1492, such as the indigenous intra-migration flows in the Caribbean region.[34]

How Dominicans came to occupy the "savage slot" in PR happened not only through migration status, race, and class (as visible marks of marginalization), but also through that particular fear of the smell of underdevelopment that the "modernity ideology" ingrained in Puerto Rican society.[35] There is urgency in the social sciences and anthropology, in PR in particular, to study *with* Dominican communities rather than *study them*; also needed are studies from cultural perspectives that go beyond transnational migration and working-class immigrants as an economic and population push-and-pull issue. Designing research projects with the humanity of Dominicans as cultural beings in mind could help us go beyond migration as a problem and, instead, help us recognize this ancient art of movement as an intrinsic formative aspect of Caribbeanness. Researching diasporic movements as part of particular groups' cultural histories allows us to rescue individuals, such as Doña Luz, as complex social subjects who "transculturate"[36] their local lives as they also help transform the societies of which they are a part.

CHAPTER 7

Queering the Chili Queens
Culinary Citizenship through Food Consciousness in the New Borderlands

NORMA L. CÁRDENAS

San Antonio's longstanding history of public food purveyors is imprinted with struggles over race, class, gender, sexuality, and nationality. Hidden from the early history of public dining are the precursors of Tex-Mex cuisine that predates the 1800s.[1] Even accounts of the colonial "San Antonio Chili Stand" at the 1893 World's Columbian Exposition in Chicago are lost to history, obliterating a culinary epistemology. The original Chili Queens, whose industry inspired the World's Columbian Expo stand, became legendary for serving chili in the public *plazas*. Little is known of their history because extant research on Texan Mexican female food entrepreneurs primarily focuses on consumption and gendered notions of reproduction. In contrast, an emerging *her*-story of micro-entrepreneurial Mexican working-class women recognizes their productive labor as everyday resistance to a history that restricts the social mobility of their bodies and denies their own desires for economic and cultural change.[2] As entrepreneur and artist, therefore, Ana Fernández fights against dominant attitudes about ethnic working-class women in business in order to reclaim *her*-stories, to mobilize collective consciousness, and to resist commodification and appropriation of their labor, as has been the case with the Chili Queens. Fernández, building upon the legacy of the Chili Queens, operates the "Institute of Chili," a contemporary food truck in San Antonio. Her food truck subverts the imperial and national mythologies that made it possible for San Antonio to eventually exclude the original Chili Queens from its landscape. Her business practices embody what Chicana feminists call the process of queering and queer-y-ing masculine, colonialist, and imperialist ideologies that historically have excluded women from rightful ownership of public spaces. In particular, Fernández engages in queer-y-ing the racist, sexist, and classist policies created to limit ethnic, working-class women's ability to make a living and create communities though their culinary knowledge. The "y-ing" in "queer-y-ing" suggests an ongoing process in a constant fight against historical and cultural erasure.

Referring to *puestecitos* (food stalls), Meredith E. Abarca recognizes the cultural-historical contributions women business owners bring to the community as "familial wealth."[3] As culinary and cultural entrepreneurs, the original Chili Queens were path breakers in using public spaces to create sites of "familial wealth" expressed in cultural exchange where food traditions were shared. The ownership of this knowledge was eventually appropriated by the industry of culinary tourism with its oppressive heteronormative culture. Ana Fernández, as a modern "Chili Queen," recreates public spaces, resists commodification, and reveals a new culinary citizenship through a "food consciousness"[4] that enables a queer-y-ing of unacknowledged histories and desires. I add to the ways and values of reclaiming public kitchens, as Abarca has done with her study, by using Chicana feminist notions of queering and queer-y-ing. My inquiry is aimed at reinterpreting and recovering the voices and *her*-stories of the "Chili Queens," both past and present, by examining gender, sexuality, class consciousness, and desires as integral to this recovery of *her*-stories.[5] Through juxtapositions of the legendary Chili Queens of the 1893 World's Fair "San Antonio Chili Stand," Fernández's Institute of Chili food truck, and the "Chili Queen Chili Cook-Off" drag show, I illustrate how the performing body and the production of food are transformed into subjects of protest. Focusing on the consumption and production of the Chili Queens, chili becomes a culinary performance about gendered and sexualized bodies, subjectivities, identities, and consciousness.

The Original Chili Queens

Between 1880 and 1937, the Chili Queens dished out chili, *picadillo* (ground meat stew), and *fideo* (vermicelli soup) to townspeople, soldiers, and tourists at night on makeshift tables in the open air at Military Plaza. The first appearance of the Chili Queens was when Spanish soldiers camped at Military Plaza. Texas Mexican women cooked chili in *cazuelas* (clay pots) at home and reheated it over mesquite wood fires. Illuminated by oil lanterns, the sights and sounds provided a picturesque night scene that marked Texas modernity. The original chili recipe, archived at the Institute of Texan Cultures, calls for beef shoulder, pork shoulder, suet, pork fat, onions, garlic, *ancho*, *serrano*, and red *chiles*, salt, black pepper, cumin, and oregano. The original recipe advised to "never cook frijoles with *chiles* and meat." The meat-bean separation was for acidic control in order to achieve the perfect consistency of the slow-cooked beef-stew delicacy. Noted was the later addition of beans to reduce the heat. In the 1920s, the Chili Queens were recognized as the originators of Tex-Mex food who modernized the process of selling food to customers in automobiles.

The open spaces of the public plazas' connoted sociality as well as "sites of power and ideology."[6] The plazas were the soul of the city where social activities and commercial businesses were forms of visibility. From memories based on oral histories, Texas historian Felix Almaráz Jr. recalls the plaza as a space to exchange news or listen to music, or to raise political consciousness. It was also a site where "[f]or a dime, you could get chili con carne, tamales, and beans, coffee."[7]

Mainstream media changed the public's perception and image of the Chili Queens. The media reflected a racist and sexist ideology that dates to the colonial tropology of American Western culture. Paradoxically, the Chili Queens were perceived as deviant from racial, gender, and sexual norms, while at the same time their image was objectified as commodities of masculine desire. According to literary critic Suzanne Bost, "Mexican queens feed alimentary and sexual desires," marking the female body as territory that is metonymically consumed.[8] The media's use of racialized, gendered, and sexualized discourse to control and subordinate Mexican bodies and femininity eventually legitimized the Chili Queens' exclusion from public kitchens as entrepreneurs. Notwithstanding, the Chili Queens still managed to negotiate some levels of agency within the patriarchal heterosexual framework. This agency was such that, among the chili vendors, they were designated the best-selling female vendor among rivals.

For a while, they managed to shift the meaning from an objectified/sexualized marker of beauty to business acumen.[9] The Chili Queens, despite the ingenious jostling display created by the media, enacted agency by conjoining the domestic kitchen, where most of the chili was prepared, with the public kitchen, where the food was served in the plaza.

The performance of femininity by the original Chili Queens challenged white middle-class feminine conventions for economic mobility. Women's roles and responsibilities were limited to domestic and private affairs. The imaginary served by the Chili Queens was self-fashioned in *China Poblana* national attire, including sequined skirts, embroidered white blouses, and *rebozos* (shawls), sartorially symbolizing the working-class feminine ideal. If the Chili Queens subversively played the feminine peasant image to disrupt Mexican nationalism, their embodied otherness transgressed the racial and spatial politics of exclusion and undermined their normalized invisibility.

San Antonio's borderlands were complicated with power and authority over space, cultural forms, and sexual censure. By requiring an inspection and license, Mayor Maury Maverick Sr. sanitized the one-hundred-year-old Chili Queen tradition to protect citizens and tourists and eventually expelled the Chili Queens from public spaces.[10] Issuing citations for "unsanitary" dishwashing methods, sanitation commissioner Henry F. Hein and his band of army inspectors permanently closed the chili stands in 1943.[11] Regulations to serve behind screened enclosures further stigmatized the Chili Queens who resisted the enforced invisibility and controlled surveillance. According to Lewis F. Fisher,[12] the San Antonio Conservation Society, which sponsored the sanitary bill, offered their white feminized domesticity to tame the Chili Queens. This society supported the mostly Anglo, middle- and upper-class women's commodification of chili and the appropriation of La Villita square, allowing the group to sell it for tourist consumption,[13] while precluding the inclusion of the racialized Chili Queens from the public sphere.[14] After unsuccessfully petitioning to keep their chili stands in Military Plaza, the defiant Chili Queens continued to serve chili in vacant lots and backyards. This action challenged their outsider status and the exclusion they faced as a result of a gendered hierarchy of culinary labor. Unfortunately, the social pressure remained to the point where most Chili Queens ultimately went to work as waitresses earning substandard wages in predominantly male-owned Mexican restaurants. With the start of the war and military employment open to men, the women eventually opened their own restaurants or found work as civilians on military bases.

Ana Fernández: A Millennial "Chili Queen"

Born in Corpus Christi to Nick, an engineer, and Rosa Fernández, a schoolteacher and artist, Ana Fernández is the eldest of four children. The family originates from the Rio Grande border between Texas and Guerrero, Tamaulipas, Mexíco. Fernández shares the same familial culinary wealth as the original Chili Queens; her paternal grandmother was an entrepreneur who peddled tamales from her home and her grandfather was a *vaquero* (cowboy) who cooked over campfires. Accounting for the limited availability of ingredients, equipment, and time, *ranchero* (ranch) food consisted of chili, cornbread, *fideo*, and brisket cooked in Dutch ovens.[15] From distinct histories and geographies, Fernández's lived knowledge of her grandmother and mother's Mexican home cooking and her grandfather's cowboy cooking are intertwined in her own Tex-Mex cooking that reflects their collective complex identities. This familial complexity is reflected in the hybrid Tex-Mex cuisine, as it is an amalgamation of Spanish, Mexican, Tejano, African American, Native American, and Anglo influences.

A 1989 graduate of Roosevelt High School, Fernández attended San Antonio College. She left Texas to earn her BFA from the esteemed School of the Art Institute of Chicago in 2000 and earned her MFA from the University of California at Los Angeles (UCLA) in 2004. While living in Los Angeles, she worked at Stamps.com. When the economy tanked, she was among those let go. She returned to San Antonio in 2009 to find employment. While working as a river barge driver on the River Walk with San Antonio Rio Tours, she was involved in a barge accident for which she was terminated from her employment. However, it was while working as a river barge driver that she learned about the original Chili Queens. In her hopes to revitalize the cultural heritage of chili created by the Chili Queens, she turned to cooking as a form of self-employment.

After purchasing a 1978 Frito-Lay truck, Fernández, in an effort of queer-y-ing its industrial past, transformed its physical appearance, the food items sold from it, and the "food consciousness" served through its routes.[16] With no personal capital, she relied on her ingenuity to invest in her food truck by selling her own car and accepting the limited financial support her family could offer. She paid less than $15,000 for the delivery truck and invested another $3,000 in a grill and other improvements, such as butane burners, a flat grill, a steam table, and a barbeque pit. She still plans to add an exhaust vent to complement the small air conditioner. Fernández works six nights a week, from 5:30 p.m. until midnight on weekdays and until 2 a.m. on Friday and Saturday, in addition to the hours spent shopping, cooking, opening, and closing. Operating her food truck, which she named Institute of Chili, requires a high degree of self-dedication and commitment.[17] From a critical labor perspective, she valorizes domestic reproductive labor (cooking, cleaning, shopping, etc.) by reorganizing the structures of food production to defy patriarchal capitalism through her spatial intervention as a self-employed businesswoman. Her reconfiguration of the Frito-Lay truck, part of the queer-y-ing process, enables her to regain social and creative wealth, to reclaim resources from the state, and to control public space, all while transforming the nature of her work and subjectivity.

Fernández debuted her food truck on March 1, 2012. Even with no professional training as a chef, she considers her role to be one of cultural stewardship. As a representative of the new generation of "Chili Queens," she refashions the new with the old in a veritable market niche that, ironically, was opened by tourists in search of authentic foods. Inspired by the chili's working-class culinary roots and cultural affiliation, she rewrites the script of femininity, as her gender is not culturally and socially associated with meat consumption. Her chili recipe calls for two meats: brisket and ground beef. Her condiments reflect a slight deviation from the original Chili Queen's recipe as hers include *guajillo, ancho, chile de arbol,* salt, pepper, onion, garlic, and cumin. What she does follow of the original recipe is that she does not add beans. Her chili fuses the urban culture of Texas Mexicans with a Mexican *ranchería*, or small rural town. By transforming the space of the former delivery truck to a kitchen, she adapts the Chili Queen's cooking methods with gas appliances, a blender, her grandmother's spoons, measuring cups, and butcher knives. She improvised the use of her grandmother's vintage coffee pot to melt butter and found an eighty-eight-year-old cast-iron waffle maker. Furthermore, she repurposed the stainless steel countertop to create a series of miniature knife pendants with red accent liner between the blade and the handle.[18] With her knife in hand, she cuts through the myths and fantasies of masculine heroes such as the fighting "bowie knife" purportedly invented by the Alamo's James Bowie. Fernández's lesbian identity, her recipe and her actions defy the notion of the kitchen as a limited feminine space, while queering the meaning associated with chili.

Fernández queers chili as a culinary performance of difference to resist and reject heteronormative myths and archetypes of white supremacy. Chili becomes the site for the (de)construction of meanings, knowledge, identities, and the transformation of patriarchal structures and culinary imaginings. As a new "Chili Queen," she fashions a theory from personal and collective identities, knowledges, and histories through spatial practices that insist on nonstatic and nonessentialized subjectivities. This theory speaks to the "food consciousness" that Abarca and Pascual Soler define as a "pragmatic embodied epistemology, wherein knowledge is acquired through the sensations and emotions that food awakens in the body," and it also is a consciousness that "demands an analysis of the material conditions surrounding food production, distribution, and consumption."[19] Fernández finds membership in active Tex-Mex food production and consumption, where the mobility of bodies, sexuality, and desire are central to subjectivity and agency and provide a vehicle toward culinary citizenship.

Spectacle of Spiciness

As documented by historian Jeffrey Pilcher,[20] the stereotypes and discourse of what I call the spectacle of spiciness were rampant in travelogues and the local press during the 1900s. Using objectifying language, "pungent" aromas were conflated with immigrants and women, eroticized by the racial and sexual difference, and thus excluded from the space of whiteness. The strongly cumin-spiced aroma, a Berber

Ana Fernández.
Courtesy of Mark
Greenberg.

Ana Fernández, owner of the Chamoy City Limits and Institute of Chili food truck
in San Antonio. Courtesy of Mark Greenberg.

flavor, which the Canary Islanders brought to San Antonio in 1731, was symbolic of racialized sexual excess that aroused the discomfort of miscegenation. Ethnobotanist Gary Paul Nabham explains that the cumin spice signals "imperialism, cultural competition, and cultural collaboration, religious belief, and social status."[21] Thus, chile, cumin, and oregano were signs of imperial desire for "the other." Scent as an erotic art, as "sound[,] can become its own form of sexual pleasure," and "function[s] as another kind of embodied gesture."[22] Because of the spices used, the food cooked by the Chili Queens may have had this association; however, the *mestiza* Chili Queens' embodied knowledge and movements resisted the limits of a male desire and objectification.

The spectacle of spiciness that racialized Latina sexuality also conveyed anxieties about national identity that led to efforts to contain the threat of ethnic difference. A critical reading of an early drawing of an archetypical Chili Queen smoking a cigarette presents bodies as racialized, gendered, classed, and sexualized. The hyperbolic threat is peopled with "some of the Chili Queens' friends," "including a tourist from back east sporting a monocle and boat hat, an African American with outlandishly thick lips, and a 'trans-San Pedro dude'—a diamond studded gangster who crossed over to the Mexican side of town for his business dealings ... [and] an aged crone, who served as procuress for the young woman."[23] As they are depicted here, the interracial encounters with migrants, *mestizos* (mixed-race peoples), and working girls in public illustrate the sexual anxieties about race that inspired the exclusion not only of the Chili Queens, but also of Texas Mexicans from visible public spaces in order to restrict interracial interactions and censure sexual pleasure.

La Prensa, a Spanish-language newspaper founded in 1913 by Ignacio E. Lozáno Sr., portrayed all Texas Mexicans as ignorant and men as upholding the patriarchal ideal of domesticity that views women as only maternal beings. Such attitudes both justified the subjugation of the Chili Queens and simultaneously defamed chili. What *La Prensa* was publishing were the attitudes held by Mexican national elites, who migrated to San Antonio to escape the Mexican Revolution in 1910, toward Texas Mexicans and their food, specifically chili con carne. These Mexicans reviled the urbanized chili con carne as an affront to their national traditions. Mexican linguist Francisco

J. Santamaria scorned chili con carne as an inferior "detestable food with [a] false Mexican title that is sold in the United States."[24] This disdain for the dish was extended to ethnic Texas Mexicans in the United States. The rhetorical representation of chili using the Nahuatl name *chilmolli*, sauce made of chile, further invoked linguistic links of indigeneity, which were subordinate to Mexican nationalism. The modern view of mestizaje as whitening and a neocolonial paternalistic attitude toward Texas Mexicans consolidated a whiteness for US politicians and Mexican-born elite.

Representations in popular culture echoed the markers of a racialized class of chili and the racialized sexuality of the Chili Queens. Intersecting race, gender, and sexuality, the stereotype of "Hot Tamale" (a reference for "hot-blooded, volatile, sexually promiscuous") was synonymous with Chili Queen for the alluring spiciness.[25] In response to such portrayals, *La Obrera* newspaper criticized the League of United Latin American Citizens (LULAC) for advocating a "rigid patriarchal notion that relegated women to the domestic sphere and demanded considerable more modesty of them."[26] By endorsing the government's ban, LULAC simultaneously criminalized the Chili Queens by sexualizing them and by institutionalizing exclusive racial spatial boundaries.[27]

Spiciness Demystified

If the original Chili Queens subverted the limitations of racialized sexual representations, Ana Fernández, then, queers the body and femininity in order to revise historical representations and to question notions of desire and objectification. She demystifies the spectacle of spiciness as ambiguous to reveal how remixing chili recipes can alter identities, bodies, and desires. Offering a thematic menu inspired by *guajillo, arbol, ancho*, and *serrano chiles*, Fernández resignifies chili by calling it "street food plus gourmet." Using tropes as dish names, she offers an alternative and queer-y-ing discursive space of belonging from which to critique Spanish colonialism, US imperialism, and Texas masculine nationalism.

Her first invention was "The Bomb," which is street vernacular for "the best." The Bomb is a sandwich made of brisket, chili, fried egg, sharp cheddar, and jalapeños that has become her signature dish. Perhaps interpreted as faddish, Fernández posted on Facebook, "I refuse to use the following words in the marketing of my business or when composing status updates: 'Boom,' 'Booya,' [sic] or, 'this just happened.'"[28] Her queer-y-ing consumptive and performative practices uses a rhetoric that embeds the act of consumption with new historical and political awareness. Against a backdrop of imperialist military bases, missions, presidios, and nationalist associations, including the symbol of the Alamo, she subverts ideologies of militaristic nationalism by poignantly using language as a source of agency. Echoing the Food Not Bombs movement, Fernández rewrites narratives of empire and citizen making.

From Fernández's menu, a customer can order "The Roosevelt" plate, which also is known as the "Frito pie deluxe." It consists of two pork tamales, homemade Texas chili, fried egg, and *Cotija* cheese.[29] Lieutenant Colonel Theodore Roosevelt, the dish's namesake, visited San Antonio in 1898 to recruit and train Rough Riders for the Spanish-American War. Famously known as the "Cowboy of the Dakotas," the leader of the Rough Riders is renowned for his military heroism, defense of the US empire, and adherence to the Monroe Doctrine. By employing this Roosevelt motif in a satiric fashion, Fernández queers the unsettled conquest—both militarized masculinity and global tourism—in protest against imperialism, heteropatriarchy, and racialized gendered citizenship. She appropriates the white masculine cowboy trope to undermine the expansion of the domestic sphere of empire and rebrand desire through embodiment and epistemology.[30] Furthermore, by outsourcing the tamales from Ruben's Homemade Tamales, a San Antonio family-owned tamale institution located on the south side, she is queer-y-ing consumption and production from a competitive and individualistic model by offering an alternative to global capitalism and neoliberalism. Through a creation of a "food consciousness," she exposes colonial and imperial history to reimagine postnational identities and provides a map to reshape the borderlands in a global capitalist economy.[31]

At $8 for both "The Bomb" and "The Roosevelt," three tacos for $8 or $2.50 each, $7 enchiladas, and $6 Frito pie, Fernández strives to keep her food accessible. By keeping the menu to a select few items, she maintains sustainable practices that trickle down the food chain. Cost prohibits frying her own Fritos for her Frito pie, so she resorts to using store-bought Fritos, which she claims are light and retain crunchiness. She rotates her menu items seasonally. During the summer, she offers fish tacos, shrimp tostadas, and a salsa verde made with tomatillos. The rest of the year, she offers waffles with *costillas*, brisket, tacos *al pastor*, enchiladas made with chicken and chili cheese, a *chimichurri* steak *torta*, and homemade pecan cheesecake pie. She also makes gluten-free burgers and vegan chili. She recently added *tacos de mollejas* (sweetbreads) with chimichurri and pineapple pico de gallo to replace an earlier food item she called "The 210," San Antonio's area code.[32]

The Three Battles of the Chili Queens

Using Fernández's culinary story, we can map out three distinct battles in relation to the historical and cultural appropriation of chili and the marginalization of the Chili Queens. The first battle is the transformation of chili itself. Chili has become an iconic artifact in Texan and American culture; it is a veritable symbol of Texas ethnonationalism and US nationalism, much like the contested Alamo as a "master symbol."[33] The mythologized images of chili as masculinized nationalism, which is evoked with the Wolf Chili brand, gain new significance in Fernández's food business by which she creates a new social imaginary. The current battle over the "symbol[ism] of Anglo masculinist heroism," which I have dubbed "The Battle of the Chili Queens," is over the commodification and gentrification of chili that is used to legitimatize the racial order. To contest this appropriation that minimizes the contributions of the original Chili Queens, she reclaims the Chili Queens in her contemporary formation: naming her truck the Institute of Chili and using the original recipe with just a few modern modifications. Her development of a "food consciousness" was amplified when her craft and role as a modern "Chili Queen" was silenced in the struggle for representation, which led to the second battle.

The second battle relates to the Drag Chili Queen Cook-Off that takes place at the Bonham Exchange, a gay nightclub located behind the Alamo. Here, drag queens appropriate the Chili Queens as icons using palatable racialized tropes and masculine symbols. Within the spatial practice of the San Antonio Fiesta celebration that commemorates the Anglo-Texan military battle at the Alamo and San Jacinto, the Drag Queen Chili Cook-Off is a modern fantasy that performs comic indifference to showcase white masculine identity and taste. Furthermore, this cook-off reflects a revival that incorporates sexuality while also vacating questions of race, class, gender, space, and nationality. Since 2006, the Bonham Exchange has sponsored the Drag Chili Queen Cook-Off to benefit the San Antonio AIDS Foundation Kitchen, and it describes the cook-off as "a modern and eccentric interpretation of a historical event."[34] The problem with parodying the original Chili Queens, in an attempt to create a hyperfeminine gender and sexual performance in full or partial drag, is that gay men humorously transgress gender norms of Texas Mexicans only to reinscribe nationalist identities of domination. Donning folkloric *papel maché* (paper mache) costumes, the counter-history of drag Chili Queens reifies the frontier myth where women are marginalized; this takes an ironic turn, as the actual cook-off is a public and highly visible event. From a presumed gay male homonormative palate, both chili and the symbol of the original Chili Queens' bodies represent the homoerotic fantasy as depoliticized: "exotic but disinfected."[35] Affectations and the irreverent nicknames of drag performers elide a critical understanding of the politics of desire and solidarity that denies female sexual agency even as the self-fashioned bodies and mobility of the drag "Chili Queens" appropriate the Chili Queen persona.

Latina/o camp drag, according to Ramón García, is an expression of aesthetic practices of "stylizing marginal social space in order to construct a queer Chicano identity [and it] is not only and always a form of resistance."[36] While sharing an alliance in the desire and pleasures of gay tourists, the drag "Chili Queens" affirm a hypernationalism while excluding contemporary female "Chili Queens" from the nation as being from the "tacky" past. The drag queens' cultural appropriation is "expanded to not just the belle of the ball, but [also to] the tackiest of the tacky!"[37] In a parody of the cult of domesticity and femininity, tacky is invested in a working-class "excess" aesthetic for a tourist audience. The tacky pun here, masquerading as a slur, refers to a cultural taste that reifies a stigmatized stereotype and maintains hierarchies through a privileged gay masculine culture that is inaccessible to women. The middle-class aesthetics and sensibilities that represent the Chili Queens, reimagined in the gay nightclub as "queer," are in contradistinction to the spatial public plazas where the original Chili Queens were deemed abject subjects. Forgotten are the meaning and histories of the Chili Queen tradition in hegemonic culture and the subversive potential in gay culture. The drag "Chili Queens" queer the archive as modern; however, the tourist performance signifies an ahistorical view of subjugated working-class Chili Queens through an erasure of identities.

The third battle deals directly with the very use of the name "Chili Queen." Because of drag cultural politics that have allowed for the appropriation and institutionalization of the designation for the Drag Chili Queen Cook-Off, Fernández was denied the right to use "Chili Queen" as the title for her business identity. Despite this rejection, her trademark registration application signified an intervention in the mythological imagery of the original Chili Queens. As a self-proclaimed bona fide "Chili Queen," she strategically reconfigures the heteronormative image the original Chili Queen has come to represent by deconstructing the boundaries between public/private, local/national, rural/urban, individual/community, feminine/masculine, and high/low culture. Mobilizing and politicizing the Chili Queen icon and legend, her use of the title stirred up controversy and confronted hegemonic norms.

The rejection of her trademark name did not diminish her conviction to politicize the Chili Queen icon. In a press release, as a performative act of identity, she announced the Institute of Chili as her new business name.

> The original Chili Queens were street food pioneers who we owe a cultural and culinary debt of gratitude. Our new name will allow the business to grow unencumbered by literal, historical associations. The new name more clearly defines our attitude and unique culinary vision, while still paying homage to the original [C]hili [Q]ueens. The "Chili Queens" is not a place or geographical location. The Chili Queens were entrepreneurs, Mexican-American women of San Antonio who sold chili in open-air markets for over 200 years. That is my culinary heritage. I am honored to carry on the tradition in 2012 as a bona fide [C]hili [Q]ueen.[38]

The Institute of Chili has become a site, subjectivity, and practice of resistance to counter the commodification of women's bodies and knowledges by creating and affirming a broader citizenship and collective consciousness. As such, the gender ambiguous name, Institute of Chili, functions to create a complex identity regarding the interrelationships of race, ethnicity, class, gender, sexuality, and nationality. Furthermore, Fernández resists dominant meanings of domesticity and femininity by regarding cooking as a source of pleasure and identity. In the process, her daily operation of the Institute of Chili politicizes the representation of the original Chili Queens on the culinary borderlands. The juxtaposition of the San Antonio Conservation Society's commodification of the original Chili Queens at La Villita against the Drag Chili Queen Cook-Off as part of "A Night in Old San Antonio" (NIOSA) at the Bonham highlights the position of Texas Mexicans as Others for tourist consumption. Without forgetting the original Chili Queens, Fernández's Institute of Chili, as both performance and discourse, resignifies Tex-Mex food production and consumption from racialized sexual abjection.

The Chili Queen's Revenge, or Remember the Chili Queens

Much like the Alamo has served as "a powerful impetus for U.S. revenge against Mexico," for Fernández, the Institute of Chili serves as a retribution agent in public spaces to vindicate the original Chili Queens from a repressed collective nostalgia and forgotten history.[39] She also queers her performance by the art designs on the food truck, the subversive creativity of the menu, and the use of social media as her marketing device. The holistic aspect of her performative act ruptures the patriarchal heterosexual romance via the production of chili, which is traditionally considered a highly masculinist food. By reappropriating chili, the state's dish, from its symbolism of white rugged masculinity, she reverses the gendered norms to express feminine desire and to question exclusion. She transforms the heteronormative meaning and ideologies of chili by "[engaging] in the debate about the acceptability of female masculinity" through her presence as a modern female lesbian food truck operator.[40]

Fernández has found subtle revenge, literally for herself and symbolically for the original Chili Queens, in garnering recognition from the local press and Spanish-language television. One such recognition was winning The Twisted Taco Truck Throwdown in 2013 for her tacos al pastor made with pork shoulder and chili paste rub that established her legitimacy. She was visited on April 2013 by Fox's Spanish-language Utilisima travel-food series called MotoChefs, with Chefs Aquiles Chávez and Aarón Sánchez.[41] *Food & Wine* magazine recognized Fernández for the "Best Chili in the U.S." in 2013, as did *Travel + Leisure*.[42] She has been featured in various TV venues: PBS's *The Daytripper* with Chet Garner; *Noticiero Univision*; "Good Day SA with Shelly Miles"; and FOX TV's *Daytime @9*. In spite of these accolades, her food truck has been all but ignored by mainstream food critics. The Institute of Chili has been reviewed by a local alt-weekly newspaper in San Antonio, *The Current*, which shows how the dominant press reproduces difference in the culinary economy.

Following the success of the Institute of Chili, her newest endeavor is an ice cream truck: Chamoy City Limits, which features frozen comestibles, or shaved ice, for $5. The following is a snippet of the press release that announced the new venture:

> The truck has been outfitted with vintage ice cream truck music and a special high-capacity Japanese shaved ice machine that can quickly turn 300 pounds of block ice into light, fluffy snow . . . Our goal at Chamoy City Limits is to take the classic experience and crank it up [not to a 10 but] to 11 with our house specialty chamoy and pickled fruits.[43]

Awarded "Best Shaved Ice" by *News 4 San Antonio*, her creations tantalize and satisfy desire and pleasure, especially during the hot summer. Drawing inspiration from traditional and diverse cuisines, she recreates chamoy, which is an Asian-influenced and chile-based snack made with fruits. The spatial metaphor evokes the liminal space that restricts difference and constructs hybrid identities. Her chamoy is prepared from pickled apricots, plums, and peaches, is strained, and then separated from the brine. The brine then doubles as a sauce or spice and the taste is sweet, salty, and spicy. Used on a bag of chips for *tostilocos*, Fernández predicted that her brine would be the next

Sriracha sauce; her prediction was made before the *Houston Chronicle's* restaurant critic Alison Cook tweeted, "It's the Sriracha of 2014."[44]

Expanding her spice repertoire (and hashtags), Fernández's #IcySpicy comestibles contain whole ingredients including anise, hibiscus, and tamarind. Using Twitter's hashtag feature to describe flavors and ingredients, she entices her loyal customers to visit the ice cream truck to cool off. She tweeted, "Whole fruits, peppers, spices, and cane sugar is what's in our #Chamoy," thereby emphasizing that she uses no preservatives or artificial coloring.[45] Through their use of chamoy as a chili paste, "Chamoyadas" with limeaid, chili, and chamoy render a palatable refreshing taste. The customer favorite is the "Mangonada Supreme": a layered treat with mango sorbet, red and green chamoy, with *chango* or pickle brine, and topped with chili salt. Featuring the south Texas classic, the "Piccadilly" is a Cherry Kool-Aid powder and chamoy with Best Maid pickle wedges. In another hashtag, Fernández speaks about a childhood favorite shaved ice: "Pink Leche." She states, "the elusive classic from the Rio Grande Valley. This is our secret recipe."[46] Another flavor is "El Diablito" made with "Tamarindo, fresh key lime, house chili syrup, salt."[47] The "Komodo Dragon" includes "pickle brine, house jalapeno syrup, chili salt, cucumbers, and chamoy."[48] The newest flavor is "Fabuloso" and the "secret blend includes hibiscus #SoFreshSoClean."[49] She self-designs marketing hashtags and acronyms, such as #IcySpicy and #GSG for Go Spurs Go, that enables her to create a community with followers.

The Institute of Chili on the Twitter Trail

The metaphor of the trail evokes the intertwined histories of Texas Mexicans on cattle drives and migrant trails on the frontier. The Twitter personas @TheChiliQueens and @HouseOfChamoy build on the industrial lunch truck concept to remap exclusionary spaces in the city and establish a trail of Twitter followers.[50] Asserting her visibility as a "Chili Queen," Fernández transforms the discursive and material spaces using hashtags that add context and metadata to create trails for added agency and pleasure. Leveraging the historical and political consciousness of followers, she negotiates racialized class divisions, desires, food gentrification, and consumer culture. According to

Richard Gambitta, gentrification is "viewed as domestic imperialism, [where] outside forces occupy their territory and cannibalize their folkways."[51] Fernández counters gentrification by expanding the frontiers of downtown and traveling to consumers, both with her truck and her tweets, to help mitigate social inequalities.

By navigating new discursive spaces and negotiating tensions, the Institute of Chili is creating sites and practices for new identities. Operating among visible sectors, Fernández affirms the right to occupy suburban sites such as The Point Park and Eats on Sunday from noon to nine, and the RackSpace for lunch on Fridays. She also occupies urban venues such as TacoLand, a live music bar, every Friday, and the Alamo Street Eat Bar. She seeks to serve low-income customers at marginalized locations by vending on weeknights at public parks including Miller's Pond, Mission Park Library, and Mission Drive-Inn on the south side, and Lion's Field on Broadway across from Brackenridge Park. The Golden Gloves Social House at the Pearl Complex near downtown, Culebra Creek Park near the west side, and The Block SA at UTSA are also spaces she engages. One customer pleads, "Come to the west! Alamo Ranch or somewhere! Broadway is so far away."[52] Building a following with her customers, even naming a dish, Maricela's Combo, after one of her regular customers, shows her investment in the community.

Disrupting the capitalist economy with its private land use restrictions and addressing the lack of food accessibility in urban food deserts, Fernández offers free food every first Monday of the month at Haven for Hope where she feeds about 125 people. Serving democratic dishes without "the alienating and exploitative effects of capitalism," she finds ways for the food truck to serve a food consciousness.[53] Blending ethics and compassion, she imagines a Food Truck Justice League committed to public service every month to restore food consciousness to the community.

Queer-y-ing Aesthetics

The Institute of Chili encourages sentiment and identification in food consumption and production as grounded in a historical-materialist approach. Fernández has expanded her customer reach by using digital spaces such as Twitter and Facebook as well as word of mouth to reverse the specter of her chile-based dishes. Her tweets are a way to form community and identity, both virtual and actual, and bring a queer consumerism of relating to others. More than transgressing spatial borders, she alters the way bodies are represented through communal relations. Her public performances include Facebook, Pinterest, LinkedIn, Instagram, Tumblr, YouTube, and Google+. On Twitter, she unveiled photographs of her new truck remarking, "I really think our truck belongs in a museum."[54] Her photographs are sharp contrasts to early travelers' photographs and journalists' drawings that both racialized and sexualized the original Chili Queens. As an ambulant museum, the food truck features a minimalist black print font on white background that makes a topographical statement exposing "an experience that creates multiple layers of community, consumption, and interaction through street food."[55] Using pastiche, her "T Queen" vintage vanity plates, where T stands for Texas, simultaneously forge a visible title and place on the performance space of the street.

With a digital food community, Fernández harnessed the corporatized knowledge of savvy marketing learned while working at Stamps.com to use on social media platforms. She peppers her posts with humorous status updates alongside photos of food shared by and for customers. The juxtaposition between the physicality of the original Chili Queen and the digitality of the modern "Chili Queen" allows for increased interracial interaction, albeit often anonymous and across time and space. As I write this, the Institute of Chili has 2,964 likes and Chamoy City Limits has 30,427 likes on Facebook. On Twitter, @TheChiliQueens has 1,803 followers and @HouseOfChamoy had 963 followers.

Fernández's performativity, as a process to recover the Chili Queen archive, reimagines relationships of power and the politics of gender, sexuality, and historical relations. By building an intergenerational network and profile on social media to promote her food truck, she is creating an alternate genealogy and collectivity. Challenging invisibility and silence, she equalizes the power of official histories with her Twitter feed that expands the discourse beyond individuals to include a social community with their devices. Her visibility also sustains the working-class Chican@ community against their forgotten culture and across contexts. Through affective archives, she compels remembering the Chili Queens as the matrilineal heritage of Tex-Mex food while challenging masculinity, nationalism, and heteronormativity, whereby the Chili Queen lineage is self-reflectively queered.

As a contemporary artist, Fernández's self-fashioning is a hybrid aesthetic that is low maintenance, yet high technology. Her artistic training and standpoint from the chef's seat on the food truck give her a unique view of the city and its residents. From her food truck, as an artist residency, her oeuvre shows how families as a collective use domestic space, the most private domain, to enact identity through use and design. Her paintings in large scale recognize the beauty of ordinary houses in San Antonio, decorated and maintained by families over generations. In her rendering, the non-enclosed space of the house challenges notions of modernization and prosperity otherwise considered marginal, and connects indoor and outdoor spaces. She reinterprets housescapes through props such as cars, piñatas, balloons, lights, flags, dogs, and the use of numbers such as 210 that represents San Antonio's area code. Her paintings of houses are queered to individualize the people who live in them and who control the collective space of the neighborhood in order to fuse public and private spaces.

Conclusion

Neither remembered as "foreign" nor forgotten as "domestic," culinary citizenship is invoked by Fernández to reclaim public space in an effort to recreate a narrative that shows how memory fortifies history. She reimagines and reappropriates the original Chili Queens from male bureaucrats, women boosters, drag queens, and hipsters. With her entrepreneurial spirit and culinary heritage, family support, adapted modern technology, strategic visibility, and a honed market niche, she challenges the homogenization, commodification, and appropriation of chili. Expanding her culinary reach to disrupt the racially sexualized structure that appropriated the Chili Queens, her recipes materially flesh the body and sustain the community. Through queer and queer-y-ing possibilities, she creates empowering images to challenge the perception of the Chili Queens as passive and abject.

Beyond preserving the historical memory of the Chili Queens, she disrupts contemporary nationalist constructions of chili and engages in spatial praxis to construct a new identity and consciousness.

The historical continuity of the chili wars perpetuates a struggle for culinary citizenship, as the right to signify chili shows what and who merits protection. Resisting multiculturalism and the politics of marginalization, Fernández is serving more than decolonized food to the people. She is using identity and aesthetics to forge an inclusionary foodscape with implications for social relations in San Antonio. Unsettling a culinary tourist economy built on ideologies that maintain women's marginalized status, she performs flexible gender as a queer Chicana entrepreneur. She continues to research new recipes and dishes so that her future desire of a food truck tour that reimagines the 1893 Chili Queen Columbian Exposition tour one day becomes a reality.

CHAPTER 8

More Than "Just a Waitress"
The Waitress as Artist and Activist in Contemporary Chicana Literature

CRISTINA HERRERA

I have carried food out and brought it back. I've lifted trays and put them back on the shelf. I've worked so hard that at night my legs have flailed and twitched. I haven't slept at times, I was so tired, and I've also overslept, overeaten and slipped on salad dressing, wet lettuce and God knows what the hell was that, and I've known what food smells like on an unwashed uniform. And I have always appreciated the hard work food servers do. I salute all waitresses, waiters, busboys and cooks. Where would we be without the nourishment of food? Food is necessary to fortify and replenish. Bendiciones/blessings and a hearty thank you to all who work with food on a daily basis. Your work is important, it matters, it is the basis of all community.[1]

In her 2006 memoir, *A Taco Testimony: Meditations on Family, Food and Culture,* Denise Chávez draws attention to the cultural, social, and political implications of eating Mexican food, particularly her mother Delfina's delicious Mexican entrees such as tacos. Throughout the text, Chávez marks the connection between the consumption of her mother's Mexican cooking and the development of her own sociopolitical identity as a Chicana writer and artist, but she does not stop there.[2] In passages such as the epigraph I cite, Chávez takes her critical discourse on food a step further by making visible those individuals who not only prepare the food we eat at restaurants and at home, but those very same who bring food to table, refill our water glasses, and wipe our table without "disturbing" our dining experience. Chávez's insistence on recognizing the worthiness and the humanity of food servers, especially waitresses, given her own experiences waiting tables as a young woman, must be read as an oppositional, critical stance against dominant norms that relegate food service employees to the margins. For Chávez, the work performed by waitresses and others within the food industry not only is "important" but, in addition, their work creates a sense of unity at a time when divisions across gender, racial, sexual, and class lines have never seemed so prominent. Employees within this labor force, according to Chávez, are valuable human beings despite dominant power structures that render them as faceless workhorses and little else.

Research conducted by Chicana/Latina labor historians has worked to uncover the ways in which working-class Chicanas/Latinas have contested systems of power that relegate them to marginalized, silenced places and turn them into useful, cheap sources of labor. While this research is highly significant for challenging the historiography of Chicana/Latina laborers, many of these studies have tended to center on women in agricultural, cannery, domestic, or garment work.[3] Research on Chicanas/Latinas in other sectors, in particular as food servers, is lacking despite the prevalence of food, restaurants, and dining in literature by contemporary Chicana writers. I aim to broaden the critical literary scope of Chicana labor by examining the representation of the waitress in three contemporary texts by Chicana writers: Diana López's novel *Sofía's Saints*, the very recent novella by Demetria Martínez, *The Block Captain's Daughter*, and Denise Chávez's novel *Face of an Angel*. While Chávez's well-known novel has been the subject of several studies, the novels by López and Martínez have not been investigated, marking this chapter's simultaneous effort to expand literary criticism on these writers.

In this chapter, I will begin by briefly discussing the literary representations of women laborers in Chicana writing to ground my investigation of the Chicana waitress as worker, critic, artist, and activist. This chapter will introduce studies on the waitress in US culture and society as a mode to contextualize my reading of the three texts. On the one hand, many of these studies have largely examined the waitress's role as a surrogate maternal, even wifely, figure, an idealized nurturer, and a server of food to the hungry; on the other hand, some investigations have pointed to the very real, daily threats of sexual and/or racial harassment and class exploitation that belie romanticized images of the cheerful waitress. As I argue, the three novels feature intelligent, socially conscious Chicana/Mexicana waitresses who challenge the food industry's systemic erasure of their humanity and identities as brown, working-class women. Although these female characters are aware of sexist, racist, and classist discourses that render them only as anonymous replaceable cogs, they challenge degrading views by constructing empowered identities as critics, activists, and artists. In an intriguing manner, while the character Soveida Dosamantes from *Face of an Angel* critically elevates her work as a waitress to a spiritual level as a mode to overturn the stereotype of waitresses as passive and servile, the protagonists Sofía Loren Sauceda, from *Sofía's Saints*, and Guadalupe Anaya, from *The Block Captain's Daughter*, construct their empowered identities outside their labor as waitresses as they choose to identify as artists and activists. However, even as these two characters attempt to separate themselves from their occupations as waitresses, the novels reveal their critical reflections on life, community, social justice, and art that occur while working in restaurants. The three narratives insist on not only making visible the Chicana waitress within the food industry, but also fusing the women's activism, art, and waitressing into a working-class Chicana feminist sensibility embodied in their waitress occupation.

"Women's Work":
Literary Representations of Chicana Laborers

> *I am a waitress who knows what it is to serve others and a woman who knows what it is to work hard.*[4]

Chicana literature is ripe with images of working women. In novels such as Ana Castillo's *So Far from God* and *The Guardians*, Bárbara Renaud González's *Golondrina, why did you leave me?*, or Sandra Cisneros's *Caramelo*,[5] to name only a few, Chicanas, often mothers, are engaged in paid and unpaid labor to support and sustain their families. Yet, what is significant in these texts, and others that feature Chicana laborers, are the novels' insistence on highlighting the humanity of the women characters, as well as depicting characters who at times are frustrated with their seeming invisibility and often desire not only to labor with their hands and bodies, but with their minds as well. In other words, these Chicana workers are artists and activists whose lives are, however, constrained by the difficulties of working-class womanhood that reduces the will to create and think to a mere fantasy rather than an actual possibility. In these texts, then, the writers demand attention to working-class Chicana artists and activists whose words and images may never be conveyed on paper or canvas. Yet, in a well-known passage that calls on the working-class Chicana to write no matter her financial limitations or domestic responsibilities, Gloria Anzaldúa names those spaces inhabited by Chicanas as legitimate material for the creation of art: "Forget the room of one's own—write in the kitchen, lock yourself up in the bathroom. Write on the bus or the welfare line, on the job or during meals, between sleeping or waking . . . While you wash the floor or clothes listen to the words chanting in your body."[6] As Anzaldúa correctly points out, working-class Chicanas do not hold the same economic, racial, or social privileges as writers such as Virginia Woolf, who argued that, in order to write, women must have the freedom of personal space, or a "room of one's own."[7] But what of the working-class woman-writer of color, with daily meals to prepare, a mountain of dishes to wash, and the never-ceasing piles of laundry to fold? What if her "studio," her artist's space, is the kitchen or laundry room?

For Chicana writers such as Anzaldúa, the creation of art and the practice of activism must be embodied by this working-class sensibility and experience.[8] Anzaldúa refuses to separate the working-class, daily reality of Chicanas and the creation of art. As Tey Diana Rebolledo argues in her analysis of labor in Chicana writing,

> It is not the mere representation of work that infuses contemporary Chicana literature; rather it is a new perspective toward that work, a perspective that not only values it but also ennobles it and celebrates it. This perspective is a tool, a strategy that allows contemporary Chicana writers to use their knowledge of domestic work as a way to claim authority in their writing.[9]

Significantly, the representation of labor in Chicana writing serves to valorize the work performed and the human being behind the apron or uniform. It also goes beyond that as this labor imagery simultaneously is an effort by Chicanas to fuse working-class sensibility and artistry—to connect the two rather than separate them. For many Chicana writers, the kitchen space is one such realm where "nourishment and creativity take place."[10] The kitchen does not hinder the creation of art; instead, the sensual, bodily, and political act of cooking is art in and of itself.

In her intriguing article on what she calls "pink-collar resistance," Karen Kovacik engages in a critical discussion on the poetry created by women who have been employed as waitresses and clerical workers. Rather than allow their working-class daily realities to prohibit the creation of poetry or to deny their validity as artists, these women laborers "dare to imagine alternative worlds in which secretaries and waitresses, visible and loud, speak out, talk back, assert their individuality, and, at the same time, honor collective commitments."[11] It is often during the completion of domestic chores that we glimpse instances of this "talking back" in literature by Chicanas as well. For example, in Bárbara Renaud González's novel, *Golondrina, why did you leave me?*,[12] the mother character, Amada, often counsels her daughter-writer, Lucero, throughout the text while engaged in household tasks such as ironing, cooking, or washing dishes. Chicana poets and writers have created a feminist literary tradition that overturns the dominant view that tasks like cooking are mindless or menial. In literature by Chicanas, the cook, in particular, is an artist in her own right, and thus the kitchen is transformed into an active space where Chicanas can create empowered identities.[13] However, as the three novels I examine here demonstrate, it is often difficult to demand attention as waitress-artists when such deep-seated cultural myths of the passive waitress are so prevalent.

The Waitress: Passive? Servile?

> *All women are waitresses because all women feed and nurture those around them. Waitresses are simply the "professional nurturers."*[14]

Waitressing is a physically taxing and demanding occupation. For those who have worked as servers or who have observed waitresses in action, we see that the task of taking one's order, ensuring beverages are refilled, and juggling heavy trays of steaming food while avoiding the embarrassing mistake of dropping plates and glasses is a balancing act and a job that requires timing, efficiency, and intense focus. It was table three that requested the high chair, not table four; and the woman at table one is allergic to strawberries, remember that. I have never worked as a waitress; indeed, my lone food service experience was as a nineteen-year-old college student working at Baskin-Robbins where it felt as if I scooped never-ending amounts of ice cream to impatient customers who complained of being short-changed on hot fudge or whip cream. While being an employee of an ice cream shop may seem to be an easy task, to say this job was difficult is an understatement.

Despite the importance of their labor in the restaurant industry, waitresses have often been the subject of negative myths and stereotypes constructed by the dominant culture that position this occupation in line with passivity, mindlessness, and servility. As Greta Foff Paules points out in her study, the equation of food service with servility has much to do with the "etymological nearness of the terms *service worker* and *server/servant* to *servile*, [which] contributes to the imagery of servitude by providing linguistic continuity between historically stigmatized and modern forms of service."[15] In the early twentieth-century restaurants, for example, Anglo-American women entrepreneurs quite literally capitalized on this gendered, racialized myth of the docile woman by employing African American waitresses because they were thought to be "deferential" and "passive."[16] Harking back to the racist, sexist image of the servile mammy, African American waitresses have had to battle the omnipresent stereotype that they "desire to serve whites."[17] The important point to note on this history of African American (women) servers is the apparent contradiction between their performed service and the privileged act of eating out. While these African American waitresses may historically have been tolerated because they were performing "acceptable" Black roles as servers, these same restaurants may not necessarily have granted the workers the privileged role of diners within the very walls that employed them. However, Latina/o employees within the restaurant industry have often been forced to "labor behind kitchen doors" because of the historical tendency of restaurant owners in large cities such as New York and Los Angeles to hire waiters whose features are deemed more "European."[18]

Therefore, patrons have been comfortable with female employment in the food service sector because of women's performance of such gendered activities as serving food: "In the theater of eating out, the waitress plays multiple parts, each reflecting a female role. To fulfill the emotional and fantasy needs of the male customer, she quickly learns the all-too-common scripts: scolding wife, doting mother, sexy mistress, or sweet, admiring daughter."[19] The waitress's occupation as paid laborer, thus, becomes subsumed by the symbolic, "female" act of serving food, thereby rendering her position within the restaurant as "acceptable" so long as she fulfills male, heterosexual desires. Such romanticized constructions of the waitress as happy servant are deeply ingrained in dominant discourse. According to Paules, the work performed by waitresses is deemed "low skilled," and waitresses are often portrayed by the media as "ignorant, incompetent, apathetic, lazy, and slow," which further contributes to the myth of servility.[20] In Leon Elder's and Lin Rolens's nostalgic collection of essays *Waitress: America's Unsung Heroine*, for example, the authors elevate the waitress to the esteemed height of "heroine," which may very well be an attempt to overturn the waitress's invisibility, yet passages such as the following are nevertheless troubling: "Always more intimate, [the waitress] not only conducts you through the rituals of eating, but she serves, depending upon the need, as a Geisha-Nurse-Mother figure."[21] Invoking a rather imperialist tone, the authors conflate the waitress with the geisha—easily one of the most quintessential objects of the Western heterosexual male's fantasies. In this light, the waitress's occupation is reduced merely to a server of sexual fantasies rather than a paid employee who happens to serve food for a living. Furthermore, the pitting of geisha on the one hand against surrogate "mother" on the other, also hints at the contradictory expectation for all women, waitresses or not, to fulfill the rigid, dichotomous role of sexual "server" and de-sexed, bodiless maternal figure.

Perhaps the real danger of subscribing to racialized and sexualized myths of the waitress as wife, mother, or geisha is how such normalized thinking overlooks the daily threats faced by Latinas/Chicanas and all women employed within the food industry. Beyond these degrading myths that reinforce the image of the waitress as docile, mindless, and endearing, her very occupation as food server places her within capitalist society as economically dependent on privileged diners. This dependency makes "sexual harassment . . . an occupational hazard . . . In the servant role of waitress, a woman is in a subordinate economic power position vis-à-vis the customer."[22] Within this unequal power structure, mistreatment not only is allowed, but is encouraged even, given that "degradation is part of the food service experience."[23] When we factor ethnicity into this class-based system, it becomes evident that women of color face added reminders of their "subordinate" status: "Within the food services, Latina/os experience long work hours, strenuous physical tasks, few opportunities for advancement, and low wages. High levels of poverty, low levels of education, and fear of job loss, particularly for undocumented workers, make Latina/os vulnerable to workplace injury, exploitation, and discrimination."[24] The deep-seated myth of the passive, cheerful servant belies the systemic mistreatment of waitresses, and upholding such harmful myths serves to prevent these workers from constructing empowered identities as working-class women.

Clearly, then, waitresses juggle various roles in addition to trays of food. But how can waitresses rewrite the most persistent "script" of waitressing: that of the cheerful and passive servant who attends to the customer's gastronomical (or even sexual) desires? As Kovacik argues, it is through the writing of poetry that some waitress-poets reject and disrupt "popular notions of waitresses as deferential servants."[25] In a similar vein, the three protagonists I discuss in this chapter challenge their invisibility within a food industry that positions Chicana waitresses as silent and faceless. It is to these novels that I now turn.

While Chávez's *Face of an Angel* overturns dominant constructions of wait-service by elevating it to a higher rank of spirituality, López's and Martínez's novels differ slightly in the ways they shape the waitress identity. In Chávez's novel, the protagonist, Soveida, takes great pride in claiming an identity as a waitress, viewing her occupation in a subversive mode that highlights the worthiness of the work she performs. However, the protagonists in López's *Sofía's Saints* and

Martínez's *The Block Captain's Daughter* claim their identities as artists and activists while engaged in their waitressing occupation. Although they do not actively identify as waitresses, their work performed as artists and activists must be read within the context of their waitressing.

Restaurants: Sites of Reclaiming Identity

López's novel features a thirty-year-old woman, Sofía Loren Sauceda, who works as a waitress at Pete's Mexican Restaurant in Corpus Christi, Texas. While Sofía has been employed at Pete's since the age of eighteen, following the death of her mother, and has become a surrogate daughter for the owners, Pete and Chimuelita, she admits that her true passion is her art. She creates images of saints that she burns on wood: "Drawing with my pyroelectric pen is nothing more than tracing an image already in the wood, making the saints evident . . . to the flea market shoppers who can't see the holiness in nature the way I try to see it."[26] For Sofía, wood is a natural canvas that holds sacred images for those willing to uncover them and, like the sturdiness of the wood, she seeks permanence and stability in a life that is marred by the trauma of her mother's death from a car accident and repressive memories of this same woman who engaged in numerous sexual relationships with men to avoid real intimacy. Shaping images of saints is an act of branding herself onto nature; it is a way of claiming a space for herself in the natural world when the social world around her appears to be fragile and short lived.

Sofía sells saints at the local flea market, but she refuses to sacrifice her artistic virtue by creating wood drawings that are guaranteed to bring in more profit. By claiming her identity as artist, Sofía attempts to reject the image of waitressing as an unworthy occupation, despite receiving almost daily reminders from her boss Peter that, as a waitress, she is little more than a woman who serves food: "But what do you know about art? . . . You're a waitress."[27] As Pete's classist statement suggests, Sofía has no right to proclaim herself an artist because of her working-class status, and his rigid thinking places artistry firmly among the elite. According to Pete's binary logic, working as a waitress disqualifies Sofía as an artist; moreover, artists and waitresses occupy separate boundaries that should not overlap, as he tells his wife, Chimuelita: "Sofía can't paint, . . . She's a waitress."[28] Although Pete tells Sofía that she is considered a member of the family, his condescending remarks that she is (only) a "waitress" contradict this claim and serve to place her as his economic subordinate as well; after all, the restaurant that employs her bears *his* name.

In fact, at times throughout the novel Sofía struggles to maintain a sense of her artistic and personal integrity because she risks internalizing the destructive myth of waitressing as low-level work. When she reunites with David, a former friend who later becomes her romantic interest, she admits to herself, "I worry that David's eyes are making their judgments and scoffing at my waitressing job, the same job I had when I knew him before."[29] Her fear that David is belittling her occupation, however, says more about her own anxiety over what she does for a living. Sofía is uncomfortable with claiming a waitress identity when her credibility as an artist also is put into question. Later, when she visits the local bank and unsuccessfully attempts to apply for a mortgage loan to buy the home she has been renting since her childhood, she reveals her discomfort within a privileged space that conflates one's value, literally and figuratively, with capital: "What did I expect? I'm not a businesswoman, but a waitress and a flea market clerk fighting against the urge to sneeze."[30] Within the banking system that is a product of a dominant capitalist society, an artist and waitress such as Sofía is deemed not only unworthy as a client because of her low wages, despite a consistent income and full-time employment, but, furthermore, the denial of a loan and her mere presence inside the bank suggest that she is unwelcome to even enter a space designated for a privileged group of which she is not a member, thus marking her a lesser person, or an outsider.

Despite the challenges she faces as a struggling artist disguised as a waitress, Sofía acknowledges the significance of Pete's restaurant in her shaping and understanding of family. Her mother's death and father's abandonment leave her parentless, but her inclusion in the restaurant's extended family ensures that she is not an orphan. However, while Sofía loves the Pete's restaurant family, she also witnesses a darker side to this family's intimacy. This can be seen when, during a party that Pete and Chimuelita host at their restaurant for their family members and employees, the owners discover that their son César is gay and

Pete's homophobia erupts in a violent scene: "You don't know what you want! This is your family, César, and families always stay, but fags like Parker come and go."[31] In this powerfully emotional moment, López queers the Mexican restaurant by inserting the presence of a gay Chicano character and his young lover Parker, also an employee of Pete's restaurant. Their queer presence serves to challenge Pete's patriarchal homophobia, suggesting the writer's understanding of the restaurant as a site of negotiations of sexuality, gender, ethnicity, and class. Moreover, Sofía's witnessing of this moment also hints at the novel's deliberate queering of the restaurant space. As a restaurant employee, yet also extended member of the family, her presence blurs the boundaries that she is expected to maintain while donning her waitress uniform. She quickly learns, however, that as much as she is "supposed" to please her customers by performing the role of cheerful waitress, her employers, who happen to be her surrogate family, also demand this performance. The fact that this moment occurs when the restaurant is closed to general customers points to the ways in which this dining establishment can be redefined not only as a place of business, but also as a setting for intimate family functions that reveal complex and problematic views on sexuality and identity that may be more covert while the restaurant is open to business. So, as an extended family member who simultaneously is an employee of the restaurant, Sofía's presence during a moment in which César's secret is revealed to his blood relations is all the more significant. She has an in-between status that redefines rigid boundaries of "family" and employer-employee relations given that she is viewed as both welcome and intruding on "family" business; she is a "family" member and yet also an employee.

By expressing Pete's rigid notions of "family" as blood relations, the novel's author opposes static definitions by including the presence of queer characters. Of course, Pete's earlier classist remarks to Sofía work alongside his initial rejection of his queer family member. Sofía herself learns the tenuousness of family and intimate ties when she critiques Pete's homophobia only to be reprimanded subsequently by Chimuelita, who orders her to work harder as a form of punishment for speaking out: "She points to a bucket of soapy water and I feel like an exploited Cinderella sloshing away."[32] Like the fairy-tale princess's unwelcome status as stepdaughter, Sofía sees the contradictions inherent within such narrow constructions of family. On the one hand, biological children such as César or orphans like herself may be adopted and cared for as members of a family; on the other hand, their inclusion into the family unit rests on their acceptance of rigid roles such as the ideal, heterosexual son or obedient, unresisting daughter. Indeed, that Sofía is "placed" back into the role of employee for vocalizing her discontent demonstrates the unsettled, even ambiguous position she holds. Passages such as these highlight the significance of the restaurant as a critical space in which to challenge and negotiate dominant racial, sexual, gender, and class discourses of power.

Much like Sofía, the protagonist Guadalupe "Lupe" Anaya, from Demetria Martínez's *The Block Captain's Daughter*, weaves in critical commentary on the restaurant's social world while fulfilling her waitressing duties. The novella, which is mostly epistolary in form and comprised of Guadalupe's letters written throughout her pregnancy to her unborn daughter, Destiny, also includes other character voices and alternates between first-person, second-person, and third-person narrative. Although employed at La Tropical Mexican Restaurant in Albuquerque, New Mexico, she, like Sofía, claims an identity as a Mexicana artist and activist in a post-9/11 world and is most proud of her accomplishment of being block captain for her neighborhood watch program. In her role as activist and burgeoning artist, Lupe attempts to construct a more empowered, oppositional identity, given that she is often invisible in her work as a waitress at a Mexican restaurant frequented by Anglos. Furthermore, Lupe's status as an undocumented Mexican woman provides her with a more critical, first-hand perspective on border crossing, NAFTA, and the capitalist exploitation of undocumented labor—critiques that she frequently reveals in letters to her daughter written during lunch breaks or in her second-person narrative voice.

Lupe's work as a waitress positions her as an observer of the restaurant's social dynamics and as an occupant within this space who is at once seen and unseen. Being a Mexican waitress at a "Mexican" restaurant managed by an Anglo man, Mr. Simmons, Lupe critiques what she sees as the restaurant's distortion of Mexican food to appease finicky Anglo palates:

"Bean and cheese burrito, hold the cheese." "Huevos rancheros, egg whites only." "Tortillas, the kind without lard." "That's
whole beans, please, not fried." Everyone's on one kind of diet or
another. When you take orders you feel like a doctor scribbling
out a prescription, life and death in your hands. What is the
world coming to? The gringos believe in cholesterol the way
Mexicanos believe in the existence of God. It's enough to make
you ravenous.[33]

In her sarcastic recitation of Anglo food orders, Lupe laments the ways
in which eating has become a "life and death" situation rather than a
pleasurable, self-affirming experience. Facetiously commenting on her
customers' rigid eating habits via self-denial, their lack of enjoyment
and indulgence, indeed their self-imposed starvation, is transferred
onto her body, making her hungry for "trans-fatty acids."[34] Unlike
starvation as a result of extreme poverty, Lupe's privileged customers
routinely diet, thereby making their devotion to self-denial akin to a
fierce and rigid religiosity.

Beyond that, Lupe alludes to what food scholar Lisa Heldke has
defined as "cultural food colonialism," where "the cooking techniques
of the Other become marvelous resources that can be scooped up,
'developed,' and sold to Us."[35] Rather than consume Mexican food in
its "original form," the restaurant patrons impose Anglo dieting rituals
to transform it into "healthier" fare. In another letter Lupe writes to
her unborn daughter, she states, "I am helping Mr. Simmons develop
a recipe for enchiladas with tofu and vegetables instead of cheese, as
some of our customers have gone vegan on us. Oh well, we must be
ecumenical in our customer service. But tofu enchiladas? What is this
world coming to?"[36] In her repeated concern over "what this world is
coming to," Lupe critiques what she sees as yet another form of colonization: this imposing of a Western, capitalist obsession with dieting
and often expensive, organic food items that only the privileged can
purchase. Given that the Mexican food served is constructed as inher-
ently "unhealthy," Anglo restaurateurs such as Mr. Simmons "develop"
it, as Heldke describes, through Anglicizing. The Mexican food, in
other words, is in need of improvement and metaphorical salvation
to achieve the "superior" rank of low-fat cuisine.

As a Mexican waitress, Lupe is astutely aware of the ambiguous space she occupies within La Tropical as visible yet invisible. Much like the previous novel, *The Block Captain's Daughter* also blurs these boundaries, for even as Lupe wears the exact uniform that marks her as "the help" and "servile," according to this faulty logic, her letters and inner dialogue position her as a thinking subject, which is contrary to what her customers may presume. Conscious of this, she transmits to her unborn daughter through letter writing a sense of empowerment that she cultivates through her work as neighborhood block captain, artist, and activist. In her attempts to fuse activism and artistry, Lupe, with the support of her friends, creates "prayer wheels" made of empty birth control packets to critique what she sees as waste added to land-fills. Deemed "scandalous" by the local bishop for using contraception as a *"spiritual aid"*[37] for Chicanas and Mexicanas in need of prayer, Lupe's work is nevertheless picked up by a local gallery, as she explains in a letter: "They've given to calling me an 'artist . . .' I read the review again and with a pencil circled the word 'artist.' I said it out loud, 'artist,' to see if it would fit. But in truth it felt like a too-tight pair of shoes. So I said it again, then again, 'artist.' Say it enough times, I thought, and it will stretch to fit me, big as I am, carrying you around on swollen feet day and night."[38] As an undocumented waitress, Lupe is uncomfortable claiming an artist identity at first because of dominant power struc-tures that reduce her humanity to laborer and little else. Yet, this letter is composed during her waitressing shift, and her final acceptance of herself as an artist is voiced within this context, thereby rupturing boundaries of the restaurant space that would otherwise reduce her merely to paid "worker" rather than artist. Thus, the novel challenges a reductionist perspective that denigrates the working-class artist who also works within the food industry and fuses the waitress-artist role into one. Moreover, Lupe's initial undocumented status quite literally renders her an invisible body that is unaccounted for and living "in the shadows." However, as a mother-to-be of a daughter who will be a US citizen, Lupe rejects current racist, anti-immigration rhetoric that would reduce her daughter to the epithet, "anchor baby." To counter this xenophobia, Lupe transmits a working-class Chicana feminism to her unborn Destiny:

> To think your mama had dreams of being a writer so long
> ago, but it was not to be. Maybe you will pick up on that dream

where I left off. Instead of pushing a broom here at La Tropical, you might be sitting in a booth pushing a pen. Okay, my lunch half-hour is almost up. I must report quickly: Your mama, whom God has chosen to serve as Block Captain, may have saved a life. ... Well, little one, back to work where no one knows I'm an artist *and* a Block Captain. I'm just another Mexican.[39]

Although Lupe is aware of the dominant perception that she is little more than "just another Mexican," writing letters to her daughter during breaks from work serves to fuse her artistry and activism with her working-class identity. This blurring of space, that is, Lupe's use of the work space to write loving letters to Destiny, is a critical, empowering strategy employed within the novel to resist rigid binaries that attempt to put Lupe in her "place" as faceless worker. To the Anglo patrons who do not acknowledge her humanity, she is invisible; yet, Lupe refuses to allow this dominant system to silence her unborn daughter. Through her empowered and subversive letter writing, Lupe embodies strength, activism, and dignity to her daughter despite unequal power structures that work to deny these values to those who labor with their bodies. In a beautiful letter that serves as the novella's ending, we hear the voice of the eighteen-year-old Destiny, and her touching statement to her mother reveals that she has embraced Lupe's feminist, working-class sensibility: "I cried when I read in one of the letters that you hoped someday I would be pushing a pen instead of a broom. Just remember Mama, you too pushed a pen: You pushed and pushed, writing letters to your Destiny, words that shimmer now in this pool of candlelight far from home."[40] As a working-class Chicana who has entered the privileged space of the university, Destiny refuses to reinforce dominant ideology that marginalizes people like her mother. By calling her mother an artist and by acknowledging the empowered nature of Lupe's letter writing, Destiny cultivates an oppositional identity through the maternal bond. Thus, Lupe's letters, which are written mostly at the restaurant, fuse maternal empowerment with her working-class waitressing occupation.

Like much of her fictional work, Chávez's novel *Face of an Angel* is subversive in its efforts to challenge the subordinate role placed on working-class Chicanas, embodied by the protagonist Soveida Dosamantes's waitress occupation. Chávez's feminist project is significant for its insistence on rewriting "women's work" through a "reclaim[ing] of service" not akin to passivity.[41] Narrated from Soveida's first-person point of view, her personal and family histories are also complemented by her "Book of Service," which essentially is a spiritual and life handbook written for fellow waitresses employed at El Farol Mexican Restaurant in the fictional town of Agua Oscura, New Mexico. Throughout the novel, Soveida's "embrace of service,"[42] through a critical perspective of waitressing that overturns dominant norms, is a primary theme. As Soveida recalls, her lessons on waitressing began one summer as a fifteen-year-old under the supervision of El Farol's head waitress, Milia Ocana, who instructs the young Soveida to remember that she is "to be of service" rather than a servant.[43] For Milia, the waitress provides a valuable service to humanity, but is not a slave to people's demands. According to Milia's tutelage, the task of waitressing is a form of art akin to a "dance," and rather than reduce the occupation to a mere "job," Milia teaches Soveida the necessity of critically elevating what, on the surface, may appear to be mundane.[44] In other words, the waitress is not merely "like" an artist; she is one.

Unlike Soveida, the restaurant owner and manager, Larry Larragoite, "hate[s] waiting on tables"[45] because he views the physical act of clearing dirty dishes to be degrading. In response Soveida admonishes Larry's dichotomous thinking that reduces Mexican food and subsequently Mexican people as shameful, as can be seen in the following exchange:

> "I hate to see how people eat."
> "I never think about it. You see things as good or bad, you start making judgments, you won't be able to do the work."
> "You sound like Milia."
> "I guess I do. I really miss working with her. I can't believe I'm staying on. The food's gotten to me!"
> "Call it by its real name: slime! Have you ever really looked at a dirty plate after someone has finished a meal? It's disgusting! It's full of discarded chile skins, fat globules, wilted lettuce, old beans like dry turds, soggy tortillas. Yech!"
> "I never think of it that way."
> "Pork entrails, half-chewed steak, greasy rice, tough gristle,

watery vermicelli! Go on, think about it! It's nauseating! I hate food! Especially Mexican food!"[46]

This dialogue between Soveida and Larry, while humorous, reveals the vastly different views they hold not only on food service, but also on Mexican food itself. Perhaps most important, Soveida critiques Larry's attempts at Anglicizing through his internalizing of dominant, racist views of Mexican food as "slime," which, of course, suggests that those who consume a diet of Mexican food are "slimy" themselves. In fact, Larry's description of Mexican food as "greasy" and full of fat alludes to the derogatory epithet of "greaser" commonly used to describe Latinas/os in the early twentieth century. Larry's repulsion of food service, then, is not solely aimed at the labor required to perform that work, but mostly to the service of that particular type of food. Thus, his aversion to Mexican culture is manifested in his bodily rejection of Mexican food, as Soveida explains:[47] "He avoided the food, because it gave him gas. He loved red enchiladas but they always made him sick."[48] As someone who consciously removes himself from a Mexican ethnic identity, the very food items made within his restaurant cause physical discomfort; in other words, he is unable to consume a culture that he adamantly rejects. His disparaging views of wait-service are reflective of this ethnic and cultural rejection.

Throughout the novel, Soveida defends her waitressing occupation to counter perceptions of her identity as a "servant" engaged in meaningless tasks. For example, in her "Book of Service," Soveida instructs the younger generation of waitresses to adopt an oppositional perspective on the art of waitressing, stating, "*A waitress is the observer/observed sanctified by food*";[49] moreover, the waitress must learn "*that there is more to waitressing than serving food.*"[50] As a self-reflective waitress, Soveida shapes her identity within El Farol's walls, calling the restaurant "home" and as connected to her as her "own face."[51] Rather than subscribe to the myth of the waitress as servile, Soveida consciously chooses to construct her occupation as a vital, even "holy" order.[52] In this elevation of waitressing, "woman's work is lifted from the mundane to the sublime,"[53] thereby converting the waitress and Chicana laborer into a sort of priestess or perhaps even goddess-like figure.[54] If the task of eating is of the highest order, then the server of food is elevated to the ranks of deity.

Forging an empowered identity as a sort of spiritual worker, Soveida counters disparaging views of what she does for a living, unlike characters such as Larry or her cousin Mara, who insult the waitressing profession: "Working with those wiped-out, tired-horse old women and those men—pubescent, chinless wonders—delivering half-warmed tortillas and dried-out tamales? Can't be all your life will amount to, will it?"[55] Rather than admire Soveida's work ethic and financial independence, Mara reduces the entire food service sector to a group of exhausted, used-up individuals. Interestingly, Mara's criticism of the workers and her criticism of the Mexican food are described in a similar vein, thereby illustrating her problematic relationship with food and eating, as evident in other conversations between the two women. However, for a socially conscious woman such as Soveida, it is imperative that waitresses defend an occupation that is denigrated as lowly, servile, and lacking dignity: "[S]ometimes we have to deal with stereotypical images of what people imagine Mexicans to be, as well as what they imagine waitresses to be."[56] As an astute and critical observer of the social world around her, Soveida challenges racist, sexist, and classist ideologies that construct a body of people and the work they perform as worthless.

Her critique of stereotypes reveals her nuanced understanding of the fact that she faces discrimination not only due to her occupation, but also because this working-class employment intersects with her gender and Chicana identity. These astute observations are highly visible throughout "The Book of Service," which she intends to pass on to the younger generation of waitresses. First and foremost, according to Soveida, the younger waitress, Dedea, must learn the differences between service and servitude: "In our family, men usually came first ... The first tenet of waitressing is service. The dictionary defined serve as: To render assistance, to be of use."[57] Soveida's sense of humanity and compassion combine to teach young waitresses to know the difference between servants and women who serve. Servants are held in passive states within a dominant capitalist structure, but the waitress, the woman who serves, must construct an identity as an empowered worker. While serving men in her family equates to passive servitude,

Soveida's guidance teaches Dedea that providing service is valuable for the existence of humanity. In fact, Soveida rejects the gendered view of service that places women as "natural" servers of men; of course, this gendering of service implies both the serving of food and even sexual favors. In her final chapter of "The Book of Service," she continues with this thread:

> By now you know that there is more to waitressing than serving food. More to living than being fed or feeding someone yourself. More to people than what we briefly see of them in our work. . . . I wanted to give you a little gift. It's a copy of The Book of Service: A Handbook for Servers that I've been working on for many years. I still don't think it's finished yet. It's taken me a long time to get my thoughts together, and longer to put them down. The handbook is about more than serving food. It's about service. What it means to serve and be served. Why is it that women's service is different from men's?[58]

In these parting words, Soveida urges Dedea to reject dominant views of service that subordinate the work performed by women as inferior to that provided by men; in addition, these dominant views suggest that work performed by women is only valuable if it is in service to men. Most important, Soveida questions the very gendered nature of service that differentiates between "women's" and "men's" work that renders women as servants and men as workers. In her insistence on humanizing all servers, Soveida critically works against the prevailing images of waitresses as passive and silent. The waitress occupation, like the waitress herself, commands respect.

Conclusions

The study of Chicana labor, food, dining, and consumption within Chicana literary texts is growing, but scholars must also acknowledge the presence of food servers, such as waitresses, within these works. Much as food is a critical discourse in which to study Chicana literature, so, too, does the Chicana waitress provide us with an oppositional perspective that resists dominant forms of oppression. It seems apt that as much as scholarship examines the critical implications of eating food, the significance of serving food would also resonate as an equally important mode of investigation. However, this has not been the case. If, as this scholarly collection attests, food, dining, and consumption offer unique ways of interrogating Latina/o identity and presence within the food industry, what may be said of the food server's presence (or absence, as the protagonists of this study point out at varying degrees) within the four walls of a restaurant? I am reminded of the political rhetoric surrounding contemporary immigration reform, which discusses the need to bring undocumented Latinas/os "out of the shadows." While this chapter does not engage with such a discussion, and while the use of this language may initially appear to be unrelated to the chapter's critical scope, I believe this very phrase, "out of the shadows," may also refer to the need to excavate Chicana literary waitresses. Indeed, we need not only flip the pages of a Chicana text to witness the waitress's work, for a quick meal at many restaurants will most likely be served by a Chicana/Latina waitress or busboy. What are the implications of studying this Chicana service work? What does the presence/absence of Chicana waitresses in literary scholarship tell us about the overall state of this group of women within the food industry? For the waitresses studied in this chapter, we see the ways in which they must negotiate their absence and invisibility within a larger system of power that would deny their humanity along the lines of gender, ethnicity, and socioeconomic status. Cannot serving a meal also be powerful precisely because presiding over the act of eating unsettles boundaries we deem to be rigid and unshakable? Or must this resistance be cultivated not only by serving food, but also by claiming an identity as artist outside the restaurant space? For Soveida, however, such claims to artistry necessitate the rewriting of food service as art in and of itself. Of added significance is the fact that eating a meal with another human being is an act of intimacy, yet how much of this intimacy is also cultivated by the waitress who brings food to table? As characters such as Soveida Dosamantes and Lupe Anaya observe in their monologues, the waitress blurs the lines of intimacy because of her presence within and outside the dining atmosphere. She, after all, touches the plate on which the food is served; she reaches for the water glass that is in need of a refill. And while she performs seemingly mundane tasks to ensure her customers' comfort, she hears and listens all around her to conversations taking place as if she were not there.

The novels I examine in this chapter challenge degrading assumptions about waitress work, and astute observations by these waitresses not only belie their supposed mindlessness, but indeed, they use their surroundings as critical, even humorous subject matter, unbeknown to the customers. Much of this humor is subversive, naturally, as part of the joke is at the expense of the customers who are not in on the secret. The surroundings are critical, namely because the waitress who "only" brings food to table possesses a critical voice, indeed, a life separate from her work place where she is artist. Claiming a voice, and in particular, claiming the artist's voice, is one such way to challenge waitresses' invisibility within a profession that depends on their labor but attempts to reduce their humanity merely to a body who serves. As women, as Chicanas, the challenge comes in rewriting "service," as in the case of Soveida, who refuses to abide by raced, gendered, and classed notions of service that deny her right to claim autonomy as a Chicana waitress who enjoys her work.

The novels by Diana López, Demetria Martínez, and Denise Chávez create complex Chicana characters who challenge what it means to be a waitress. Although dominant norms would have us believe that the waitress is little more than a faceless being who brings food to table, the three Chicana texts consciously challenge such a reductionist perspective. Soveida Dosamantes embraces her work as a waitress, and in her pride in constructing this waitress identity she refuses to align her food service to servility and, instead, she elevates her occupation to spiritual work of the highest order. Both Sofía Sauceda and Guadalupe Anaya identify as artists and activists, yet they also intentionally fuse their work as waitresses into a working-class artistic and activist sensibility.

PART 4 ▪ Producing and Reproducing Identities

CHAPTER 9

Conspicuous Consumption?
Eating Disorders as Nervous Immigrant Conditions in Contemporary Latina Fiction

MARION CHRISTINA ROHRLEITNER

Eating is an act laden with affect.

—Paul Rozin[1]

Immigrant bodies historically have been associated with threats to the literal and economic health of the nation. During the height of the influx of Irish, Eastern, and Southern European immigrants to Ellis Island in the late nineteenth century, figures such as the Irish immigrant Mary Mallon, better known as "Typhoid Mary," became the embodiment of the immigrant as ignorant contaminant.[2] More recently, refugees and immigrants from Haiti have to undergo extensive HIV testing and are often unjustly blamed for having brought the disease to the United States.[3] It is, therefore, not surprising that the battle over the legal inclusion of immigrants into the US body politic is fought and often inscribed on the physical bodies of immigrants.

This is true particularly for Latina immigrants due to the triple marginalization of their bodies in the US mainstream via nativist vilification, racialized exclusion, and rampant sexism. First, Latinas are frequently the victim of vicious attacks about their alleged goal to plant "anchor babies" in the United States. By virtue of being immigrants from the Southern Hemisphere, they are under constant pressure to justify and document their presence in the United States, and this is the case not only since the passing of Arizona SB 1070 and Arizona HB 2281.[4] Second, they are expected to conform to cultural norms and ideals of female behavior and racialized standards of female beauty in both the United States and their countries of origin; and third, Latinas' bodies are subject to surveillance and to being relentlessly read and interpreted as being "fit," or not quite "fit enough," for US citizenship.

Obesity has become the most recent form of singling out the Latina/o body. Obesity rates continue to be alarmingly high among US Latina/os, especially among Mexican Americans, and children are particularly at risk. In public discourse in the United States, this obesity crisis is often racialized, associated with urban poverty, and attributed to an alleged lack of knowledge about and access to nutritious, healthy meals and exercise in ethnic communities. In her speech to the National Council of La Raza in New Orleans, Louisiana, on July 23, 2013, First Lady Michelle Obama participated in this discourse and affirmed that "food is love," yet also claimed that "we are loving our children to death" by feeding them an excessive amount of unhealthy meals.[5] Even though the First Lady was careful to cross-reference her critique of Latina/o foodways with her own experiences of growing up African American in the south side of Chicago, her remarks were met with some stark criticism. She was accused of "food shaming"[6] and blaming the obesity crisis among Latina/o children and youth on "unfit" mothers whose food choices, whether out of misguided love or limited access to healthier options, turn their children into a liability for the nation.

In opposition to this narrative of, however well-intended, ignorance, I propose to read the representation of foodways and eating disorders in some Latina fiction as a response to the vilification and marginalization of Latina/o bodies as "illegal." I argue that these "nervous conditions"[7] associated with food consumption are not the result of poverty and lack of knowledge about or access to proper nutrition and exercise. Instead, I show that these phenomena reflect a larger psychological response to immigrants' experiences of violent displacement, cultural alienation, individual isolation, and xenophobia in the host country. I also highlight that these anxieties are paired with the desire to become a fully accepted member of US-American society via one of its most persistent myths: consumption of material goods, including food, as a sign of material success and, consequently, the full immersion of the immigrant into the US-American body politic. Specifically, I look at the literary representation of eating disorders such as compulsive eating, bulimia, and anorexia in the work of the Cuban American author Cristina García as reflections and expressions of some Latina immigrants' anxieties regarding their physical, legal, and cultural presence in the United States.

To show the complexity of an immigrant's anxieties to be part of the "legal" American body and to illustrate that the solution of eating disorders is not a simple matter of returning to traditional and healthy food practices, I also examine *Under the Feet of Jesus* by Chicana writer Helena María Viramontes. Here, we see the systematic challenges many Latina/o immigrant and migrant families encounter in reaching this thwarted solution to ease their concerns. These challenges are mostly the result of a lack of access to affordable fresh fruits and organic vegetables, time constraints as a result of having to work multiple low-paying jobs, and a pervasive "food shaming" that is fueled by aggressive marketing campaigns by large food-processing corporations.[8]

Retaining and maintaining food preparations, ingredients, and flavor patterns from the country of origin can provide immigrants with physical and psychological comfort and offer a reminder of belonging to a cultural community. However, this return frequently remains but a nostalgic attempt when (im)migrants have to navigate a foreign and often hostile land that keeps many Latina/os in the margins of its options for healthy food choices.

Drawing on the work of Psyche Williams-Forson, I show how representations of food choices, preparation, and consumption in contemporary Latina fiction are never mere reflections of ethnic commodification, as Ellen McCracken also suggests.[9] Instead, I argue, they are indicative of the physical and cultural "politics of location"[10] the Latina protagonists struggle to occupy in an American body politic that seems keen on excluding them from the very onset. These constant attacks and challenges to the presence of Latina bodies in the United States leads to "nervous conditions" that often take a toll on the immigrants' physical and emotional well-being via alternately overeating, excessive dieting, and disavowal of traditional ethnic foods in favor of a detrimental fast food diet full of high doses of sugar and corn syrup, unsaturated fats, and empty carbohydrates. As Raphael Dalleo and Elena Machado Sáez, drawing on Nestor García Canclini, put it, "[T]o consume in excess may signal an attempt to deal with the 'unstable social order and uncertain interactions with others' and 'make more sense of a world where all that is solid melts into air.'"[11]

In García's 1992 *Dreaming in Cuban*, Latina women's appetites are pathologized through the excessive consumption of empty calories by the protagonist Lourdes. Lourdes eats vast amounts of cinnamon rolls, chocolate croissants, potato chips, and Oreo cookies in order to consume what is perceived as a diet condoned by the American mainstream. By gaining weight, Lourdes claims and takes up more space in an attempt to increase her visible presence in the United States. Ironically, this overconsumption and the subsequent large size tragically lead to her increased invisibility in a United States public sphere that polices women's bodies and asks them to comply to often unattainable standards of thinness, fitness, and, ultimately, a fictionalized version of whiteness.

Estrella and her mother, Petra, in Viramontes's 1995 novel *Under the Feet of Jesus*, however, are migrant workers whose food choices are severely limited by their lack of access to affordable, fresh, and healthy foods such as corn, squash, beans, rice, and tomatoes, which could be the basis for a healthier diet. Their bodies are not marginalized due to obesity, but due to their precarious socioeconomic and legal status as migrant farmworkers. This family serves as another example of how the industrialization of US agriculture has made it all but impossible for farm laborers to afford and have access to healthy nutrition.

While Lourdes chooses to eat unhealthy foods as a result of a misguided sense of what it means to eat and thus *be* Cuban or American, Petra and Estrella are limited to cheap, processed foods instead of the fresh, if also heavily fumigated, produce they help harvest. Lourdes on the one hand and Petra and Estrella on the other hand thus embody two sides of the same coin: the central role food production, preparation, and consumption play in marginalizing Latina immigrants from successful integration into the US body politic and excluding them based on both external and internalized racism, sexism, and classism, which often results in immigrants' eating disorders and other food-related illnesses.

The intimate and profound connection between mind, body, and environment, both natural and cultural, becomes perhaps most tangible when looking at eating disorders. As Deane W. Curtin convincingly explains, "Anorexia nervosa is a disease made possible by the conditions of contemporary cultural life that predominantly affect women."[12] It is an illness that is conditioned by and responds to patriarchal notions of femininity that seek to contain and control female energy, especially women's sexuality and creativity. To eat close to nothing or to consume food compulsively are forms of behavior related to food that can be understood as two extremes of women's responses to such attempts at control and containment. In the context of the lived experiences of Latina immigrants, this containment is complicated by the cultural demands that are placed on women in both home and host countries. According to Curtin, the intrinsically relational quality of personhood as defined by food studies showcases how "our connections with food partially define who we are."[13] Ethnic identity, embodied personhood, and, by extension, a claim to citizenship in the daily lives of immigrants are thus made via the foods produced, created, and consumed by members of migrant communities.

In 1899 economist Thorstein Veblen coined the term "conspicuous consumption" to describe the way in which the emerging American bourgeoisie showcased and implemented its social status via a display of luxury goods, including an abundance of not-readily-available food items.[14] Consuming a large amount of expensive food could, then, be read as the immigrants' attempt to showcase their material success in the new country and, by extension, their successful assimilation into what was depicted and perceived as the American mainstream. What is crucial in this context is not only how much food is ingested overall, but also how much of a certain food is consumed based on what is considered indicative of superior social status.

The central tension associated with the protagonist Lourdes in García's novel consists of her attempt to "become American" via consumption of the kind and amount of food deemed "all-American." Ironically, this desire seems to be based on a false and perhaps outdated sentiment as many educated, upper-middle-class white Americans have either never consumed or are turning away from consuming the stereotypical post–World War II American diet largely based on processed foods. The current food movement, counter to what Lourdes believes when she first arrives in the United States, advocates eating habits that are more healthful, holistic, and environmentally sustainable, if also a lot more expensive.

The success of the grocery and lifestyle chain Whole Foods as well as the current popularity of ethnic foods, especially its most recent manifestation in urban food trucks, is representative and indicative of this new food movement. At the same time, they also highlight some of its inherent problems: Whole Foods is expensive, even for those with an upper-middle-class income, and exclusively located in neighborhoods the corporation deems profitable. Farmers' markets, which often feature organic foods, are also frequently present only in affluent neighborhoods and in regions whose climate invites home-growing fruits and vegetables. As Warren Belasco has pointed out with renewed force in his updated introduction to *Appetite for Change*, the promises of the food revolution of the 1960s have not quite taken hold in the United States due to what he calls "corporate hegemony." This type of hegemony has coopted elements of countercultural lifestyles and "employ[s] effective marketing to avoid substantial reform," which fail to change a larger underlying system.[15] In a process I call the "gentrification of ethnic cuisine," two things happen. First, traditional ethnic foods are appropriated by the food industry and sold in trendy food trucks or at farmer's markets in affluent neighborhoods; and, second, members of poor immigrant communities are kept from using the best quality product to prepare their traditional foods as these are replaced by cheap processed foods in their local grocery stores. This replacement of healthful eatables for processed goods is foregrounded in Viramontes's *Under the Feet of Jesus*.

The process of "becoming American" via consumption of abundant processed food as well as the act of "food shaming" of certain ethnic foods is reflected and addressed in García's novel. This novel speaks to the excessive consumption of unhealthy, fatty, sugary, and heavily processed foods and related eating disorders as expressions of immigrant anxiety over the constant challenge to Latina immigrants' rightful presence in the United States. In terms of "food shaming," it is important to note that it is a force not only external to immigrant communities. The long reach of the immigrants' internalized racism, which often favors a perceived "all-American" diet over ethnic foods (the great popularity of assimilated ethnic foods notwithstanding), has a great impact not only on immigrants' food choices, but, subsequently, also affects their attempt to approximate a notion of female beauty that privileges an idealized and often photo-shopped Northern European body type over all others.

The main Latina protagonist in García's narrative struggles to become an accepted member of the civic community by consuming foods she associates with and believes to be accepted by the United States. This pattern of consumption is conspicuous because it leads to bouts of bulimia, obesity, and other food-related illness, and also because it runs diametrically against the established idea of thin and fit femininity as a marker of class distinction in the United States. I suggest, therefore, that after failing to comply with the profoundly unrealistic and media-manipulated expectations of white femininity in the Unites States, Latina immigrants, such as Lourdes, use food as a psychological consolation and dissenting statement for the rejection they receive time and again. By turning her body into a manifestation of the abject, Lourdes defies rejection by the US mainstream at the price of her own health. In contrast, neither of the protagonists in *Under the Feet of Jesus*, Estrella nor Petra, is much concerned with their civic status in the United States; rather, they are more in tune with the transnational realities and demands of their immediate migratory community, even as they are hindered from living a healthy lifestyle by the very infrastructure an industrialized agriculture imposes on workers and consumers alike.

Dreaming in Cuban

In Cristina García's debut novel, *Dreaming in Cuban*, Lourdes Torres is a first-generation Cuban American whose cyclical fluctuations from an obese to an anorexic bakery owner reflect her struggles with "becoming American." Lourdes is trying to overcome, via the consumption of food, a traumatic history of rape and of suffering a miscarriage as a result of sexual violence in her home country. In spite of this tragic violent encounter with a guerrilla fighter in the early years of the Cuban Revolution, Lourdes is not a sympathetic character.

When Lourdes arrives in New York City, she immediately feels a sense of ease associated with the rebirth she has anticipated. She does, indeed, recreate herself physically, economically, and spiritually as the founder of a successful chain of bakeries. From a purely materialistic perspective, Lourdes becomes the embodiment of the entrepreneurial American Dream and the narrator lets us know, "Lourdes considers herself lucky. Immigration has redefined her, and she is grateful."[16]

Despite her sense of gratefulness, however, Lourdes does not extend her gratitude to others. Instead of showing empathy to fellow refugees and immigrants, she ruthlessly builds her bakery empire on the backs of undocumented workers—a way of doing business that makes her feel more fully American. By endorsing and capitalizing on the "from rags to riches" myth, Lourdes feels herself merge with the American mainstream, and she seals this union by putting on display and eating a vast number of sticky cinnamon rolls every morning. Enlarging her physical body alongside her business signals, or so Lourdes hopes, her full immersion into the American mainstream.

However, this redefinition equals Lourdes's full immersion in American material(ist) culture and is accompanied by an appetite for empty calories that knows no bounds. Initially, the familiar smells of sugar and cinnamon are soothing and restorative, as they offer a link to Cuba that is not tainted by her painful experiences during the revolution: "She is comforted by the order of the round loaves, the texture of grain and powdered sugar, the sustaining aromas of vanilla and almond."[17] This soothing sensation associated with Cuban-style *pan dulce* is a form of what Anita Mannur has called "culinary nostalgia."[18] Lourdes's longing for an imaginary Cuba that no longer exists, and which probably never existed as such outside of Lourdes's vivid imagination, is fed literally by foods that are equally lacking in essence and consist of mostly empty calories. In an aptly literal reading of the German saying "Man ist was man isst" (One is what one eats), Paul Rozin suggests, "Cooking and eating are transformational acts" of both ourselves and the foods we consume, and the foods that physically and emotionally sustain us ultimately become our own physical substance.[19] Thus, when Lourdes consumes sugary calories without nutritional value, her body and self in turn become an embodiment of the absence of any true essence. Lourdes has lost her essence in the act of violation she experienced in Cuba and no amount of empty calories can fill that void.

As Fred L. Gadarphé and Wenying Xu point out, "[T]he exile's foodways have the capacity to function as a cushion from displacement and homelessness, as comfort food that momentarily transports the exile to the ever elusive home."[20] This "cushion" literally manifests on Lourdes's body through the consumption of *pan dulce*, as she almost doubles her body weight, and it becomes a metaphorical cushion against a hostile patriarchal world bent on rejecting her in spite of the comparatively warm welcome Cuban immigrants, especially those from the early wave of immigration in the immediate aftermath of the revolution, have received in the United States.

Lourdes's process of mental dissociation from her body following the traumatic experience of rape initially only allows her to ingest comfort food items. Soon, however, her need for comfort turns into insatiable greed and an obsession that results in her massive physical expansion along with the expansion of her business:

> The flesh amassed rapidly on her hips and buttocks, muting the angles of her bones. It collected on her thighs, fusing them above the knees, hung from her arms like hammocks. She dreamt continually of bread, of grainy ryes and pumpernickels, whole wheat and challah in woven straw baskets . . . Lourdes had gained 118 pounds.[21]

What begins with a renewed lust for life quickly turns into a burden that begins to threaten her very survival. Initially disassociated from her physical needs, she meets them with sugary and fatty foods, only then to turn to an obsessive consumption of sex as well. This obsession provides her with another form of instant gratification, while slowly destroying her physical and mental health. Lourdes's husband is depicted as an only slightly humorous victim of her insatiable and violent advances, which his wife has constructed in her mind as a very American form of freedom mixed with an almost religious fervor for consumption: "Lourdes did not battle her cravings; rather, she submitted to them like a somnambulist to a dream. She summoned her husband from his workshop by pulling vigorously on a ship's bell he had rigged up for this purpose, unpinned her hair and led him by the wrist to their bedroom."[22] Lourdes's sexual appetite is depicted as predatory and emasculating and is as equally unidirectional as her excessive consumption of empty calories. As Abarca and Pascual Soler show in their introduction to *Rethinking Chicana/o Literature through Food*, sexual appetite and craving food are intricately connected sensations in Latina/o and Latin American literary representations, perhaps most famously in Laura Esquivel's 1989 novel *Como agua para chocolate*.[23] It is worth noting that specifically female sexual desire often is cast in food imagery, and the sexual act frequently is represented metaphorically in the act of cooking.[24] However, Lourdes's sexual appetite is not written as a pleasurable release, but as an act of domination over her diminutive husband. Having taken on "American" dimensions, she dominates her husband, her daughter, and her employees with a greed that cannot be satisfied.

Significantly, Lourdes names her bakery "Yankee Doodle Bakery," and, in a highly performative act of patriotism, celebrates its "grand opening on the 200th birthday of America" and offers "free food and drinks" to her customers.[25] Her daughter Pilar comes to learn quickly that nothing offered for "free" is ever truly without cost. Lourdes swiftly adopts some of the uglier sides of the American entrepreneurial spirit, especially via her exploitation of undocumented immigrant workers. When one of her hired hands, a recent immigrant from Pakistan, challenges her authoritarian and often senseless rules, she fires him on the spot and "wants Pilar at the bakery after school. [She] fired the Pakistani yesterday."[26] The employee remains nameless and his identity reduced to his precarious immigrant status and country of origin, which marks him as a foreigner and potentially dangerous outsider, even in the pre-9/11 United States.

Lourdes meets her wake-up call, from her attempts to become American through her excessive consumption of unhealthy foods, in the shape of Ivanita, her nephew. When she travels to Cuba for the first time as a wealthy American tourist and businesswoman, Lourdes is struck by the slender, almost emaciated, employees of the fancy resort she booked. She decides to invite Ivanito for dinner and "was shocked to see how her nephew devoured his food at the tourist hotel in Boca

Ciega. Ivanito refilled his plate six times with palomilla steak, grilled shrimp, yucca in garlic sauce and hearts of palm salad."[27] It does not escape Lourdes that the abundance of food in the resorts and the scarcity of foods on the island, and most other items of daily need, are a result of both neoliberal practices and the ongoing Cold War because "Lourdes knows that Cuba saves its prime food for tourists or export to Russia."[28] The juxtaposition of her own excessive and unhealthy consumption of food and her nephew's starvation draws attention to the ways in which both members of the Torres family suffer as a result of the Castro regime and how their inability to control these conditions affects their eating habits.

Lourdes's appetite for both food and sex begins to wane after this sobering encounter with her nephew, and she begins to transition into buying into another American myth: that of the eternally young, perennially desirable, and endlessly slender woman. Lourdes starts to lose weight and tries to adapt to the very narrow ideal of female beauty in the United States. Upon her initial arrival to the United States as a refugee from Cuba, Lourdes had embraced excessive consumption of unhealthy foods as a sign of material success—not as a need to nourish herself, but as a consumption of luxury.

After having attained solid middle-class status, Lourdes now becomes a victim to internalized "food shaming" and begins to see her unbridled lust for food and sex as the marker of an unrefined immigrant "fresh off the boat"—an image of the immigrant she, as a wealthy, light-skinned Cuban, abhors. Lourdes comes to realize that as a member of the upwardly mobile middle class, boundless consumption is no longer the accepted manifestation of wealth and Americanness. Instead, restraint rules the day. As Paul Rozin explains,

> In the peculiar social situation of the world of food abundance in late 20th century developed cultures, the nutritive value of food has become a moral issue for some. Just as, in the past, drug use has taken on immoral status, and as currently smoking is entering into the immoral domain, we now see the beginning of the moralization of food indulgence.[29]

Lourdes buys into this very "moralization of food indulgence" the same way she initially bought into the earlier narrative of excessive consumption and lust as a marker of liberation. As she gets older,

Lourdes wonders whether it "was true that the older you get the less you can savor and that sweetness is the last taste left on the tongue."[30] Her loss of appetite also seems to indicate a waning of her ideological, sexual, and culinary fervor—again, her political convictions as a recent immigrant are intimately intertwined with her identity as a woman of color, who is struggling with her body image.

In the end, significant weight gains and losses tell us little about Lourdes's potential lack of knowledge about nutrition and a healthy lifestyle; yet, they tell us everything about her anxieties as a first-generation Cuban immigrant who escaped political violence and sexual abuse. In order to reinvent herself through buying into an accepted Horatio Alger[31] narrative of immigrant success through hard work, self-confidence, and bravado, she, in effect, lost her essence and replaced it with materialist greed and empty calories. Once Lourdes has attained a respectable middle-class status—and middle age—she is forced to adapt yet again to another ideal: that of the slender, eternally dieting, and self-restraining American woman. Lourdes's food choices and her body's subsequent radical transformations have little to do with her access to or knowledge about healthy foodways; instead, they reflect her never-ending attempts to forget a painful past, reinvent herself as a greedy, all-consuming Cuban immigrant, and her later class-based need to adjust to the Protestant self-restraint of a respectable American middle-class businesswoman.

Under the Feet of Jesus

For Abarca and Pascual Soler, "[Food] consciousness demands an analysis of the material conditions surrounding food production, distribution, and consumption."[32] In the following pages, I apply the theoretical framework of "food consciousness" to show how *Under the Feet of Jesus* succinctly illustrates the inequalities in the material conditions of foodways for Latina/o (im)migrants. Viramontes's extensive acknowledgments that accompany the novel are a testimony to the centrality of food in the conception and writing of this text. The author structures her notes around the theme of food and nourishment and the ways in which physical, emotional, and intellectual human needs are intertwined with the production and consumption of food:

The food on the table: Thanks to the piscardores, who, with weary bones and hard labor, feed me and you daily ... The food of the soul ... The field of the food ... To the blood-red pomegranate seeds of my familia ... To the oranges and palm dates ... To leaves, trees, and peaches.[33]

Here, Viramontes employs an aesthetic ideology that clearly is inspired by indigenous values, such as communal living, and respect for the interconnectivity of all of creation.

Through this aesthetic ideology, Viramontes also is affirming the connection between thinkers and doers that philosopher Lisa M. Heldke addresses when making the case for the complex knowledge that working with food entails. Heldke points out that Cartesian dualism insists on the classist bias that domestic and agricultural laborers are "doers not thinkers; users, not discoverers"[34] whose appetites and desires are simple, physical, and easily met. Yet, a turn to a relational definition of self that privileges participatory rather than individualistic notions of selfhood showcases the outstanding insights that may emerge when theory is viewed as an embodied practice, and knowledge is defined not only as intellectual, but also emotional and experiential. Curtin describes this process as developing a "healthy personhood ... through achieving the power to choose the defining relations through which one becomes a person."[35]

In *Under the Feet of Jesus*, food frequently evokes intense personal memories that are often associated with a profound sense of loss: "What Estrella remembered most of her real father was an orange. He had peeled a huge orange where they stopped to pee. They were traveling north where the raisin grapes were ready for sun drying and the work was said to be plentiful."[36] The visceral connection between the migrant farm laborers and the land they are working is inscribed literally on their bodies. This is not a distant, romanticized version of the visceral connection between humans and the territory they inhabit and cultivate, but an honest, and at times brutal, depiction of the ways in which hard farm labor inscribes itself on the farmworker's body: "His [Perfecto's] back curved like a sickle against the window and her garlic-scented fingers ran up and down the beads of his spine. He was a man with lashes thick as pine needles, a man who never whispered; his words clanked like loose empty cans in a bag."[37]

Each member of the migrant family is described in terms of the food they harvest. For instance, Petra compares her daughter's "buttocks [to] shiny garbanzo beans."[38] The workers' bodies seem to merge with the food they produce. In Marxist terms, the means of production—in this case their bodies—become, in effect, indistinguishable from the product they create: "She had bitten the muscle of her thumb, tore flesh, then reeled herself back and ran cold water in the tub to vanish the blood drops like pomegranate seeds."[39] The smell of the fields follows them into their private quarters, making it impossible to ever escape the labor that dominates and structures their lives: "Day after day, when the last row of tomatoes had been picked and the sun was low . . . the fragrance of tomatoes lingered on her fingers, her hair, her pillow."[40] Notably, the narrator uses the word "fragrance" to describe the scent that accompanies the workers from the fields to their beds. The natural scent of a healthful food local to the region, unlike the processed tomato paste they are forced to buy in the store, provides the dignity and luxury of a pleasant "fragrance."

However, the migrant farmworkers do not inhabit an idyllic rural landscape; rather, they work in an industrialized agricultural landscape that is poisoned by pesticides and processed foods for the workers.[41] The novel abounds with references to cheap and heavily processed food, and even though the farmworkers are at the very source of fresh produce, they ironically—and unjustly—have to purchase processed and canned foods since the best fresh produce is reserved for further processing and global distribution. One of the few traditional and somewhat healthy foods the family has access to is homemade tortillas, and the narrator spends a significant amount of time sharing an actual recipe and reviewing how Petra, the matriarch of the family, makes flour tortillas from scratch.

It is noteworthy that Petra engages in the time-consuming and labor-intensive process of making tortillas after the farmworkers have been exposed to pesticides and are suffering the violent physical repercussions. Flour tortillas, though not the healthiest of foods when made with lard,[42] are a comfort food to the Mexican American laborers and are a significant part of what Williams-Forson has referred to as a "symbolic but also tangible return to the homeland."[43] The narrator of *Under the Feet of Jesus* describes Petra's tortilla making in intricate detail:

Three fingers of *Clabber Girl* baking powder, sprinkle of salt
... a few handfuls of *La Pina* flour, *Rex* lard, and warm water from
the aluminum coffeepot. Knead. Let the white mound stand with
a dishcloth over it. Boil. Put the coffee grinds in the pot. Saute
the papas with diced onion and tomato and lard. Remove the
dishcloth, begin rolling the tortillas.[44]

Petra's flexibility in making tortillas from scratch with a limited set of
ingredients showcases her creativity and improvisational skills. Her
ability to go through the lengthy process also illustrates that ethnic
food is a source of both comfort and pride. As Gardaphé and Xu put
it, "[A]s demands for assimilation and inculcation of ethnic inferiority often impact the ethnic individual's alimentary desires, so does
the restoration of ethnic dignity and pride operate through culinary
enjoyment."[45] By making her own tortillas from scratch under difficult circumstances, Petra recuperates and reclaims a sense of herself
as a Mexican migrant woman illustrating a case where, as Joanna B.
Marshall states, "The immigrant's kitchen becomes the space where
ethnic identity is recuperated and nourished, and self-reliance and
creativity rewarded."[46]

The spirit of communal living and sustainable food production is
juxtaposed with the proliferation of the American fast food industry,
which makes itself incessantly visible in the novel via constant references to brands that produce food items that can be consumed quickly
in an effort to "ease" the demanding lives of migrant farmworkers, but
that also have been devoid of most nutritional value. In a thinly veiled
reference to Ester Hernández's iconic screen print, *Sun Mad*,[47] early
on in the novel Viramontes has Estrella realize this basic contradiction between the forces of advertising healthful foods with the very
unhealthy living conditions of its producers: "Carrying the full basket
[of grapes] was not like the picture on the red raisin boxes ... in the
markets, not like the woman wearing a fluffy bonnet, holding out the
grapes with her smiling, ruby lips, the sun a float orange behind her."[48]
The famous image of the company advertising "Sun Maid Raisins" also
features a Disneyesque version of an idealized peasant girl falsifying
the ethnicity of the women and girls who actually do perform the hard
labor in the fields. The omnipresence of corporate America and its
marketing machinery becomes so overwhelming that the protagonists

themselves are described in terms of ready-made products. This can be seen, for example, when Estrella's straight posture is compared to "the ARGO woman on a box of corn starch."[49]

The "gentrification of ethnic cuisine" in relation to not being able to obtain good-quality food items that would enable Petra to cook familiar meals is described painstakingly in one of the key passages of the novel:

> Petra picked up a can of *El Pato* Tomato sauce, checked the price, then checked a can of *Carnation* Milk, a jar of *Tang*, then returned each to the shelf. She decided on four cans of Spam and stacked them into Estrella's basket at $1.80 each for a seven-ounce can and made a mental calculation of $ 7.20 ... The fresh produce was dumped into small size zinc tubs and pushed against a wall and hardly resembled the crops harvested days before. The fruits and vegetables were firm and solid out in the hot field but here in the store, only relics remained[;] squished old tomatoes spilled over into the bruised apples and the jalapenos mixed with soft tomatillos and cucumber peeked from between blotchy oranges. The white onions reminded Petra of eggs.[50]

The produce available to the farmworkers are "relics" and damaged goods whose health benefits are long gone: the apples are "bruised," tomatillos "soft," oranges "blotchy," and the onions have reached a state of decay that makes them unrecognizable as such. In a similar vein, the workers do not have access to freshly roasted coffee beans or fresh dairy; instead, they are offered "*Eagle* condensed milk"[51] and "*Nescafe* coffee."[52]

When Petra first enters the temporary shelter where she and her family will live for part of their journey, she is confronted, again, with the intimate connection between an unhealthy physical environment, the pesticide industry, and fast food: "Nothing in the cabinet except the thick smell of Raid and dead roaches and sprinkled salt ... and the box of *Quaker Oats* oatmeal."[53] While oatmeal is certainly a healthy cereal, the Quaker brand, which dominates the US market, sells processed oatmeal that cooks in one minute and has a lot fewer of the health benefits of steel-cut oatmeal, which requires a much-lengthier cooking process—time that migrant farmworkers, and single mothers in particular, do not have at their disposal. Again, the branding of such potentially healthful food items is crucial in a novel about migrant farmworkers: the Quaker Oats box features an image of a sanitized pilgrim, which denies the historical realities of grain production in the United States. Parallel to the ever-popular, yet notoriously racist image of Uncle Ben's rice and Aunt Jemima's syrup, the Quaker distorts the historical exploitative nature of food production in the United States.

The pervasive and detrimental nature of corporate advertising also is addressed in the novel. For instance, the TV in the local and ill-equipped store blasts advertisements for "Swanson's TV Dinners, closest to Mom's cooking"[54] to workers whose home cooking not only would be the more affordable, but also would be a significantly healthier choice. The skillful way in which the local *curandera* attempts to heal the workers who have been exposed to pesticides and her cautious and respectful use of rice water and egg yolks stand in stark opposition to the false promises of the ready-made TV dinners.[55] For Petra and her family, healthful and nutritious food is inaccessible because of the family's location and economic status. The food industry does not value its workers, without whom we would not have access to local produce and vegetables. Petra's family and other workers in the field not only are excluded from being able to make healthy food choices, but are also, in effect, killed by their labor in the fields due to the use of heavy-duty pesticides and insecticides. In fact, exposure to these toxins not only will affect all consumers of allegedly healthy foods over time, but also will destroy the very environment that allows us to harvest fruits and vegetables in the first place. In this sense, the Latina/o migrants in Viramontes's novel are at the frontlines of a global war on healthy food production and are the first victims of an industrialization that negatively affects all of us: consumers and producers alike.

Conclusion

The French philosopher Jean Anthelme Brillat-Savarin claimed in the early part of the nineteenth century that "[t]he destiny of nations depends on how they nourish themselves."[56] Given Latina/os' crucial contributions to food production and the larger food industry in agriculture and gastronomy in the United States, immigration reform, environmental reform, and food reform have to be intertwined intimately. Only the full inclusion of Latina/os, whether they be recent immigrants or minorities as a result of US-American imperialism in the Southern Hemisphere, in the US body politic will reduce existing and prevent further anxieties about Latina/os entering and living in the United States. On the one hand, those immigrants who, like Estrella, would thrive on healthy, sustainable, and affordable foods are prevented from doing so by the pesticide/pharmaceutical industry that dominates the agricultural sector. Lourdes, on the other hand, wishes to become Americanized in an effort to disremember traumatic experiences of sexual abuse in Cuba and she falls victim to the obesity crisis by mistaking success and assimilation with boundless consumption and exploitative entrepreneurship.

As I have shown in my analysis of the protagonists' "food consciousness" in *Dreaming in Cuban*, excessive overeating and dieting are the result and manifestation of anxieties over the rightful presence of racialized and classed Latina bodies in the United States. *Under the Feet of Jesus* demonstrates how civil rights, labor rights, and environmental justice are intimately intertwined; the ill treatment of migrant farmworkers is yet another manifestation of the exploitation, economic and psychological, of Latina (im)migrants that takes a toll on the health of Latina bodies and, thus, ultimately, on the health of the nation. A reorientation of how we define productivity and valuable work must result in an appreciation of organic farming, in fair pay, and in safe and healthy working conditions for farmworkers. As Lázaro Lima put it, we need to continue the work that studies "how the Latino body has been imagined, dismembered, and reimagined anew, and how it has reconstituted itself within the National symbolic order,"[57] and Abarca and Pascual Soler's "food consciousness" offers one highly effective and illuminating theoretical framework to achieve this goal.

CHAPTER 10

Writing against Food-Based Aesthetics of Objectification
The Work of Judith Ortiz Cofer

KAREN CRUZ

Women experience subjugation in a variety of ways, and one mode is the process of objectification. That women are objectified has been bandied about to such an extent that the notion, quite disconcertingly, seems to have lost some import. So many scholars recognized this truism that it was perceived perhaps to be too obvious and no longer worthy of scholarly investigation. However, I wish to interrogate how a specific type of objectification, food-related troping,[1] functions in systems of representation. Food is a complex object for investigation, especially concerning the nearly infinite ways in which it appears in representations in popular culture, advertisements, and literary forms. Thus, reading with an eye for food reveals a great deal about culture, literature, and life. It is my firm contention that these complex attitudes regarding foodstuffs also function in systems of representation and that the social category of gender, though certainly fluid and contested, remains one of the means by which representations form a gender-based cultural practice.

The patriarchal cultural tradition, specifically its system of representation that intimately associates women with comestibles, is a system of practices that frequently figures women metonymically and metaphorically as food. This results in a subsequent fetishizing that negates women's status as fully human and reduces them to objects. This process of gendered fetishizing becomes even more pronounced when applied to women of color. One area that has and continues to make this association is, in fact, the advertising industry that makes strong use of the aesthetics of objectification. Puerto Rican author Judith Ortiz Cofer,[2] among others, is a writer whose work directly speaks back to the ways food has been used to objectify women.[3] Ortiz Cofer deploys a focus on food as she addresses and reconfigures aspects of this patriarchal tradition of representation. Moreover, she attempts to instantiate a healthy relation between women and food that emerges in representational discourse that acknowledges women's humanity, including their desires.

Some sexist and racist food-centered representations are all too familiar and deeply ingrained in the US cultural imaginary. Women scholars have begun to expose and analyze such representations. For example, Psyche A. Williams-Forson undermines the longstanding stereotype associating African Americans with chicken. She examines conventional tropes, for instance the widely disseminated gendered image of the black mammy in the kitchen "happily" donning a headscarf, and then debunks them by historicizing the ways chicken has provided autonomy and self-expression in the lives of many black women. Indeed, the title of her book *Building Houses out of Chicken Legs: Black Women, Food and Power* refers to the ways some African American women in Gordonsville, Virginia, who called themselves "waiter carriers," would prepare and lift up trays of food for sale, including chicken, to the open windows of a passenger train. "Bella" Winston notes that her mother purchased their home "with chicken legs,"[4] thereby illustrating the resourcefulness and independence of these African American women, and the improvement of the material conditions of their lives achieved by the women's knowledge of how to prepare and market delicious chicken.[5] Williams-Forson's work brings to the forefront the sociohistoric significance of this image that is forgotten when it is used as a stereotype to represent African American women. Salas and Abarca present a similar analysis in the final chapter of this collection, where they focus on the stereotypes the food industry creates to sell food.

In *When I Was Puerto Rican*, Esmeralda Santiago challenges a different kind of stereotype that eroticizes women as fruit by juxtaposing such metonymic images with a food-centered memory.

> Today, I stand before a stack of dark green guavas, each perfectly round and hard, each $1.59. The one in my hand is tempt-

ing. It smells faintly of late summer afternoons, and hopscotch under the mango tree. But this is autumn in New York and I am no longer a child . . . the guava joins its sisters under the harsh fluorescent lights of the exotic fruit display.[6]

Displaying the guavas as an "exotic fruit" contrasts sharply with the memory of youth that speaks to who she is. Santiago describes her method of eating a guava in this way:

> When you bite into a ripe guava, your teeth must grip the bumpy surface and sink into the thick edible skin without hitting the center. It takes experience to do this, as it's quite tricky to determine how far beyond the skin the seeds begin . . . I had my last guava the day we left Puerto Rico. It was large and juicy, almost red in the center, and so fragrant that I didn't want to eat it because I would lose the smell. All the way to the airport I scratched at it with my teeth, making little dents in the skin, chewing small pieces with my front teeth, so that I could feel the texture against my tongue, the tiny pink pellets of sweet.[7]

Santiago's description of eating a guava signals the intimate connection between the foods of Puerto Rico and her identity.

Indeed, an important characteristic of Santiago's prologue points toward the deep connection between food and self-knowledge.[8] Principally responsible for her own pleasure, the speaker's understanding of how *precisely* to savor a guava at its most desirable level of ripeness and with a refined approach demonstrates her proficiency in eating well and articulates her own desires and awareness of the gustatory satisfactions in the world. In this female-authored and female-centered text, Santiago is not troped as food, but rather thoroughly enjoys this fruit as she displays skill and a willingness to share her knowledge with others. Furthermore, nibbling the guava while heading for her flight to New York City, she is critically aware of the transience of this pleasure and anticipates that eating the guava will engender loss as she wishes not to lose its beautiful fragrance.

My critical interpretive focus on the guava may be labeled with an especially apt phrase that describes this kind of theoretical and critical practice that Meredith E. Abarca and Neives Pascual Soler coin as "food consciousness." Abarca and Pascual Soler explain "food consciousness" as a mode of awareness that "speaks to a theory of pragmatic, embodied epistemology, wherein knowledge is acquired through the sensations and emotions that food awakens in the body."[9] And although Abarca and Pascual Soler productively apply this perspective to examine postnationalism in Chicana literary texts, I believe the notion is pliable and can enhance the reading of other texts as well since this insistence on the epistemological import of food as a source of knowledge about the self and others can be discovered in much of Latina literature.

"Food consciousness" helps reveal social attitudes, values, and relations of power, especially about the gendered self and ethnonationalism that representations of food produce. Carole M. Counihan writes about how social power is communicated and potentially stratified through food experiences: "Men's and women's attitudes about their bodies, the legitimacy of their appetites, and the importance of their food work reveal whether their self-concept is validating or denigrating. We are concerned with how their relationship to food may facilitate gender complementarity and mutual respect or produce gender hierarchy."[10] Counihan's observation links notions of "self-concept" to the ways people perform food work, which might relate to dynamics such as who cooks, how often, and under what kinds of pressures and expectations, as well as who serves whom at meals or even who eats first.

Such cultural patterns have sometimes produced more "gender [and ethnic] hierarchy" than "mutual respect" in the lives of most Latinas, thus reinforcing the historic and longstanding weight of oppression. Food tropes and attitudes toward consumption in cultural expressions can function in especially poignant ways: to liberate in some instances, but also to exoticize, to racialize, and to subjugate Latinas in other instances. Much of Ortiz Cofer's writing attends to the struggles of women in the face of both gender and ethnic subjugation. She critically assesses the kind of expressly exoticized troping of women of color that occurs both in mainstream American popular culture and the food marketing industry, as well as in the Western literary tradition. Consequently, this prevents healthy and egalitarian gendered relationships between men and women and compromises ethnic relations between Anglo-Americans and Latina/os. As some of her autobiographical accounts attest to, Ortiz Cofer identifies how this systemic use of objectifying food metaphors results in harmful effects in the lived experiences of Latinas.

Ortiz Cofer's "food consciousness" makes visible female, and particularly Latina, human agency. Indeed, much of her writing promotes a healthy relation between women and food that popular culture and the food industry, particularly advertisements, insist on rupturing. Her writing offers a model of artistic production that encourages a full appreciation of Latinas' self-worth as fully human[11] and as legitimate subjects.[12] In *The Latin Deli: Telling the Lives of Barrio Women*, as well as *Woman in Front of the Sun*, Ortiz Cofer examines how food expresses the complexities of Latina/o culture and identity, specifically within the context of migration and the Puerto Rican diasporic experience.

Women and Food

Ortiz Cofer shifts the representations of women and food away from the aesthetics of objectification. Her texts treat food as a major motif presented through a feminist lens about the self and community that makes visible various relations of social power, especially in the terrain of gender, ethnicity, and the transnational. By the transnational, I mean a dynamic through which she engages with different locales, specifically Paterson, New Jersey, and Puerto Rico. In *Woman in Front of the Sun*, Ortiz Cofer describes her family's experience shopping in Paterson, New Jersey. Her family would shop first at the A & P supermarket and then the *bodegas*, which were Puerto Rican grocery stores in the barrio where her mother purchased the ingredients for her favorite Puerto Rican dishes. Ortiz Cofer remembers that in the *bodegas*, because of her father's relative success as a navy officer, her family was rather too visible and often seemed out of place and overdressed by barrio standards. She explains, we "were suspect to the other customers. Little pockets of silence would form around us as my mother examined the yuccas, plantains and other *viandas* she would need for the week's meals."[13]

This alienation was ameliorated by retaining a strong connectedness with Puerto Rico through her frequent visits and, in significant measure, through food—both eating it and writing about it. In

"Woman in Front of the Sun," an excerpt from a short eponymous volume, Ortiz Cofer describes a return trip to Puerto Rico. As the plane touches down in San Juan, she recounts a visceral reaction upon deboarding the plane: "Immediately I can feel the strangely physical way I am changed when I arrive on this island. It is a flutter in my chest, an excitement, a feeling of joyful anticipation. It's almost like falling in love, or maybe the start of a fever."[14] Ortiz Cofer insists that this response is biological as her body "is desperately trying to adjust to the heat and humidity."[15] As she waits for the next flight to Mayagüez, the primary order of business is eating. She makes a beeline for the *fritura* (fried food) stand:

> The man at the counter waves to me; my order is ready: cod fritters, rice and red beans. My health-conscious daughter would lecture me sternly if she could see what I am about to consume. She would point out that the grease is the fatal flaw in Puerto Rican cuisine ... Though I know the sermon verbatim, I dig in. My adipose cells yell, *¡Ole!* My body celebrates the orgy of oil and fat and spices. The taste and aroma of the meal take me back to my primal Puerto Rican self.[16]

What is at work here is a dynamic with a generational, transnational, and epistemological conflict; it is a kind of transcultural and inter-generational tension in respective ways of knowing and experiencing the world.

In Ortiz Cofer's epistemology, this occasional splurge and the sheer satisfaction of consuming this delicious grease-laden meal trump any US "progressive" health concern about cholesterol that her daughter's sermon might espouse. In this moment of "food consciousness," the meal she savors signifies her identity, her cultural affiliation, and her place on the island. The cod fritters and rice and beans are powerful social symbols with a historical and cultural resonance that her daughter just might not comprehend. Ortiz Cofer relishes every bite as they bring her back to her "primal Puerto Rican self." The current US concerns about Latina/os obesity, as Marion Rohrleitner's chapter in this volume illustrates, ignores the importance that certain foods have for a person's "primal self." Ortiz Cofer uses this description of eating in the service of her own self-definition to emphasize the physical nature of the pleasure of food as she gives voice to "her adipose cells," which apparently remember this gustatory, embodied enjoyment, and exclaim "¡Ole!" One can speculate that Ortiz Cofer's delight in this Puerto Rican cuisine is all the more intense as a result of typically not eating this food after her migration to the continental United States.

Food historian Miguel Cruz Ortiz Cuadra notes that, with the extraordinary influx of many different types of food to the island, whether from the United States or even elsewhere in the Caribbean, some foods, like codfish, have come to

> retain their familiarity and come to stand for durability and permanence. They have nothing of the provisional or fleeting about them; on the contrary, they have helped shape a collective memory of the palate, an emotional response that evokes a world of food practices and habits and calls up experiences associated with particular flavors, textures, colors, food shortages, survival strategies, festivals, religious rules, and pleasures and displeasures.[17]

Thus, for Ortiz Cofer, such a long-held culinary tradition demonstrates both a corporeal dimension and a social aspect as the pleasurable meal at the airport evokes a collective memory of the palate. Although she relishes the consumption of the cod fritters and illustrates her joy upon returning to the island, the nostalgia she feels does indeed invoke Puerto Rico's own history of colonialism, as that "primal self" is a colonized self.

For Ortiz Cofer, the experience of exile provides the impetus for writing in terms of her own sense of a transcultural self as she explores many of the dynamics of complex transnational issues such as dislocation, hybridity, bilingualism, and el vaivén (coming and going).[18] The Puerto Rican migrant, who is officially a United States citizen and enjoys great mobility between the US mainland and Puerto Rico, is unlike other migrants whose presence in the United States may or may not be legal and who are not afforded such mobility between the United States and their country of origin. Lidia Marte explores this migrant status in terms of Domincans in Puerto Rico in her study of Doña Luz's gallintas rellenas included in this volume. Significantly, the Puerto Rican is forced to engage with a dominant US culture and, at the same time, typically may wish to retain a sense of the past and remember her homeland traditions. What may be called the vestiges of that "primal self" is a self that Ortiz Cofer is clearly able to feed with each subsequent return to Puerto Rico. These connections are always degraded when the relationship between women and food reflects more of an aesthetics of objectification.

In significant measure, a sense of loss and hybrid identity is inscribed in Ortiz Cofer's writing, not solely but frequently, through representations of food; these representations function as signs about identities in formation and in flux. However, uses of food in her texts also articulate moments of pleasure, joy, and liberation from constraining aspects of gender and ethnic oppressions. Under close inspection, the social significations of consumption present Ortiz Cofer's readers with important insights into Puerto Rican culture and identity. Her work encourages a renegotiation of gendered subject positions regarding Puerto Rican women in relation to their desires and their autonomy, as well as an articulation of Puerto Rican identity positions, in a more general sense, as they relate to a white, Anglo-American, hegemonic culture.

Systems of Representation and Food

Depicting women as food is a transhistorical and transcultural phenomenon that has informed the Western literary tradition.[19] Latino writers deploy this type of depiction. In *Bodega Dreams*, Ernesto Quiñonez describes the New York streets where "young girls strutted their stuff, shaking it like Jell-O."[20] In *The Brief Wondrous Life of Oscar Wao*, Junot Díaz writes "what [The Gangster] wanted to do was to suck Beli's enormous breasts, to fuck her pussy until it was a mango-juice swamp, to spoil her senseless so that Cuba and his failure there disappeared."[21] These representations, among others, comprise an aesthetics of objectification. Indeed, there is a deeply entrenched connection in the male cultural imaginary between women and the oppressive metaphoric potential of food tropes. Admittedly, there exists a strong connection linking women and food, most profoundly in the fact that through their lactating breasts mothers often are the first form of food for their children. Nonetheless, as with other biological factors, culture has inflated this biological reality as a means to a cultural logic that produces highly problematic representations of women that pervade both literature and popular culture.

In *The Latin Deli* Ortiz Cofer articulates *la lucha*, the struggle, of a range of Latinas. In her essay "The Myth of the Latin Women: I Just Met a Girl Named Maria," she explores what it means to be stereotyped in a cultural framework regarding sexuality that views the "Latina" as "Hot Tamales and sexual firebrands."[22] Regarding the circulation of such representations in popular culture, specifically the food marketing industry, she explains, "[I]n their special vocabulary, advertisers have designated 'sizzling' and 'smoldering' as the adjectives of choice for describing not only the foods but also the women of Latin America."[23] Indeed, "sizzling" might as well describe either a Latina or a fajita. This kind of language exoticizes women of color. It supports and promotes colonizing gestures toward all women of color as wild and exotic that often appear in popular media, are promoted by the food marketing industry, and consequently contribute to an oppressive cultural milieu that disseminates a sexist and racist aesthetic.[24]

I offer the following example to show how women of color are subjugated to aesthetics of objectification when they are deployed within food/beverage advertisements. The beer known as "Sexual Chocolate," by Foothills Brewing Company, is described on the company website as a "cocoa infused Imperial Stout. Opaque black in color with a dark brown head. Big chocolate aroma with notes of espresso, blackstrap molasses, dark sweet toffee and dark fruit."[25] Most poignantly, the striking image on the label of the bottle depicts a beautiful woman of color. The outline of her full head of hair and "the dark brown head" of the beer evoke the iconic hairstyle of the Afro. Her red dress is strapless and tropical; the fiery red lettering of the beer's name, the red background, and the woman's rather thick, red lips provoke the appetite. Her simple naturalistic necklace conjures the primitive. The seductive label and the beverage marketing industry provoke the desire to taste this liquid black beauty. The label's visual representation and metonymic logic arouse the beer consumer to their imaginative pleasure seeking. This is comparable to when a Latina is seen as a "Hot Tamale" or seen as "sizzling" like a fajita. Ortiz Cofer, in her work, challenges this aesthetics of objectification.

According to bell hooks, "Cultural taboos around sexuality, desire and ethnicity are transgressed and made explicit,"[26] and the language about food that Ortiz Cofer points out certainly reverberates with sexual innuendo. Perhaps, hooks suggests, it is an interest in the exotic, or a desire to taste a "bit o' the other," to use her phrase, that reveals the West's fascination with the primitive, which actually has to do with its own crisis in identity. Thus, in contemporary cultural politics, consuming the other can take the form of eating exotic foods or sexual activity, or both.

Food philosopher Lisa Heldke elaborates on the notion of tasting the Other as she coins the phrase "cultural food colonialism" to describe the type of eating experiences she sought in graduate school. Heldke was captivated with ethnic cuisines, or a world she describes as "culinary Disneyland."[27] After years of happy, but unreflective, consumption, Heldke contemplates the motivations underlying her adventure eating. Interrogating the ethical implications of her ethnic eating, Heldke concludes: "I could not deny I was motivated by a deep desire to have contact with, and somehow to own an experience of, an Exotic Other, as a way of making myself more interesting"[28]; such an admission supports hooks's assessment of these types of desires as exposing one's own "crisis in identity."[29] Unfortunately, this degree of self-reflection and philosophical awareness is a trait that evades most consumers. Furthermore, it is not a quality of thought encouraged by the food and beverage marketing industries in the United States.

An example of exoticizing, specifically in regard to food, also occurs in a biographical anecdote in *The Latin Deli*. A boyfriend kisses Ortiz Cofer sloppily and then resents her insufficiently fiery response—he spews, "I thought you Latin girls were supposed to mature early."[30] She addresses this invidious comment with wit and mild indignation as she explains, this was "my first instance of being thought of as a fruit or vegetable—I was supposed to *ripen*, not just grow into womanhood like other girls."[31] And though much has been done examining the role of meat in connection to representations of women,[32] less consideration has been given to fruit. Ortiz Cofer presents these autobiographical incidents to challenge the Latina myth, and the construction of female identity more generally, but these myths and associations have circulated widely and for some time.

Carmen Miranda, the famous Brazilian who sported a basket of tropical fruit as a headpiece, is one embodiment of the sexual representations of women paired with fruit. Peter Chapman, in *The United Fruit Company*, explains, "[I]n the US Carmen Miranda danced and sang with bananas to great acclaim in her films of the 1930s and 1940s. In one, *The Gang's All Here*, her female chorus laid around her waving huge make-believe bananas between their legs. The scene ended with an explosion of fruit from her tutti-frutti hat."[33] Whereas such an exotic, suggestive, and fruity representation using a blonde Anglo-American beauty in the 1930s and 1940s might have been unacceptable to the mainstream American viewing public, as a Portuguese-born Brazilian, even if she was quite fair, Miranda's Iberian/Latin American status as "not quite white" made it acceptable for such a graphic sexual depiction with food. The phallic connotations of the "bananas" and the orgasmic intimations of the "explosion" are so obvious as not to require comment, but clearly, as a Brazilian Latina, Carmen Miranda was fetishized and became a desirable object for mainstream Anglo-American consumption. The spectacle of the dancing Latina with her banana-laden headpiece and fruit-covered costume, as well as the catchy lyrics of the tune she sang, is yet another media representation that reinforces this exoticized and consumption-driven dynamic. This representation creates a heightened visibility, which Eleanor Ty has described as "the politics of the visible" that in turn often incite unsolicited and undesired attention to women of color.[34] Latinas are characterized in terms of a specifically tropical mystery and desirability.

Another entry from *The Latin Deli* entitled "The Myth of the Latin Woman: I Just Met a Girl Named Maria" contains two autobiographical accounts that demonstrate how such stereotypical representations alter perceptions of Latinas. Ortiz Cofer tells of an awkward experience she had while a graduate student at Oxford. On a bus trip into London, a rather drunk young man got down on bended knee and sang the song "María" from *West Side Story*. Thus, through physiognomy, with her olive skin, and dark hair and eyes, Ortiz Cofer is hyper-visible as a Puerto Rican in London. As a result of this hyper-visibility, she then is made a spectacle of as she is waylaid by this social aggression.[35] This encounter demonstrates a logic that renders her hyper-visible and leaves the male with the misperception that she is available. Certainly, widespread media representations of Latinas inform the presumptions of some men.

The exoticizing of Latinas as fruity, as in the case of Miranda, or as "hot tamales" as Ortiz Cofer recounts, partakes of a system of alimentary representations that operates in the collective imaginary in pernicious ways. Such representations reflect a dynamic, indeed an aesthetic, that allows and perhaps even encourages males to believe they have the right to taste a "bit o' the other" or to imaginatively pleasure seek, even if only through serenades, at the expense and public humiliation of the Latina. I posit that some men's assumption of such license, particularly in relation to women of color, can lead to far more violating encounters. Thus, Latinas are both hypersexualized and ethnically stereotyped as such notions pervade the US cultural imaginary.

Ortiz Cofer's life stories demonstrate some of the intersections between representation and actual experience, and they validate the importance of ethnic and gender identity in embodied, lived experience. It seems the racialized, sexualized female cannot evade the meanings and realities generated by her marked body. These realities are not merely "descriptions" but rather hard facts of Ortiz Cofer's experience and embodiment as a Latina, which certainly entail some painful moments. With a burgeoning awareness of self and her own visibility as a Latina, she muses: "María had followed me to London, reminding me of a prime fact of my life: you can leave the Island, master the English language, and travel as far as you can, but if you are a Latina, especially one like me who so obviously belongs to Rita Moreno's gene pool, the Island travels with you."[36] Through her writing, and especially her food motifs, Ortiz Cofer attempts to alter the social perceptions and meanings attached to the Latina body.

Revising the Aesthetics of Objectification in "Corazón's Café"

Ortiz Cofer offers a healthy remedy to the system of oppressive food-centered troping of women so prevalent in the Western tradition with her oppositional representational strategy in the short story "Corazón's Café."[37] Rather than conceding to the inevitability of misogynistic discourse and an aesthetics of food-based objectification, she focuses instead on the use of food references as a vehicle for liberatory possibilities for Latinas as she debunks both gender and ethnic-based myths and stereotypes.

This tale commences after closing time in the bodega where Corazón and Manuel built their life together. Now Corazón finds herself grieving and utterly alone. Distraught by Manuel's death from heart valve disease earlier that day, she sits behind the counter and reflects over the events of their history and their love story. Back on the island, her mother died while she was very young and her father thereafter retreated into severe alcoholism. Remembering their initial encounter, Corazón recalls meeting Manuel at the market where she is instantly and powerfully attracted to him. From its inception, their love affair is connected to food. The aromatic trace of coffee he leaves on her skin after handing a package to her haunts her for the remainder of the day. Afterward, she leaves her father's abusive household to find refuge with Manuel and his elderly mother, Doña Serena. Their early life together is pleasant. After Corazón's miscarriage, when she learns that she will never be able to bear children, and then the death of Doña Serena, the narrative takes a transnational turn as the young couple relocates to New Jersey to open a bodega, a grocery store, of their very own that sells ethnic, specifically Latina/o, foodstuffs. There are several instances in which Ortiz Cofer's treatment of gender and ethnic food argues convincingly for new subject positions for Puerto Ricans and, most poignantly, for Puerto Rican women.

Literary critic Carmen S. Rivera comments on a remarkable split in gender roles in Puerto Rico. Rivera writes about how Ortiz Cofer addresses these gender roles during an interview with Acosta-Belén:

> During her stays on the island, she [Ortiz Cofer] notices that the two worlds are very definitely demarcated and that one is not to cross over the boundaries. Gender roles are specifically defined. Cooking, childbearing, child rearing, housekeeping and the preservation of morality and local traditions are the realm of women. Working, drinking, sexual entertainment, traveling and wandering are the men's.[38]

On the contrary, in "Corazón's Café," the gender politics between Corazón and Manuel challenge the cultural fictions of femininity since it is she who controls the finances, pays the bills and keeps accounts, and Manuel prepares the meals he "learned to cook, by helping his mother in the kitchen."[39] Manuel is the one who is intimately connected with food, both its preparation and aesthetics, thereby basically transposing and decisively reversing traditional gender roles regarding the social positions of men and women.

Manuel, hoping to inspire creativity in his patrons, follows his own intuition about how best to display their products. A description of the layout of their bodega is as follows:

> *Habichuelas rojas*, the cans of red kidney beans they stacked in a little pyramid. There were little sacks next to it holding the long grain rice that Puerto Ricans like to eat. The only logic that Manuel followed in stocking his shelves was based on his idea of what most people wanted to see in a barrio store.[40]

Corazón trusts his instincts and knowledge derived from his close connection with the culinary desires of Puerto Ricans.

Next, Corazón reflects on their rather unusual courtship and several intimate interactions. At their first liaison, "Manuel was waiting for her on the back steps of the store. Her own daring had made her feel reckless, and she leaned down and kissed his mouth. It tasted like a sweet, moist fruit straight from the tree of summer."[41] Ortiz Cofer's use of simile is an instructive reversal that calls attention to the need to take a full account of the use of food in this narrative. Food metaphors abound, as in another example, Corazón recalls the smell of the "warm milk sweetened with cinnamon" that he drank each night as she and Manuel embraced each other in his room.[42] When describing Manuel's appearance, Ortiz Cofer gestures to the Renaissance blazon:[43] "Manuel had a little beard then too . . . But the beard only framed and softened his features. His eyes were almond-shaped with long eyelashes that made shadows on his cheeks when he looked down to figure an account for a customer. His lips were an invitation for a kiss: full and sensuous."[44] Ortiz Cofer portrays Manuel as food as she describes his mouth like "sweet, moist fruit straight from the tree of summer" and his "almond-shaped" eyes. She also feminizes him in significant ways as well with his "little beard," "softened" features, and "long eyelashes." These representations undermine conventional notions of masculinity, yet, ostensibly do not compromise his status as a lover or what a "real man" might be. This dynamic might usefully relate to Frances Aparicio and Susana Chávez-Silverman's concept of tropicalization as it intersects with gender in that Ortiz Cofer is deploying tropes in such a way that they accentuate "the transformative cultural agency of the [female] subaltern subject,"[45] including her own desires.

In contrast to the examples of conventional misogynist representations in "The Latina Myth," Ortiz Cofer in "Corazón's Café" portrays Manuel in accord with her own vision and desires about masculinity that clearly challenges the fairly pervasive discourses of hypermasculinity and machismo in Puerto Rican culture. In the description, Manuel becomes tropicalized and feminized as a "sweet, moist fruit." Ortiz Cofer enacts "the transformative cultural agency" of the female Puerto Rican subject as she decolonizes both the kitchen and the bedroom and interrupts the oppressive food-focused objectifications of women. Furthermore, she does not merely effect a turning-of-the-tables, but rather writes toward a revision of marital relations in which reciprocity is a sexy, highly desirable, and important relationship dynamic.

Ortiz Cofer then writes an entire segment of the short story replete with the poetics of food as she revels in the enticing aromas and delectable foods of the island:

> They made love with the window thrown wide open to the
> smells of the Island, all concentrated on Doña Serena's property
> —her little garden of herbs with the pungent oregano over-
> whelming all the other aromatic plants, the cayenne peppers,
> the cilantro, the tasty Puerto Rican coriander, the *pimientos y
> ajíes* that went into her condiments and permeated even the
> naked wood of the house with the smell of the food cooked in
> her kitchen every day.[46]

Ortiz Cofer uses the olfactory sense as a means to create metaphors for the mutuality of the love Manuel and Corazón shared as the text surrounds the lovers with the sensual beauty of Puerto Rico. The reader delights in these sensuous and sensual images that link the foods of the island with the sexual intimacy, mutual pleasure, and respect between the lovers as they give themselves to each other as gifts.

The narrative continues explaining how very special foods in Puerto Rican cuisine are wrapped in banana leaves "to add the final touch of taste and also to make food a gift to be unwrapped in cel-ebration."[47] The qualitative attributes of some of the items in this passage suggest a kind of gendered, revisionist aesthetics. Unlike so much of the aesthetics of objectification in which representation has framed women as items for consumption, Ortiz Cofer disrupts this as she recasts and recognizes female desire using the agency of her own food-focused aesthetic. She offers moments that favor the olfac-tory sense, such as the heady aromas of the redolent herb garden and "the special fragrance of the papaya"—scents that permeate the room during their lovemaking. The love scene continues: "Manuel whis-pered these things to her as they lay in each other's arms at night. She laughed gently at his love of cooking and his amazing knowledge of plants and food; not long before, she had thought these interests were strictly feminine, but his hands caressing her body were also a reve-lation of what a real man could be."[48] The tactile sense is celebrated as the delicious feeling of his hands on Corazón's body solidifies their bond through touch. Ortiz Cofer manipulates and inverts tradition to produce a strikingly different kind of aesthetic: one that explores female sexuality and gendered relationships from a refreshing per-spective, and one that offers insight into the creative mind and life of this Puerto Rican female writer.

Ortiz Cofer succeeds with her food play and gender reversals in making these delectable smells and scrumptious tastes of food an inte-gral part of the experience of their lovemaking. Nowhere in the text are women exoticized and likened to fruit. The dynamics of conven-tional, asymmetrical, male-female relationships become reconfigured as interdependence as she plays with the politics of the kitchen and the bedroom. She achieves this interdependence largely through the use of a kind of gastro-poetics[49] that deploys an aesthetic of sensual, sexual, and representational liberation for women. As male domi-nance is deconstructed and subverted by her woman-centered writ-ing, she effectively uses culinary knowledge and practices to mediate the meanings and power relations between the sexes, and she may well succeed in teaching and encouraging women to articulate, interpret, and explore their own perspectives and desires.

Much of the US discourse on Puerto Rico, and Latin America more broadly, relies on a rhetoric of tropical exoticism and primitivism with its concomitant derogatory descriptions of the inhabitants of such places as primitives, as mongrels, and as lacking in any "real" culture. For Renato Rosaldo, this reveals an attitude "where civilized nations stand duty-bound to uplift the so-called savage ones."[50] In contrast, Ortiz Cofer's description of the lovers reveals a human relation of mutual desire and affection, rather than a wild, exotic, animalistic encounter. Furthermore, the careful cultivation of the beautiful little garden and its variety of plants and herbs suggest culture in one of its most fundamental forms and original senses, namely that of agri"culture" (consider Virgil's *Georgics*) as the small property yields a bounty of the earth's good products. Lastly, the mention of the daily cooking and how the fragrant smells of the kitchen pervade the very wood of the house, as if the house itself retains the memories of Puerto Rican cooking, indicates established practices in culture in an ethno-national cuisine, so to speak, replete with "the cilantro," "the tasty Puerto Rican coriander," "oregano," and "*pimientos.*" These ingredients are ubiquitous in Puerto Rican recipes.

Conclusion

Ortiz Cofer revises patriarchal systems of representation that include popular culture, the food marketing industry, and the Western literary tradition. She embraces the ongoing project of reshaping culture and reinventing gendered and ethnic identities by deconstructing convention and reconstructing new models for Puerto Rican, transnational womanhood. By encouraging women to greater "food consciousness," she invites her readers to perceive things anew and view food systems more critically as she challenges a demeaning gender-based aesthetics of objectification through food tropes. Ortiz Cofer emphasizes a mode of reading culture that entails greater "food consciousness." She makes visible the ways Latinas are subjugated in a variety of media: from early examples of the Latina body being represented as tropical fruit for consumption, as in the case of Carmen Miranda, to her own explicit objections to Latinas being described as sizzling. Her work encourages us to speak back to other forms of objectification such as women of color being portrayed as "liquid black beauties."

Ortiz Cofer's "Corazón's Café" is a narrative that makes evident the agency, subjectivity, and full humanity of Latinas. One of Ortiz Cofer's persistent endeavors is to emancipate women from a system of objectification. Such a system finds expression within food advertisements, which often inform popular culture ideals that derive primarily from male perspectives and desires, and we often find such representations in literary texts. Ortiz Cofer aims at cultivating a more ethical aesthetics through her writing that speaks against the aesthetics of objectification. She opens a space for women to move toward empowerment and the fulfillment of their own desires, perhaps leading to greater liberation and satisfaction. Ultimately, Ortiz Cofer's work may foster an epistemological shift—one that transforms how we think about Latinas and about food.

CHAPTER 11

Food Marketing Industry
Cultural Attitudes Made Visible

CONSUELO CARR SALAS
AND MEREDITH E. ABARCA

> *"Laden with cultural meaning food is always more than matter.... Food is rife with metaphor."*
> —W. B. Park[1]

On May 13, 1899, the *Los Angeles Record* ran a story about the near-death experience suffered by Miss Maude Hufford, "one of the most handsomest girls in Los Angeles . . . a most pronounced blonde [with] beautiful flaxen hair, a pearly complexion and large expressive blue eyes." According to the reporter,

> Miss. Maude Hufford . . . had been lying at the point of death since early last Sunday morning . . . due to ptomaine poisoning, produced by a tamale that was composed of putrified [*sic*] meat. . . . Bad meat is often used in . . . tamales, the offensive taste being disguised by the fiery condiments which are used.[2]

In their reading of this report, published in one of Los Angeles's "most liberal newspapers," food journalists Victor and Mary Lau Valle state that while "[t]here's no proof that a 'putrified' tamale was responsible for Hufford's poisoning," the reporter makes a strong effort to "convict a cuisine by means of racist analogy." The description of the girl, according to Valle and Valle, captures "the image of Anglo racial purity [which] was stricken by deceptive spices and 'bad meat,' the reporter's shorthand for racial defilement."[3]

That Mexican food was once rejected or seen with suspicion as being poisonous for consumption, at least for non-Mexicans, might strike contemporary American consumers as unimaginable. Mexican food has become as ubiquitous as hotdogs and hamburgers from coast to coast and border to border. However, culinary history tells us this has not always been the case. After the US invasion of Mexican territory in 1846, the Gold Rush of 1849, and the expansion of railroads to western territories, the once majority Mexican population in what is now the US Southwest, Texas, and California was quickly becoming a minority—if not in numbers, certainly in economic, political, and cultural power. The new immigrants with European ancestry saw themselves as racially superior; therefore, anything associated with Mexicans (and Native Americans) was rejected and classified as un-American.

One way of enacting such a sense of superiority manifested in attitudes toward Mexican (and Native American) food practices. Some of the first public records of the possible contamination and rather questionable eating practices of Mexicans were newspaper accounts, such as the one mentioned above, personal letters, and diaries of Euro-Americans traveling into the newly annexed territories.[4] These attitudes toward their food practices were used to justify classifying Mexicans as "noncitizen," therefore denying any legal or social rights. Mexicans' consumption of *chiles* was a central source of a racial division that declared that only those with low morality could possibly tolerate their consumption.[5]

Charles Fletcher Lummis, a journalist for the *Los Angeles Times*, is worth mentioning here for his small role in perpetuating the rejection of certain Mexican (and Native American) food practices and his substantial role in promoting the lifestyle of the elite Spanish class. While making his way to California from Ohio, he experienced his first consumption of chile in New Mexico on December 19, 1884, and wrote: "This was my first venture on chili colorado [*sic*], and will be my last. One not used to eating fire might just exactly as well chew up a ripe red pepper raw and swallow it."[6] Once in California, however, Lummis became smitten with what he conceived was the fading lifestyle of the "original" elite landowners of California who traced their ancestry to Spain. Lummis, who changed his name to Don Carlos, not only founded the Landmark Club to "preserve the missions from further decay," but also romanticized the lives of the Spaniards as the "loftier aspects of Western civilization: leisure, refined literary tastes, sartorial formality, and well-bred social graces, including courtliness."[7] His writings in the mythological recreation of the golden Spanish days, and his interests in seeing the missions as a "symbol of loftiness," became known as the Spanish Mystique.[8]

Lummis's mythologization of the golden Spanish days was a key influence in one of the rhetorical marketing mechanisms controlling and rejecting Mexican food: the process of labeling it. While several racial and class tensions were at play during the late nineteenth and early twentieth century "to effectively demonize or distort the image of Mexican culture and cuisine," Euro-Americans "called it 'Spanish' when they wished to appropriate what they liked, and 'Mexican' when they needed to disparage it."[9] Restaurant owners, whose menus served enchiladas, tamales, tacos, and tostadas, made these foods more desirable to non-Mexican eaters by calling them "authentic" Spanish cuisine.[10]

The Spanish Mystique began to wear off, according to historian George F. Sánchez, when a quasi (Mexican) Harlem Renaissance began to take place with the influx of Mexican immigrants to the United States during periods of political unrest such as the Mexican Revolution and World War I and II. Prior to these events, the majority of Mexicans in the United States lived in rural and agricultural settings; however, many of the new immigrants established themselves in urban settings making their culture more visible. New immigrants who were from middle and upper socioeconomic ranks began to establish businesses, many of which were in the food industry.[11] "Mexican" rather than "Spanish" began to appear on food labels in commercial settings. Two chapters in this volume, Mendoza Guerrero's "Mexican Food in El Paso, 1880–1940" and Cárdenas's "Queering the Chili Queens," point out how the acceptance of Mexican food began to change in the late nineteenth and into the twentieth century. This change occurred to the degree that, by 1908, William Gebhardt and then, by 1921, Lyman Davis popularized *chile con carne* with Wolf Brand Chili. La Misión Café in

Los Angeles, California, also began to advertise Mexican dishes in the 1920s. In the 1930s the popular staple of Mexican food, the tortilla, gained popularity at such a visible scale that the *tortillería* industry began to grow significantly. Patio Mexican Foods, founded by Henry E. Stumberg Sr. and his sons in the 1940s, sold frozen tamales and chili diners. El Paso based companies, Ashley and Old El Paso, also began to sell "Mexican" food at a national level as early as the 1930s, and Old El Paso now sells "Mexican" food at a global scale. Food historian Donna Gabaccia argues that the phenomena of conceiving ethnic foods as "unfit" for American consumption to embracing them as part of American foodways is achieved by the very process by which food becomes a symbol of American efficiency: mass production and distribution which is made possible through strategic visual marketing techniques. The commercial and industrial explosion of Mexican food helped alter Americans' attitudes regarding foods sold under the banner "Mexican."[12]

Representations of Mexican food in the public domain to entice its consumption inform our central inquiries. The entrance of Mexican food into the realm of mass production and commercial advertisement helped transform the attitude from rejecting it as "unfit" to eat to accepting it as "American" as apple pie. Yet, what does this transformation suggest about the complexities of cultural appropriation and representation embedded within certain images and language used to make Mexican food appetizing to the consuming eye? What social and cultural dynamics are reflected by the relationships created by those providing an image, those consuming the food, and those that are symbolically and/or metaphorically represented through such foods? How are we to read which cultural meaning is intended for us with certain symbols used to represent food?

Food advertisements project and often promote a perceived cultural context. According to Judith Williamson, advertisements "translate statements from the world of things . . . into a form that means something in terms of people."[13] This translation between image and consumer creates an "exchange value" for the product.[14] Advertisements make use of food's communicative power, which social scientist Roland Barthes has defined as food's ability to function beyond something edible and sustaining. Food and representations of food are venues by which cultural information about a society can be gathered. According to Barthes, the expressive venues of food's communicative capacity can be teased out "by direct observation [of food] in the economy, in [cooking and serving] technique, in [ritual] usages and [commercial] advertising."[15] Barthes argues that not only an actual food item or culinary practice has the power to speak of, or reflect on, aspects of a people's culture, but also the visual images used to represent food communicates cultural and social attitudes. However, while most of us accept food's communicative power to express invaluable cultural aspects of our lives, oftentimes we do not pause long enough to consider critically the complex cultural implications conveyed through food-related images, particularly when used as advertisements. Our concern in this chapter, therefore, is how the food marketing sector tends to select images that frequently communicate cultural representations of Mexican food outside its historical and social context, while in the process reinforcing *acceptable* stereotypes of the "ethnic other."

We examine food images because they are the most visible "node" within the "web of meanings" created at the intersections of the production, distribution, and consumption of food.[16] The examination of these intersections is best understood through a "holistic culinary approach."[17] The complexity and power dynamics vested in food should always involve an interdisciplinary paradigm that looks at food practices within the private and public kitchens, the personal and collective, and the local and global levels of food systems. A holistic culinary analysis involves a dialogue across and between the humanities, social sciences, health sciences, and economics to create a more complex, complete, and nuanced study of food precurment. We use this simultaneous analyzing of multiple food narratives first to *see* and then to *question* the kinds of cultural representations the food marketing industry projects and promotes with its selection of images.

We concern ourselves with images that have been and continue to be promoted by the marketing sector of the US food industry. Food images project "commodified perceptions of culture" that offers a narrow view of the symbolic cultural and historical meanings embedded in foods.[18] Commodification of culture is a result of mass production, which is the very process by which Mexican food has been accepted into the American palate and beyond,[19] and reflects what Arjun Appadurai has called "cultural hijacking."[20] Here the appropriation of (some) Mexican foods, perhaps better defined as working-class Mexican foods[21]—the eternal tacos, enchiladas, flautas—reflects two sides of the same coin. On one side, industrialization and modernization defines the terms by which the foods of an ethnic other are accepted as American. On the other side, increased capital gain seems to depend on the very act of appropriation and redefinition of a food's cultural meaning.

The food marketing industry's representation of Mexican food, and by extention Mexican people, relies on what Chimamanda Adiche calls a "single story"[22] (i.e., a single image). She defines "single story" as the process of having only one version of an image, metaphor, or symbol, which leads to a single essentialized interpretation. This process of essentialization, within the realm of food, we reframe as commodified perceptions of culture, since the (single) visual image is removed (hijacked) from its historical and social context and paired with food products in order to entice conusmers' palates.

An example of this commodified perception of culture is Frito-Lay's widely distributed image of Frito Bandito in the early 1960s. Frito Bandito is short and overweight, with a long handle-bar mustache that covers half his face. He has a gold tooth and uses a bullet-hole straw hat that is one-third his body size. He also carries two bullet belts across his chest. Furthermore, he speaks Spanish and broken English and robs bystanders (of their corn chips). Considering that this image was created in the 1960s, the same decade when much of the Chicano civil rights movement was taking place, what cultural representations of Mexican and Mexican American people (children and adults) could Frito-Lay have intended to project with a caricature-like revolutionary peasant man? Was this image supposed to be a symbolic representation of their version of a Pancho Villa or Emiliano Zapata?[23] Clearly a particular group of Mexican Americans, perhaps the parents of the intended targeted consumer of Frito Bandito, did not consume this cultural representation lightly. Whatever cultural message the marketing team had in mind backfired when "the Mexican-American Anti-Defamation Committee accused Frito-Lay of insensitivity, stereotyping, and racism."[24] The company eventually remade its image of Frito Bandito and finally stopped using it. Yet, this image left a strong enough impression on Americans' collective imaginary that even those too young to have eaten a bag of Frito Corn Chips have a notion of who this "Mexican" man was and what he looked like. A Google search of Frito Bandito can assist in continuing to project this commodified perception of Mexican people or, more specifically, Mexican men as short, fat, violent, and inarticulate.

The Sleeping Mexican Man:
His *Sombrero, Zarape,* and *Tequila*[25]

Another image of a Mexican we all have seen is the "sleeping Mexican man." He is the big-bellied man sitting on the floor leaning against a cactus, a wide-brimmed sombrero on his head, a zarape wrapped around his shoulders, and a bottle of tequila next to his feet. Its pervasiveness is such that it is found in numerous restaurants across the United States, on Mexican food packaging, and even has a transoceanic presence from Europe to Australia. The ubiquitousness of this visual is such that as consumers we do not explore what cultural, gender, and class messages it communicates. In part, we might not concern ourselves with what possible significant messages such an image could suggest because its commercialized "single story" has come to reflect nothing more than a kitschy representation. However, we call into question the situation and condition that led to this kitschy representation and ask: How do we as consumers read and dissect the "single story" we are being fed with this image?

The "sleeping Mexican man" has maintained a symbolic cultural and class currency for almost two hundred years. Some scholars traced the origin of this representation to Mexico's *Porfiriato* era.[26] As was documented by investigative reporter John Kenneth Turner, during Porfirio Díaz's dictatorship there was an explosion of homelessness experienced by Mexico's poor. Many could not seek shelter in Mexican *fondas* (inns) because they were often overcrowded, and at times the charge for the night was too expensive.[27] Those that could not afford the cost were forced to sleep outside huddled in doorways with only their zarape to shield them from the cold.

If Turner's account is correct, then a necessity due to poverty became a cultural stereotype of laziness. Historian David J. Weber traces the attitudes informing the representation of a Mexican man sleeping on the floor to conflicts Anglo-Americans had with Spanish colonial Mexico. Weber writes that "the negative attitudes toward Catholic Spaniards which Anglo-Americans had inherited from their Protestant English forebears" transferred to people of Mexican ancestry. Furthermore, Anglo-Americans believed "that the Spanish government was authoritarian, corrupt, and decadent" and that "Spaniards were bigoted, cruel, greedy, tyrannical, fanatical, treacherous and lazy."[28] Weber illustrates how such attitudes moved to the borderlands particularly after the annexation of Mexico's territory as a result of the US-Mexican War of 1846.

Foreigners traveling through Mexico in the late 1800s were the first to describe Mexican men sitting wrapped in zarapes (shawls).[29] Decades later, Nevin O. Winter documented his travel through Oaxaca in 1913 and wrote, "The *Indios* living in the hills took undisturbed possession at night, and groups of tired *Indios* wrapped themselves in their *sarapes* or shawls, and stretched their tired limbs out on the cold stones; or propped themselves against the walls of a building to rest."[30] In addition to his written account, Winter presented his audience with photographs of Mexican men leaning against walls, wrapped in zarapes, and with the wide-brimmed sombreros casting a shadow so that their faces cannot be seen. While Winter demonstrates that the supine or huddled resting position is a result of an understandable exhaustion, he still characterized the Mexican "peon" as having a "natural laziness, ignorance and a lack of interest [that] will probably always keep down [his] efficiency as a worker."[31] Eventually the depiction in this era's travel logs became a symbol "associated with the despised (yet necessary) labor force of the Mexican peon, and [the derogatory] association to laziness, lack of initiative, and the 'mañana syndrome.'"[32] The visual representation of the photographs and written accounts of Mexican men huddled in doorways then resonated with and reinforced the held stereotype of Mexican men as lazy. This stereotype simply continued to be perpetuated due to the lack of understanding of the sociocultural meaning of a man resting.

While there is contestation to the origin, this image, used at times as a symbol and at others as an icon, carries substantial currency within the food advertising industry.[33] The image of "the sleeping Mexican man" as a whole is a signifier, but its parts, the palm fiber sombrero and the zarape, also allow the image to hold its significance. Since commodification takes a representation outside its historical and social context, the significance of these components and cultural symbols can be lost on consumers when they encounter the "sleeping Mexican man" wrapped with his zarape, head tilted, and sombrero covering his face.

The type of sombrero used in the image points to a class attitude as it is not just any sombrero, but a palm fiber sombrero. By the late sixteenth century, Mexican *vaqueros* (cowboys) wore sombreros made of leather, felt, or palm fiber.[34] Sombrero derives from the Spanish word *sombra* (shade).[35] Mexican vaqueros and *campesinos*[36] developed the wide-brimmed hat as protection from the intense heat and sun. The design of the sombrero eventually led to the modern-day Stetson.[37] The felt and leather sombreros were ornamented and used by *mariachis* and *charros* (rodeo horsemen).[38] The palm fiber hat that most often is associated with the image of the "sleeping Mexican man," however, was a marker for the working class or the poor.

The term zarape, while debated, is thought to have derived either from the Arabic word *zarābiy* or the Nahuatl word *tzalanpepechtli*, which translates to "*tzalan* to interweave and *pepchtli* a course quilted cloth used as a covering."[39] The zarape originated as a part of the dress of the rural population, who were mostly indigenous or mestizos. The woven zarape is created using a weaving tradition that is native to Mexico, but that has indigenous and Spanish influences. By 1840 the artisan loom weaving tradition of the zarape began to be noticed and taken up by wealthy landowners: "There was tremendous range in quality and hence in the cost of sarapes, and only the rich could afford the very finest."[40] By the early 1900s, in part due to the effort during the *Porfiriato* to modernize Mexico's industries, the importance of the hand-woven zarape began to fade as the Mexican textile production became mechanized. Despite these changes, William Wroth argues that the zarape "became an essential part of the national costume and came to symbolize in a stereotypical way both the dress of the typical Mexican man, and more generally, the colorful ambience that foreigners were inclined to associate with Mexican life."[41] While the zarape expresses Mexican culture and tradition, its representative use by the US food advertising industry erases that artisan tradition and, instead, makes a symbol of perpetual working-class status.

While the image of the "sleeping Mexican man" does not always have a bottle of tequila next to him, the inclusion of the liquor most poignantly plays into the image of the lazy and drunk Mexican. This representation, however, leaves out the prominent historical development of tequila and mescal. Tequila is a national drink of Mexico and, as such, it was the first Mexican product "to receive a Denomination of Controlled Origin from the World International Property Organization, meaning that any product bearing the name tequila must be produced in accordance with a specified process in one of five Mexican states."[42] Tequila fuses both indigenous knowledge of the production of *pulque*[43] with the Spanish process of distillation. Pulque and tequila are fermented *agave*, but the fermented agave is then distilled to create tequila. According to Marie Sarita Gaytán, "tequila is among the earliest *mestizo* products to have emerged from the encounter between colonizers and native inhabitants [of Mexico]."[44] While tequila production is a source of pride for the Tequila region of Mexico,[45] much like champagne is a source of pride for the Champagne region of France, "across the border in the United States, drinkers and nondrinkers alike associate *tequila* with rowdiness and fiesta fueled excess."[46] By associating the artisan craftsmanship involved in the production of tequila with excess, drunkenness, and laziness, a derogatory icon has been created out of a symbol of national pride.

The zarape and the plam-fiber sombrero, even when they are not used with the image of the "sleeping Mexican man," still project a commercialized identity of "Mexican." This is in large part due to various marketing schemes from the Frito Bandito of Frito-Lay to the Taco Bell boy of the original owners of Taco Bell. The US food industry often uses these two items to stand for a symbol of Mexican.[47] But these representations limit the vastness that is the Mexican culture. Advertisements that neglect this rich history are examples of what Oaxcan painter Francisco Toledo calls "*commercializacion salvaje*" (savage commercialization), or the "reckless disregard for the unique and irreplaceable."[48] According to a restaurant owner interviewed by Gaytán, "symbols such as *sombreros, zarapes*, and *piñatas* ... presented a limited version of Mexican identity, one that neglected to consider the 'huge history of great art' produced and appreciated by Mexicans on both sides of the US-Mexican border."[49]

What value and purpose does a potentially derogatory icon or symbol have, especially when it is used in different locations for different purposes? For example, at Leo's Mexican Food Restaurant in El Paso, Texas, what is the "sleeping Mexican man" on the business's marquee telling its customers? Is this a reflection of a kitsch culture[50] or is it a subconscious reflection of the nineteenth-century stereotype? On a package of "Las Cruces Brand" corn tortillas, manufactured out of El Paso, Texas, there is a marketing stamp with "Mexi-Snax products" written on a scroll that includes a person wearing a large-brimmed sombrero sitting behind the scroll. What is Mexi-Snax attempting to communicate with this image as part of its label?[51] The examples of the image are not isolated to the Southwest region of the United States as the road stop South of the Border located in Hamer, South Carolina, also exploits the images of the sombrero and zarape as its company logo. How should travelers on US highway 301/501 interpret the rest stop's logo? Additionally, how should this image be read when one encounters it outside of the United States, in places such as Poland?

The only Mexican restaurant in Lodz, Poland, in 2007 was appropriately called El Mexicano. The Mexican flag flying outside the restaurant was the first announcement to distinguish this establishment from the four other eating places surrounding it. However, upon stepping into the restaurant there were mixed cultural signifiers provided by the waitresses, waiters, and décor. The waitress was wearing a traditional Spanish flamenco dress, confusing for a moment a Mexican restaurant for a Spanish one. The waiter was dressed as a Texas cowboy. His attire harks to the US presentation of Tex-Mex as Mexican food. But the walls covered with photographs and posters of famous Mexican figures, such as Pancho Villa, Benito Juárez, Porfirio Díaz, María Félix, Jorge Negrete, and Ricardo Montalbán, reassure customers that they are in a Mexican restaurant. To create fully this spatial transformation from Poland to Mexico, immediately to the right as one enters the restaurant was a three-foot statue of the classic nineteenth-century "sleeping Mexican man."

An analysis of El Mexicano demonstrates that the Polish have displayed the complexity of Mexican cuisine via three avenues: the history between Mexico and Spain; the relation the United States has had with Mexico; and a US food industry invention. First, the display of the waitresses' flamenco dress visualizes the history of Mexicans and their intertwined roots with the history of Spain and Spanish culture. Second, the Mexican food served in El Mexicano is a product of Mexican migration north to what eventually became the United States Southwest, particularly Texas, and what is known as "Tex-Mex." Finally, the transoceanic adaptation and display of the drunken, siesta-loving, Mexican man is a commercialized stereotype obtained via the food marketing industry within the United States, and not necessarily Mexico. Even though the "sleeping Mexican man" is used as a signifier that the contents, either in the packaging or within the establishment, represent Mexican food, a dissection of its history shows more of a commodified presentation of a culture whose origin resides with the US food industry.

While one may question why a Polish Mexican restaurant would not bypass such a stereotype, we suspect that the US marketing industry's vast and global economic influence accounts for the image being seen as representative of Mexican culture. The US food industry's fascination with the "sleeping Mexican man," regardless of its negative stereotypical implications, produces the global familiarity with this image. We have encountered this representation in our hometown of El Paso, Texas, USA; in Prague, Czech Republic; in Adalaide, Australia; and in Lodz as well as in Krakow, Poland, and the very presence of the "sleeping Mexican man" in these diverse locations is proof of the US food industry's far-reaching influence, which Theodor Adorno and Max Hokeimer call the "culture industry."[52]

The culture industry within the realm of food advertisements is significant because it controls the projection of Mexican food through its packing and restaurant logos. The industrialized creation of Mexican culture through the "sleeping Mexican man" attempts to translate to the audience an experience of "authentic" Mexican food. However, Gaytán reminds us of the power dynamics inherent in defining what cultural authenticity is. In the US food advertising industry this often gets further complicated when those creating the icon to signal Mexican authenticity are outsiders to the Mexican culture.

According to Gaytán, "in spite of its socially constructed character, practices of authenticity have real-world implications that illustrate the limits and constraints that less powerful populations face in the marketplace—especially when it comes to accessing the conditions that enable the production and consumption of their identities."[53] What is at the root of this concern of authenticity is the link that usually is made between a people's food and the people. In essence, the "sleeping Mexican man" is one that came into existence as a symbol of Mexican food and by extension Mexicans based on stereotypes. Weber argues that attitudes about Mexicans projected into the "sleeping Mexican man" image carry a history that combines "a belief in the inferiority of mixed-bloods [that] enabled Anglo Americans to predict erroneously what Mexicans would be like ... even before coming into significant contact with them."[54]

Weber's final observation about stereotypes associated with Mexicans throughout the US Southwest merits quoting at length as it underscores central concerns of our chapter, which are also addressed in other chapters in this collection.

> This discussion of the historical roots of Anglo-American stereotypes ... have had an impact on Mexican-United States relations and on the treatment of Mexicans and Mexican Americans in the United States. The stereotype of the inferior Mexican lay behind the arrogant stance of cultural and political superiority, known in the United States history as Manifest Destiny ... The stereotype of [the] inferior Mexican has been used to the present to justify efforts to "Americanize" Mexicans in the Southwest of the United States, replacing their "folkway" with "superior" Anglo-American culture. Stereotypes have also helped Anglo-Americans rationalize their exploitation and mistreatment of Mexican and Mexican American workers in fields and factories.[55]

Weber's statements regarding the Americanization of Mexicans, the appropriation of their "folkways" and foodways, and the treatment of workers in the fields and factories are themes central to a number of previous chapters of this volume. For example, Perales, Cárdenas, Rohrleitner, Menodza Guerrero, and Fitting examine the Americanization process, the appropriation of food and food practices, and Mexican and Mexican Americans' labor used in the fields.

The Illusion of Farm-to-Table

While agribusiness has replaced agri*culture* and mechanized/industrialized aspects of farming have replaced the farm, the food marketing industry still attempts to sell the illusion of consuming food that goes directly from the field of agri*culture* and, consequently, from farm to table. This narrative makes invisible people's labor in the food industry, and these laborers' presence at the table is ambiguous at best.

For example, Tyson, the biggest manufacturer and distributor of meat products, would never convey the reality that workers face in meat factories, as does Chicano poet David Domínguez. In his collection *Work Done Right*, he depicts the modern process of a pig slaughter factory:

> Open vats of red vinegar fermented outside:
> 108° of Del Sol heat and black asphalt.
> Guillermo and I choked on the vinegar's vapor
> as we threw cardboard boxes,
> still ripe with scraps of guts, into the dumpster.
> Pig blood poured from the boxes,
> ran under my smock, and down my skin.
> "This is no way to live," I told Guillermo.[56]

Here Domínguez speaks to what Carol J. Adams calls the "absent reference"[57] as a result of the great lengths the food industry has gone to keep consumers from making a concrete association between a meat product wrapped in saran wrap and the actual animal. Domínguez goes one step further by showing the physical labor and working conditions of those who are made responsible in creating the illusion that a pork chop does not come from a living pig. Furthermore, with the reference to the burning 108-degree heat of "Del Sol," he brings readers' attention to the global packaging and distributing company, Del Sol Food, LLC, that mainly targets consumers in North, South, and Central America and Asia. Del Sol Food claims to meet all of their customers' needs beginning with the packaging of the products they sell. On Del Sol Food's web page it states,

> we control the integrity of packaging from colors to materials design. Our creating team assures that all of our packages

stand out, inform and demand the customer's attention. By using the packaging as a communication tool, we create a connection between the consumer and the product, which ultimately helps sell those products. For us it is not just a box, it is the first interaction consumers have with our products.[58]

Clearly there are no references made by Del Sol Foods to the working conditions of the people that produce the foods they sell. Awareness of such details would not increase sales.

Thus, the illusion of farm-to-table, because of how much it leaves out and what it replaces it with, hides the structural vulnerabilities faced by workers in the food industry and offers consumers erroneous assumptions. On the one hand, it obliterates the reality of the labor conditions; and on the other, it presents a food narrative that aims to promote a way of growing and raising food that is declining on a global scale.[59] In the context of this chapter, we must ask, then, due to these powerful and persuasive marketing narratives of the seemingly harmonious transitions from farm to table, what narratives about Mexican food—but most importantly about Mexican people—come to the forefront, which, at best, stay in the background, and which, at worst, remain unknown?

The bright red, yellow, and white box of "Sun Maid Raisins," manufactured by Sun Maid Company, is a classic example of a commodified preception of culture. Within the context of grape harvesting in California, the company's marketing team dismisses the labor realities that affect the lives of migrant fieldworkers who in their majority are Mexican or Mexican American. Instead, consumers are offered the pleasant image of a girl, Lorraine Collette Peterson,[60] in a red bonnet with her long brown hair flowing down over her shoulders, a wide smile, and wearing a clean white blouse. Offering consumers a bushel of grapes, the image evokes a feeling of happiness, hospitality, and anticipation for the sweetness of freshly harvested grapes.

A recollection of the history of grape farming and harvesting in California quickly begins to suggest a narrative drastically different from the image presented by Sun Maid Company. The narrative of grape harvesting, as was poignantly displayed by César Chávez, Dolores Huerta, and the United Farm Workers, is not a sunny, clean, and pleasant experience. Chicana artist Ester Hernández has created renditions of this all too familiar food-related image. As a child of farmworkers, Hernández grew up in California's San Joaquín Valley. She and her family, as well as other farm-working families, "unknowingly bathed in and drank polluted water and worked in an environment contaminated by pesticides."[61] These experiences are not isolated to Hernandez's community, as many farmworkers experience such working and living conditions—a fact that is highlighted in Marion Rohrleitner's analysis of Helena María Viramontes's novel *Under the Feet of Jesus* in this collection. As a result of these conditions, Hernández's entire family became heavily involved with the United Farm Workers. These personal experiences initiated for her a "food consciousness" that she evokes in her art.[62]

Two of Hernández's most well known art pieces are based on counter-images to "Sun Maid Raisins." In 1982 she created *Sun Mad* and in 2008 *Sun•Raid*. Collectively, these two screen prints tell the historical reality farmworkers face. By making small but significant alterations to the *official* representation of Sun Maid, Hernández sends a powerful message by using this commonplace icon to call attention to a complex story about ethnicity, human and environmental health, migration, and labor agricultural politics that are intertwined with harvesting.

In the 1982 *Sun Mad*, Hernández replaces the pretty girl with a skeleton dressed in a white blouse and wearing a red bonnet covering part of her long brown hair, which flows down perfectly over her shoulders. In her arms she carries a basket of presumably just-harvested green grapes, which she offers with a wide smile. Underneath the slogan announcing the raisins, the following statement is made: "Unnaturally Grown With Insecticides-Miticides-Herbicides-Fungicides." Hernández states that the inspiration for her creation was a visit to her mother in 1979. During this visit, her mother shared newspaper articles she had saved about "water contamination in the *barrio*." Hernández decided to visually expose the dangerous practices used in the cultivation of grapes in the San Joaquín Valley. She expresses the motives of her rendition of the Sun Maid box by stating: "Slowly I began to realize how to transform the Sun Maid and unmask the truth behind the wholesome figures of agribusiness. *Sun Mad* evolved out of my anger and my fears of what could happen to my family, my community, and to myself" if such practices of growing crops were not exposed.[63] This concern can and does extend to consumers, as such substances affect the crops and not just the soil where they are grown.[64]

Twenty-six years later, in 2008, Hernández produces *Sun•Raid*. She continues to use a skeleton farmworker, but this time wearing a *huipil*, a native Mexican dress. To address the current anti-immigration political and cultural climate set off by the economic crisis of 2008 that was directed toward Mexicans and other Latin American people, this skeleton wears a security-monitoring bracelet labeled "ICE," which stands for Immigrations and Customs Enforcement. To further signify the constant fear of deportation, right below the slogan "Sun•Raid Raisins" it reads "Guaranteed Deportation." In smaller print underneath the declaration of deportation is a list of indigenous peoples from Oaxaca, México—"Mixtecos, Zapotecos, Triques, Purepechas"—who make up a large number of farmworkers in the United States. This list is followed by the last caption in the painting that reads, "By-product of NAFTA."

The last three captions announcing deportation of Mexican indigenous groups acts as a triple irony. First, indigenous Mexican people are the labor force most heavily responsible for harvesting the fruits and vegetables Americans eat. Second, it is the very neoliberal capitalist system that under rides the NAFTA agreement that creates the need for a cheap labor force within the United States, which is generally filled by documented and undocumented immigrants from Mexico, Central and South America. Third, the import of cheap GMO corn from the United States into the Mexican consumer economy has affected both the large-scale production of corn in Mexico for national consumption and for smaller farmers' subsistence cultivation.[65] Elizabeth Fitting's chapter in this volume, "From Working the Farm to Fast Food and Back Again," underscores this triple irony, but also allows us to hear stories of displaced campesinos and their desires.

Hernández's visual food narratives are an attempt to provoke awareness about the daily realities experienced by those working on the frontline of food production in the fields that, for most of us, remain invisible. Her work, while focused on raisins, is about creating a cultural, social, political, economic, and environmental "food consciousness"[66] for food consumers: *all of us*. Her work demonstrates a counternarrative to the commodified perceptions of cultures fed to consumers through advertisements. The fact that her 1982 *Sun Mad* is part of the permanent collection at the Smithsonian American Art Museum is a constant reminder of the need for such forms of "food consciousness."

Conclusions

Mexican food at one time was rejected by non-Mexicans in the United States as unfit for "human consumption." As illustrated by Cárdenas's analysis of the Chili Queens in this volume, Mexican food was associated with a lack of hygiene and its spiciness suggested low morality. The rejection of Mexican foodways transferred to Mexican people, or perhaps it was the other way around: Eurocentric feelings of superiority tainted attitudes toward Mexicans and their cultural food practices. In the last 150 years, these attitudes have certainly changed; or have they? Advertisements have been a key factor in the reorientation toward the consumption of this food. Some visual representations that have been used to entice consumers leave us wondering about the trajectory of this acceptance.

Eurocentric rhetoric in the mid- to late nineteenth century was the first step in changing attitudes toward eating the cuisine of an "ethnic other" seen as culturally inferior by announcing tacos and enchiladas as Spanish and not Mexican. With the increase of Mexican nationals during the first half of the twentieth century, Mexican restaurants and small manufacturers of Mexican foodstuffs became noticeable in urban settings. Small, often localized, Mexican-run businesses soon became visible to food entrepreneurs, who were generally outside of Mexican community enclaves, and who began enterprises for the mass production of Mexican food. Mendoza Guerrero, in chapter 2 of this volume, points out this trajectory in his study of Mexican food in El Paso, Texas. After entering into the US food industry's system of mass production, visual food narratives were created to further enhance the trajectory of accepting Mexican foods as another regional/ethnic cuisine of the United States. This *acceptance*, oddly enough, does not seem to have had much effect on the early Eurocentric discourses. The

visual narratives created by the marketing industry have been heavily influenced by a "single story" grounded in a historical perspective
based on racial, class, and gender stereotypes.

Visual food narratives read through a "holistic culinary approach"
that looks to the intersections among disciplines allows the complexities of these images to be made visible. That Mexican food has
become a part of American cuisine owes much to the "single story"
that the marketing industry has promoted in selling this food to a
non-Mexican palate. This narrative is not far removed from the attitudes that Mexican food and Mexican people have been subjugated to
throughout the US-Mexico asymmetrical relationship. The depiction
that the marketing industry consistently uses is based on a representation that either hides or takes away people's cultural subjectivity and
knowledge.

In the case of Frito Bandito, Mexican men are presented as an
emasculated, ignorant, violent, and dishonest caricature. The "sleeping Mexican man" works and is successful as a symbol of Mexican
culture because it is a way of having a relationship with the other, but
the portrayal presents the other as submissive and demonstrates an
asymmetrical relationship of power. The asymmetry presents Mexican
men as lazy, drunk, and always taking a siesta. This ignores the fact
that Mexican immigrants make up 68 percent of farmworkers in the
United States.[67] Anthony Bourdain, in a recent blog post, smartly
notices the stark hypocritical view Americans possess of Mexicans
when he remarks,

> We consume nachos, tacos, burritos, tortas, enchiladas,
> tamales and anything resembling Mexican in enormous quantities.
> ... Despite our ridiculously hypocritical attitudes towards immi-
> gration, we demand that Mexicans cook a large percentage of the
> food we eat, [and] grow the ingredients we need to make that
> food ... As any chef will tell you, our entire service economy—
> the restaurant business as we know it—in most American cities,
> would collapse overnight without Mexican workers.[68]

Stereotypical presentations of Mexican culture through depictions
such as the "sleeping Mexican man" are representative of how the
US food industry continues its appropriation and redistribution of
Mexican food and culture. Additionally, the artisan knowledge of the

zarape weaving tradition, the creation of the design of the sombrero that was used to create the first Stetson, and the mestizaje of scientific knowledge of tequila production remains hidden. How our food travels from farm to table also involves a process of hiding stories. The Sun Maid image hides the structural vulnerability experienced by farmworkers who labor in the practices of agribusiness, particularly those picking the crops. Neoliberal policies such as NAFTA, as Fitting cleary illuminates in her chapter, augment such vulnerabilities that Hernández's art brings to our attention.

It could be said that the visual food narratives we have drawn attention to here could simply be dismissed as "kitschy" representations.[69] We question, however, if these images allow for an *acceptable stereotype* and level of racism that can be traced back to the early nineteenth century. It must not be forgotten that these visual advertisements create static, essentialized images framed outside historical and cultural context. Nonetheless, advertisements do create meaning. As Judith Williamson succinctly asserts, "Advertisements' role is to attach meanings to products, to create identities for the goods (and service providers) they promote."[70] Additionally, Stuart Hall argues that mass media does not simply *reflect/represent* characteristics of groups, but instead *creates/presents* an idea of them.[71] The concern remains when an image is connected to food. It becomes difficult to sustain the argument that people can be removed from the food that speaks to their culture because food represents a group's culinary identity. By interrogating instead of dismissing the presence and ubiquitousness of these commodified perceptions of cultures, the complex cultural implications of *representation* and *presentation* can be made visible. We can only hope that this interrogation leads us to paths that change the way we think about food.

NOTES

Introduction

1. The Juarez family does not use an accent in the spelling of their name.

2. In recent years this demographic has changed to some degree. During the summer months of 2014, the southern border of the United States saw a larger number of immigrants crossing from Central and South America. For the first time, the immigration category of OTM, Other than Mexican, surpassed Mexican immigrants. U.S. Congress. House. Committee on Homeland Security, Field Hearing: Crisis on the Texas Border: Surge of Unaccompanied Minors: Message from Governor Rick Perry State of Texas, 113th Cong., Field Hearing, 2014, http://docs.house.gov/meetings/HM/HM00/20140703/102439/HHRG-113-HM00-Wstate-PerryR-20140703.pdf.

3. Enrique C. Ochoa, *Feeding Mexico: The Political Uses of Food since 1910* (Wilmington, DE: Scholarly Resources, 2000), offers an illustrative analysis of how the basic necessity to feed citizens, especially those in the poorest sectors of society, has been used as a tool of political and economic governmental power. During the first major devaluation of currency in the early 1980s and into the 1990s, the effort to feed the population via the State Food Agency created during Lázaro Cárdenas's presidency (1934–1940) saw its total dismantle. While Ochoa's work does not address what most poor people did to feed their families and themselves, this same period was one of a particularly high influx of Mexicans crossing the border (without documents) into the United States.

4. Immanuel Wallerstein, "Latin@s: What's in a Name?" PDF, March 21, 2005, accessed March 11, 2015, www.sociologistwithoutborders.org/essays/Latinos.pdf.

5. While the majority of articles in this collection are centered on Mexican and Mexican American experiences, and only three deal with other national/ethnic groups, this does not diminish our inclusive use of Latin@s. What this mostly reflects is that Mexican and Mexican American have had a longer and consequently more visible history within the context of the binational relations affecting the food industry. Some people of Mexican origins living in what is now the Southwest and California predate the inclusion of these territories as part of the United States. The food industry (i.e., agribusiness), however, has relied on their labor, and binational government agreements have been created (i.e., the Bracero Program) to ensure sufficiently low-paying labor to maintain a profitable business. Beyond labor, the history of Mexican and Mexican Americans within the layers of the food industry includes efforts to change these groups' eating habits (see Perales in this collection) and appropriate their culinary knowledge. All of these themes/histories are addressed in this collection. However, the NAFTA agreement and neoliberal economic policies (also addressed in this collection) of the food industry have had a substantial impact on the daily lives of other Latin American and Caribbean people.

Lidia Marte's chapter in this collection addresses this newer impact. Currently, emerging food studies research is exploring the new impacts of the US food industry in other Latin@s' groups. See Hanna Garth, ed., *Food and Identity in the Caribbean* (New York: Bloomsbury, 2013); Candice Goucher, *Congotay! Congotay!: A Global History of Caribbean Food* (New York: M. E. Sharpe, 2014); Richard Wilk and Livia Barbosa, eds., *Rice and Beans: A Unique Dish in a Hundred Places* (New York: BERG, 2012).

6. Quesada et al. defines structural vulnerabilities as "the process [by] which the vulnerability of an individual is produced by his or her location in a hierarchical social order and its diverse networks of power relationships and its effects ... [and] requires an analytical stance that examines the forces that constrain decision making, frame choice, and limits life options." James Quesada, Laurie K. Har, and Phillippe Bourgois, "Structural Vulnerability and Health: Latino Migrant Laborers in the United States," *Medical Anthropology* 30, no. 4 (2011): 339–62, 340–41; also, see the film *Rape in the Fields*, directed by Lowell Bergman (2013).

7. Don Mitchell, *The Lie of the Land* (Minneapolis: University of Minnesota Press, 1996); Seth M. Holmes, *Fresh Fruit, Broken Bodies: Migrant Farmworkers in the United States* (Berkeley: University of California Press, 2013); Deborah Cohen, *Braceros: Migrant Citizens and Transnational Subjects in the Postwar United States and Mexico* (Chapel Hill: University of North Carolina Press, 2011).

8. To examine further this lack of acknowledgment, see Florence E. Babb, *Between Field and Cooking Pot: The Political Economy of Marketwomen in Peru* (Austin: University of Texas Press, 1989); Meredith E. Abarca, "*Charlas Culinarias*: Mexican Women Speak from Their Public Kitchens," *Food & Foodways* 15 (2007): 183–212; Sonia Hernández, *Working Women into the Borderlands* (College Station: Texas A&M Press, 2014).

9. Meredith E. Abarca and Ramona Lee Pérez, eds., "*Cocinas Públicas*: Food and Border Consciousness in Greater Mexico," *Food & Foodways: Explorations in the History and Culture of Human Nourishment* 14, no. 3–4 (2007): 137–290.

10. Ibid., 138.

11. Ibid., 139.

12. *Fast Food/Slow Food: The Cultural Economy of the Global Food System*, ed. Richard Wilk (New York: Alta Mira Press, 2006).

13. Elizabeth Fitting, *The Struggle for Maize* (Durham, NC: Duke University Press, 2010); Gary Paul Nabhan, *Arab/American: Landscape, Culture, and Cuisine in Two Great Deserts* (Tucson: University of Arizona Press, 2008); Jeffery M. Pilcher, *¡Que vivan los tamales!* (Albuquerque: University of New Mexico Press, 1998); Jeffery M. Pilcher, *Planet Taco: A Global History of Mexican Food* (New York: Oxford University Press, 2012); Vadana Shiva, *Stolen Harvest* (Cambridge, MA: South End Press, 2000). Much of Vandana Shiva's work discusses the food industry's hijacking of an environmentally and culturally sustainable food system in India that has been in place for thousands of years.

14. Sidney Mintz, "Food at Moderate Speeds," in *Fast Food/Slow Food: The Cultural Economy of the Global Food Systems*, ed. Richard Wilk (New York: Alta Mira Press, 2006), 9.

15. Marion Nestle, *Food Politics* (Berkeley: University of California Press, 2003), 11. Nestle defines food industry as "the companies that produce, process, manufac-

ture, sell, and serve foods, beverages, and dietary supplements. In a larger sense, the term encompasses the entire collection of enterprises involved in the production and consumption of food and beverages: producers and processors of food crops and animals (agribusiness); companies that make and sell fertilizer, pesticides, seeds, and feed; those that provide machinery, labor, real estate, and financial services to farmers; and others that transport, store, distribute, export, process, and market foods after they leave the farm. It also includes the food service sector—food carts, vending machines, restaurants, bars, fast-food outlets, schools, hospitals, prisons, and workplaces—and associated suppliers of equipment and serving materials." Also see Tim Lang, "Food Industrialization and Food Power: Implications for Food Governance," *Taking Food Public: Redefining Foodways in a Changing World*, ed. Psyche Williams-Forson and Carole M. Counihan (New York: Routledge, 2011).

16. Mintz, "Food at Moderate Speeds."

17. Karl Webber, *Food Inc.: A Participant Guide: How Industrial Food Is Making Us Sicker, Fatter, and Poorer—And What You Can Do about It* (Los Angeles: Participant Media, 2009).

18. Overproduction/wastefulness of food is the focus of much of Michael Pollen's work. Nestle, *Food Politics*, 10. Michigan State University, "Food and Beverage Background," *Global Edge*, accessed March 11, 2015, http://globaledge. msu.edu/industries/food-and-beverage/background.

19. Ronald Mize and Alicia Swords, *Consuming Mexican Labor: From the Bracero Program to NAFTA* (Toronto: University of Toronto Press, 2010).

20. Warren Belasco, *Meals to Come: A History of the Future of Food* (Berkeley: University of California Press, 2006); Alexander Nützenadel and Frank Trentmann, eds., *Food and Globalization: Consumption, Markets and Politics in the Modern World* (New York: Berg, 2008).

21. Carole M. Counihan and Valeria Siniscalchi, "Ethnogragraphy of Food Activism," in *Food Activism: Agency, Democracy and Economy*, ed. Carole M. Counihan and Valeria Siniscalchi (New York: Bloomsbury, 2014), 3–12.

22. Teresa M. Mares, "Engaging Latino Immigrants in Seattle Food Activism through Urban Agriculture," in *Food Activism: Agency, Democracy and Economy*, ed. Carole M. Counihan and Valeria Siniscalchi (New York: Bloomsbury, 2014), 3–46, 43.

23. Mintz, "Food at Moderate Speeds," 10.

24. Meredith E. Abarca, "Culinary Encounters in Latino/a Literature," in *Routledge Companion to Latino/a Literature*, ed. Suzanne Bost and Frances R. Aparicio (New York: Routledge, 2013), 251–60, 252.

25. Pysche Williams-Forson, "Who's in the Kitchen with Dinah?: Intersectionality and Food Studies," *Food, Culture, and Society* 14, no. 1 (2011): 8–17, 11.

26. Wilk, "From Wild Weeds to Artisanal Cheese," in *Fast Food/Slow Food: The Cultural Economy of the Global Food Systems*, ed. Richard Wilk (New York: Alta Mira Press, 2006), 20.

27. Psyche Williams-Forson, "Food Studies as an area of research for students in the Humanities" (Roundtable Discussion, The University of Texas at El Paso, February 6, 2014). During a roundtable discussion with university students, Williams-Forson discussed her concept of "eating in the meantime." She asserted that this concept, while controversial, is a hard reality for people who cannot afford to purchase organic produce or who have time constraints due to extenuating

circumstances and therefore cannot always prepare meals at home. Additionally, she added that Food Studies should not shame individuals who are in this situation.

28. Annette Weiner, *Inalienable Possessions* (Berkeley: University of California Press, 1992). The gist of this idea is that foods cannot thoroughly be made into just a commodity. People's cultural connections to certain foods only have meaning through the exchange of family recipes, which are often presented as a gift.

29. Culinary subjectivities, as a way of speaking of self and collective identities, transcend national/regional spaces as well as singular ethnic/cultural notions of self. Using food as the marker of who we are involves an interethnic connection and sense of time that marks present, past, and future. This form of identity is made up of interconnecting moments of exchanges—methods of growing, sharing, and preparing food—that simultaneously maintain a cultural and historical continuity that expands to incorporate new social, economic, and geographical realities that reflect peoples' migratory patterns. Culinary subjectivities are lived, expressed, and recognized viscerally.

30. Elizabeth Fitting, "Cultures of Corn and Anti-GMO Activism in Mexico and Colombia," in *Food Activism: Agency, Democracy and Economy*, ed. Carole M. Counihan and Valeria Siniscalchi (New York: Bloomsbury, 2014), 175–92. Fitting in "Cultures of Corn" addresses a similar topic of how campesinos' agency manifests within the context of two Latin American contexts.

Chapter 1: *Desde el corazón*: Nourishing Bodies, Feeding Souls

1. What my ancestral women and my mother's cooking taught me is a "food consciousness" that speaks to the power implicated in food practices. Meredith E. Abarca and Nieves Pascual Soler introduce "food consciousness" to capture the ways in which material and symbolic food meanings inform our knowledge of selves and the ways in which we are included or excluded citizens from a particular culture, social class, and a nation. See *Rethinking Chicana/o Literature through Food: Postnational Appetites*, ed. Nieves Pascual Soler and Meredith E. Abarca (New York: Palgrave Macmillan, 2013).

2. Meredith E. Abarca, *Voices in the Kitchen: Views of Food and the World from Working-Class Mexican and Mexican American Women* (College Station: Texas A&M University Press, 2006), 23.

3. Ibid., 23.

4. Ibid.

5. Ibid., 79.

6. *Like Water for Chocolate*, directed by Alfonso Arau (1992; Mexico, Arau Films Internacional), DVD.

7. Abarca, *Voices in the Kitchen*, 79.

8. Ramona L. Pérez and Meredith E. Abarca, "*Cocinas Públicas*: Food and Border Consciousness in Greater Mexico," *Food & Foodways* 15 (2007): 137–51.

9. See Josie Méndez-Negrete, *Las hijas de Juan: Daughters Betrayed* (Durham, NC: Duke University Press, 2006) to place in context the relationships of control under which we lived as Juan's family. It is in the context of our lived experience that we learned to understand the meaning of nurturing and emotional care through culinary preparation practices.

10. Carole M. Counihan and Penny Van Esterik, eds., *Food and Culture: A Reader*, 3rd ed. (London: Routledge, 2013).

11. Carole M. Counihan, "*Mexicanas'* Food Voice and Differential Consciousness in the San Luis Valley of Colorado," in *Food and Culture: A Reader*, ed. Carole M. Counihan and Penny Van Esterik (New York: Routledge, 2013), 173–86, 173.

12. For more on this form of *testimonio* (testimony), see Latina Feminist Group, *Telling to Live: Latina Feminist Testimonios* (Durham, NC: Duke University Press, 2001).

13. Counihan, "*Mexicanas'* Food Voice and Differential Consciousness in the San Luis Valley of Colorado," 175.

14. Ibid.

15. Chela Sandoval, *Methodology of the Oppressed* (Minneapolis: University of Minnesota Press, 2000), 183. Sandoval's work provides me with an understanding of love as a liberatory strategy in "food consciousness" and as a means of creating social change in the home. It is in the fluid space of the home that we gained an understanding that love becomes a strategy for creating alliances to contest patriarchal powers.

16. Abarca, *Voices in the Kitchen*, 12.

17. Ibid., 17.

18. Meredith E. Abarca, "Families Who Eat Together, Stay Together, But Should They?" in *Rethinking Chicana/o Literature through Food: Postnational Appetites*, ed. Nieves Pascual Soler and Meredith E. Abarca (New York: Palgrave Macmillan, 2013).

19. Abarca and Pascual Soler, introduction in *Rethinking Chicanoa/o Literature through Food*, 8.

20. Migration or *migrante* not *inmigrante*—words I learned from Rosita, *mi supermaestra de elementaria*, who often clarified when we spoke about California or Texas. After all, she would often remind us that México was taken right from under our feet. So, in our view, Amá's movement was a migratory one because of her back-and-forth life.

21. David Montejano, *Anglos and Mexicans in the Making of Texas, 1936–1986* (Austin: University of Texas Press, 1987). In his discussion about the organization of labor in south Texas, Montejano shows that while Mexicans worked the fields to produce varying agricultural products, the crops they harvested were not often consumed by the workers.

22. Various qualities of cheese: *queso cotija* or dried and salty cow-milk cheese; *queso panela*, also known as basket cheese, is similar to mozzarella; *y queso de chiva* or goat cheese.

23. Gloria Anzaldúa, *Borderlands/La Frontera: The New Mestiza*, 1st ed. (San Francisco: aunt lute, 1987), 134.

24. While the meaning of the word *milpa* translates to cornfield, we easily bandied around to mean orchard and parcel.

25. As migrant fieldworkers, we were often limited to shop for basic provisions in the grocery store owned by the farm's owner, *el patrón*.

26. Carole M. Counihan, *The Anthropology of Food and Body: Gender, Meaning, and Power* (New York: Routledge, 1999).

27. In *Las hijas de Juan*, I address Juan's arrest for his abusive behavior. He was released after serving his prison sentence, and never returned to our family.

Chapter 2: Mexican Food in El Paso, 1880–1940:
Its Path and Discordant Voices

1. Two books required to understand the issue of Anglo appropriation of Mexican food in the United States are Jeffrey M. Pilcher, *Planet Taco: A Global History of Mexican Food* (New York: Oxford University Press, 2012), and Gustavo Arellano, *Taco USA: How Mexican Food Conquered America* (New York: Scribner, 2012). Historically, one by one, and for commercial purposes, the most popular dishes were not going to or being made Mexican hands. This was the history of chili, tamales, tacos, enchiladas, and even Mexican food recipes. Cultural appropriation is a correct concept because it implies that members of the dominant society took cultural elements such as cooking recipes, names of dishes, and ways of cooking from the Mexican American culture.

2. *El Continental* (El Paso, Texas), 3 de julio de 1937, 6.

3. Oscar J. Martínez, *Ciudad Juárez: el auge de una ciudad fronteriza a partir de 1848* (Mexico: Fondo de CulturaEconómica, 1982), 28. The few testimonies about Mexican food in mid-nineteenth-century El Paso talk about a simple meal of corn tortillas, red chile, cheese, goat meat, and wine. See *Newark Advocate* 8, no. 52 (July 27, 1859): 1.

4. Reynolds R. McKay, "Texas Mexican Repatriation during the Great Depression" (PhD diss., University of Oklahoma, 1982), 80. For a discussion of Mexican immigrants' regional origin, see Mónica Perales, "Smeltertown: A Biography of a Mexican American Community, 1880–1973" (PhD diss., Stanford University, 2003); Daniel D. Arreola, "Mexico Origins of South Texas Mexican Americans, 1930," *Journal of Historical Geography* 19, no. 1 (1993); Mario T. García, *Desert Immigrants: The Mexicans of El Paso, 1880–1920* (New Haven, CT: Yale University Press, 1981).

5. Martínez, *Ciudad Juárez*, 56.

6. Earl W. Heathcote, "Business of El Paso," in *El Paso: A Centennial Portrait*, ed. Harriot Howze Jones (El Paso County Historical Society, 1972), 203.

7. *Las Dos Repúblicas* (El Paso, Texas), March 7, 1888, 3.

8. *El Defensor* (Houston, Texas), January 27, 1895, 4, and October 15, 1894, 4; *El Latino Americano* (El Paso, Texas), January 21, 1891, 1; *La Justicia* (El Paso, Texas), September 5, 1893, 4; *El Paso del Norte* (El Paso, Texas), March 12, 1904, 3; *Las Dos Repúblicas* (El Paso, Texas), June 17, 1901, 4.

9. *La Patria* (El Paso, Texas), October 17, 1919, 4; *Atalaya Bautista* (El Paso, Texas), March 5, 1908, 8; *El Continental* (El Paso, Texas), June 24, 1937, 1; *El Eco Fronterizo* (El Paso, Texas), October 3, 1896, 2.

10. Romulo Z. Escobar, *Eslabonazos: relatos y escenas de la vida campirana (de 1896 a 1936)*, 2nd ed. (Mexico: Gobierno del estado de Chihuahua, 2003), 17.

11. *El Continental* (El Paso, Texas), January 21, 1935, 4, and November 29, 1935, 6. This did not mean that *chalupitas*, along with other foods or ingredients, were no longer consumed. In fact, foods like *eslabón* appeared in El Paso in 1935, this time accompanied by Coors beer.

12. *Newark Advocate*, 8, no. 52, July 27, 1859, 1; and *El Monitor* (El Paso, Texas), January 26, 1900, 3.

13. David Montejano, *Anglos and Mexicans in the Making of Texas, 1836–1986* (Austin: University of Texas Press, 1987).

14. In 1883 a newspaper note appeared with a very harsh review about menudo consumption. It pointed out that this food is not something to be ingested by humans, or even by dogs. *El Paso Herald* (El Paso, Texas), August 5, 1883. However, it can be ascertained that there were restaurants, like those of Juana Hernández, located on El Paso Street, that specialized in this dish. See *Las Noticias* (El Paso, Texas), October 14, 1899, 3.

15. *Sunday Herald* (El Paso, Texas), February 24, 1889, 6.

16. *Forth Worth Star*, October 23, 1916, 4; *The Continental* (El Paso, Texas), February 18, 1935, 6; April 15, 1935, 6; April 20, 1935, 1; December 17, 1937, 1; and October 27, 1937, 1.

17. *Atalaya Bautista* (El Paso, Texas), August 4, 1910, 15. The pressure to adopt new technologies at home came not only from advertising that emphasized backwardness for those who did not have a stove, a refrigerator, or an oven at home, but also from employers of domestic workers in El Paso who demanded that domestic Mexican women know how to use modern kitchen appliances.

18. *El Paso Herald* (El Paso, Texas), October 5, 1881, 2, and *La Prensa* (San Antonio, Texas), January 18, 1914. These kinds of responses were possible after many middle-class Mexican immigrants arrived to El Paso due to the Mexican Revolution. This group brought economic and intellectual resources to the city, and this allowed them to found newspapers, open food shops, and participate in the local civic and political life. Many of these individuals, through letters and newspaper articles, maintained an ongoing discussion about the vicissitudes of Mexican food.

19. In the early twentieth century, El Paso already had 16,000 inhabitants and had regained its place as the US city with the most Mexican population after having been exceeded in 1890. This demographic majority would remain until 1940, reaching a record high in 1930 when 7 out of 10 were Mexican citizens. See Martínez, *Ciudad Juárez*, 212.

20. This prejudice of the triad, by the way, was wrongly brought from Mexico to communities in the United States. It is clear that the American Southwest has always had its own culinary traditions, where corn, chili, and beans were not necessarily basic foods. Unlike Pilcher's view of Mexico, in El Paso the association of corn with indigenous and mestizo people was only in discourses because wheat flour was a crucial component of Mexican diet. See Jeffrey M. Pilcher, "Josefina Velázquez de León: Apostole of the Enchilada," in *The Human Tradition*, ed. Jeffrey M. Pilcher (Wilmington, DE: Scholarly Resources, 2003), 203; also see *La Prensa* (San Antonio, Texas), July 5, 1926, 4.

21. United Daughters of the Confederacy, Texas Division, Robert E. Lee Chapter, *El Paso, How We Cook in El Paso (Including Mexican Dishes)*, Tested Recipes / Compiled by The Ladies of the Robert E. Lee Chapter, UDC (El Paso, TX: McMath Co., 1926), 7–21. Besides what Gamio said about meat consumption, during the 1920s there was an increase in meat consumption among Mexicans in El Paso, especially pork, and it was during this time that Mexican *carneseca* became popular.

22. *El Continental* (El Paso, Texas), February 20, 1927, 6.

23. *Wordley's Business Directory of the City of El Paso*, 1901–1920.

24. *El Paso Morning Times* (El Paso, Texas), September 26, 1910, 2, and *El Paso Herald* (El Paso, Texas), April 13, 1910, 13. The most popular products were canned chili and tamales.

25. *La Patria* (El Paso, Texas), January 2, 1920, 2. For a broad discussion about Mexican American fast food in the United States, see Jeffrey M. Pilcher, *Planet Taco: A Global History of Mexican Food* (New York: Oxford University Press, 2012), 16.

26. *El Paso del Norte* (El Paso, Texas), September 18, 1904, 1.

27. *La Patria* (El Paso, Texas), July 1, 1919, and Américo Paredes, "The Problem of Identity in a Changing Culture: Popular Expressions of Culture Conflict along the Lower Rio Grande Border," in *Views across the Borders: The United States and Mexico*, ed. Stanley R. Ross (Albuquerque: University of New Mexico Press, 1978), 79, 81–82.

Paredes points out that besides "Frijolero," Mexicans contemptuously were called "Pepper belly," "Taco Choker," and "Chili Picker," while in response, the Mexicans called Anglos "Repollero" (people who eat cabbage) or "Jamonero" (people who eat ham).

28. *La Patria* (El Paso, Texas), November 2, 1921, 3–5.

29. Manuel Gamio, *Mexicans Immigration to the United States: A Study of Human Migration and Adjustment* (Chicago: University of Chicago Press, 1971 [1930]), 144.

30. Democrats of El Paso (Compilers), *Olé El Paso Border Gourmet Recipes* (Collierville, TN: Fund Craft Publishing, 1971), K, L, and N. One could think that the reason why Mexicans were not the authors of their own recipes was because Anglos were better able to preserve the culinary memory or maybe felt the responsibility to do so. However, it would have still been possible to give some credit to Mexicans as creators of their food. Authors of recipes have a knowledge and authority since they are a source that defines content and originality of the preparation of a meal. In this sense, signing (or not signing) a recipe could be a controversial issue.

31. Patricia Bowman, "History of Ashley's Incorporated and a Sketch of its Founder, George N. Ashley, Sr." (History class seminar paper, Western Texas College, May 1955), 3.

32. Ibid., 4–6.

33. José R. Iturriaga, *La cultura del antojito* (Mexico: Editorial Diana, 1993), 148; Donna R. Gabaccia, *We Are What We Eat: Ethnic Food and the Making of Americans* (Cambridge, MA: Harvard University Press, 1998), 165; Zilkia Janer, *Latino Food Culture* (Westport, CT: Greenwood Press, 2008), 10.

34. *La Patria* (El Paso, Texas), September 15, 1920, 4.

35. *The Continental* (El Paso, Texas), September 6, 1935, 3; September 25, 1936, 3; and July 1, 1937, 8.

36. Ibid., September 15, 1936, 2; and September 18, 1937, 8.

37. Ibid., March 20, 1958, 3; March 24, 1958, 3; December 4, 1958, 3; and January 9, 1959, 3.

38. Ibid., November 11, 1937, 2. This kind of reaction against industrialized food was not only rooted in cultural and national groups fighting for cultural autonomy, but also unbelievers in technical progress. The writer Upton Sinclair, and others, criticized the damage caused by the industrialized food and its elimination of the nutritional properties of the raw materials with which it had been produced.

39. *La Prensa* (San Antonio, Texas), January 7, 1940, 35 and 41.

40. *El Continental* (El Paso, Texas) June 19, 1927, 5.

41. Ibid., June 24, 1936, 4. People like Teresa Rosario Sansores Escoriaza, as well

as writers at *El Continental*, internalized this supposed feminine fault, admitting that women had forgotten that the kitchen was the center of a happy marriage and the institution that prevented empty households. See *El Continental*, July 1, 1936, 2, and September 5, 1937, 5.

42. *The Continental* (El Paso, Texas), June 24, 1936, 4.

43. *The Continental* (El Paso, Texas), August 12, 1952, 3.

44. *Odessa American* (Odessa, Texas), February 1, 1955.

45. Gustavo Arellano, *Taco USA*, 9; Meredith E. Abarca makes a similar argument on the use of originality and authenticity. Abarca argues that claiming something is authentic eliminates the right to the creative energy of the next generation. For Abarca, it is best to use "original" as a concept rather than "authentic." This ensures that the "production always belongs to the person who creates it"; "authentic or not, it's original." in *Food & Foodways: Explorations in the History and Culture of Human Nourishment* 12, no. 1 (2004): 4 and 10.

46. This generational cohort of the 1920s is known in the Chicana historiography as the immigrant generation whose political discourse was returning to Mexico instead of incorporating into the American society. This generation was perhaps the most patriotic generation and, along with Mexican consulates, boosted the use of the Spanish language and the retention of Mexican customs and traditions.

Chapter 3: The "New Mexican Way": The New Mexico Agricultural Extension Agency, Hispanas, and Making a Regional Cuisine

Thank you to the editors of this volume, members of the Texas Food Writers Salon, the UH Center for Public History Colloquium, and Marisela R. Chávez for their thoughtful feedback on various drafts of this essay.

1. Edith M. Lantz, "Nonfat Dry Milk Solids Improve Tortillas," no date, MS 300 New Mexico Extension Homemakers Council Records, box 6, folder 3, 2, Rio Grand Historical Collection, Special Collections, New Mexico State University, Las Cruces, NM. Hereafter, "NM Extension Homemakers Council Records, NMSU."

2. I have opted for the use of *Hispana/o* and *nuevomexicana/o* in reference to people of Mexican heritage in New Mexico. This term highlights the historical emphasis of many of its residents, most notably those of economic means and social standing, on a Spanish identity. On New Mexico history and terminology, see Deena González, *Refusing the Favor: The Spanish-Mexican Women of Santa Fe, 1820–1880* (New York: Oxford University Press, 1999); Laura Gómez, *Manifest Destinies: The Making of the Mexican American Race* (New York: New York University Press, 2007); John M. Nieto-Phillips, *The Language of Blood: The Making of Spanish-American Identity in New Mexico, 1880s–1930s* (Albuquerque: University of New Mexico Press, 2004); Pablo Mitchell, *Coyote Nation: Sexuality, Race, and Conquest in Modernizing New Mexico, 1880–1920* (Chicago: University of Chicago Press, 2005).

3. According to food studies scholar Warren Belasco, cuisine refers to a group's "set of 'protocols,' usages, communications, behaviors, etc." about food. A group's cuisine consists of the basic foods consumed, manner of preparation,

seasoning, and etiquette for eating. Warren Belasco, *Food: The Key Concepts* (New York: Berg, 2008), 15–18.

4. On the limits and opportunities of the NMAES, see Joan M. Jensen, "Crossing Ethnic Barriers in the Southwest: Women's Agricultural Extension Education, 1914–1940," *Agricultural History* 60, no. 2 (Spring 1986): 169–81; Jensen, "Canning Comes to New Mexico: Women and the Agricultural Extension Service, 1914–1919," in *New Mexico Women: Intercultural Perspectives*, ed. Joan M. Jensen and Darlis A. Miller (Albuquerque: University of New Mexico Press, 1986), 201–26; Anne Goldman, "'I Yam what I Yam': Cooking, Culture, and Colonialism," in *De/Colonizing the Subject: The Politics of Gender in Women's Autobiography*, ed. Sidonie Smith and Julia Watson (Minneapolis: University of Minnesota Press, 1992), 169–95; Virginia Scharff, *Twenty Thousand Roads: Women, Movement, and the West* (Berkeley: University of California Press, 2003). On Americanization and domestic instruction among Mexican women in the Southwest, see Monica Perales, *Smeltertown: Making and Remembering a Southwest Border Community* (Chapel Hill: University of North Carolina Press, 2010); George Sánchez, "Go After the Women: Americanization and the Mexican Immigrant Woman, 1915–1929," in *Unequal Sisters: A Multicultural Reader in U.S. Women's History*, 2nd edition, ed. Vicki L. Ruiz and Ellen Carol DuBois (New York: Routledge, 1994), 284–97; Peggy Pascoe, *Relations of Rescue: The Search for Female Moral Authority in the American West, 1874–1939* (New York: Oxford University Press, 1990); Sandra Schackel, *Social Housekeepers: Women Shaping Public Policy in New Mexico, 1920–1940* (Albuquerque: University of New Mexico Press, 1992).

5. On women's agency and food, see Meredith E. Abarca, *Voices in the Kitchen: Views of Food and the World from Working-Class Mexican and Mexican American Women* (College Station: Texas A&M University Press, 2006); Carole M. Counihan, *A Tortilla Is Like Life: Food and Culture in the San Luis Valley of Colorado* (Austin: University of Texas Press, 2009); Psyche A. Williams-Forson, *Building Houses out of Chicken Legs: Black Women, Food, and Power* (Chapel Hill: University of North Carolina Press, 2006).

6. Maria E. Montoya, "Home on Earth: Women and Land in the Rio Arriba," in *Home Lands: How Women Made the West*, ed. Virginia Scharff and Carolyn Brucken (Berkeley: University of California Press, 2010), 22.

7. Sarah Deutsch, *No Separate Refuge: Culture, Class, and Gender on an Anglo-Hispanic Frontier in the American Southwest, 1880–1940* (New York: Oxford University Press, 1987), 54.

8. González, *Refusing the Favor*, 45.

9. Stella M. Drumm, ed., *Down the Santa Fe Trail and into Mexico: The Diary of Susan Shelby Magoffin* (Lincoln: University of Nebraska Press, 1982, rpt.), 90, 94.

10. Mitchell, *Coyote Nation*.

11. Katherine Massoth, "'Her Many Duties in the Home': Spanish Mexican Women Constructing Identity in Territorial Arizona and New Mexico" (Paper presented at the Newberry Seminar in Borderlands and Latino Studies Fall Mini Conference, Chicago, IL, November 9, 2013). For more on women's roles in accommodating Anglos to Spanish Mexican society, see González, *Refusing the Favor*.

12. "Twenty Five Years of Extension Work in New Mexico," Extension Circular No. 162, June 1939, box 6, folder 3, 2. NM Extension Homemakers Council Records, NMSU.

13. Jensen, "Canning Comes to New Mexico," 201.

14. Wilbur Zelinsky, "Changes in the Geographic Patterns of Rural Population in the United States, 1790–1960," *Geographical Review* 52, no. 4 (October 1962): 497; Jensen, "Canning Comes to New Mexico," 202.

15. "Twenty Five Years of Extension Work in New Mexico," 2.

16. Jessica Mudry, "Quantifying the American Eater: USDA Nutrition Guidance and a Language of Numbers," in *Food as Communication, Communication as Food*, ed. Janet M. Cramer, Carlnita P. Greene, and Lynn M. Waters (New York: Peter Lang, 2011), 235–54; Harvey Levenstein, *Revolution at the Table: The Transformation of the American Diet* (Berkeley: University of California Press, 2003).

17. "3rd Annual Report of the Extension Service of the College of Agriculture and Mechanical Arts for the year ending June 30, 1917," box 7, folder 7, 45, MS UA 154 Cril, Hobson-Hunsinger University Archives, Records of the President Austin D. Crile (1917–1920), Special Collections, New Mexico State University, Las Cruces, NM. Hereafter "Crile Papers, NMSU."

18. "Twenty Five Years of Extension Work in New Mexico," 20.

19. Jensen, "Crossing Ethnic Barriers," 169.

20. Ibid., 171–72.

21. Tura A. Hawk, Lilian Randall, and Lura Dewey Ross, "Salads," Extension Circular 37, July 1918, 2–3, College of Agriculture and Home Economics, Agricultural Extension Service Circulars, vol. 1–90, Special Collections, New Mexico State University, Las Cruces, NM. Hereafter "AES Circulars, NMSU"; Jensen, "Crossing Ethnic Barriers," 172.

22. Letter from Austin D. Crile to Sue Hutchinson, August 21, 1917, Crile Papers, NMSU. Note here that by "native" Crile did not mean the indigenous population of the state, a notable omission given the state's history and demographics.

23. "Monthly Report of State Home Demonstration Leader," September 1918, box 7, folder 17, 10, Crile Papers, NMSU; "4th Annual Report of the Extension Service of the New Mexico College of Agriculture and Mechanic Arts for the year ending June 30, 1918," box 7, folder 5, 92, Crile Papers, NMSU.

24. "4th Annual Report," 92.

25. "Report of the State Leader of Home Demonstration Agents," November 1917, box 7, folder 17, 4, Crile Papers, NMSU; "Report of the State Leader of Home Demonstration Agents," December 1917, box 7, folder 17, 6, Crile Papers, NMSU.

26. "Report of the State Demonstrator in Home Economics," September 1917, box 7, folder 5, 3, Crile Papers, NMSU. Although not within the scope of this paper, the report also included an update from the assistant state demonstrator who spent a week in September 1917 at the Navajo Indian School in McKinley County, working with them to can fruit and vegetables.

27. See Schackel, *Social Housekeepers*, 367; Suzanne Forrest, *The Preservation of the Village: New Mexico's Hispanics and the New Deal* (Albuquerque: University of New Mexico Press, 1989).

28. Merrihelen Ponce, "The Life and Works of Fabiola Cabeza de Baca, New Mexico Hispanic Woman Writer: A Contextual Biography" (PhD diss., University of New Mexico, 1995), 47–49.

29. Maureen Reed, *A Woman's Place: Women Writing in New Mexico* (Albuquerque: University of New Mexico Press, 2005), 131.

30. Fabiola Cabeza de Baca Gilbert, "New Mexican Diets," *Journal of Home Economics* 34 (1942): 669.

31. Fabiola Cabeza de Baca Gilbert, interviewed by Ruleen Lazell, Good Shepherd Manor, Albuquerque, NM, February 9, 1983. RG-T153, Rio Grande Historical Collection, Special Collections, New Mexico State University, Las Cruces, NM.

32. Cabeza de Baca Gilbert, "New Mexican Diets," 668.

33. Tura A. Hawk, Lilian Randall, and Lura Dewey Ross, "Pinto Bean," Circular 38, July 1917, AES Circulars, NMSU.

34. Ibid., 9–10.

35. Montoya, "Home on Earth," 17.

36. Lilian Randall and W. T. Conway, "Food Preservation in the Home: An Outline on Canning, Preserving, Pickling and Drying of Fruits, Vegetables, and Meats for the New Mexico Home and Boys' and Girls' Clubs," Extension Circular 48, March 1919, p. 29, AES Circulars, NMSU.

37. Grace Long Elser, "Home Drying of Fruits and Vegetables," Extension Circular 132, September 1935, 3, AES Circulars, NMSU.

38. Veda A. Strong, "Home Canning," Extension Circular 120, June 1932, 25–6, AES Circulars, NMSU. By 1937 the same recipes were slightly adapted—the first being called "Chili con Carne" and the second "Chili con carne con frijoles." Veda A. Strong, "Canning and Curing Meats," Extension Circular 131, Rev. March 1937, 12, AES Circulars, NMSU.

39. Donna R. Gabacia and Jeffrey M. Pilcher, "'Chili Queens' and Checkered Tablecloths: Public Dining Cultures of Italians in New York City and Mexicans in San Antonio, Texas, 1870s–1940s," *Radical History Review* 110 (Spring 2011): 109–26; Jeffrey M. Pilcher, *Planet Taco: A Global History of Mexican Food* (New York: Oxford University Press, 2012); Gustavo Arellano, *Taco USA: How Mexican Food Conquered America* (New York: Scribner, 2012); Mikaela Selley, "The Melesio Gómez Family: Mexican Entrepreneurship in Houston's Early Twentieth Century" (MA thesis, University of Houston, 2013); Thomas H. Kreneck, *Mexican American Odyssey: Felix Tijerina, Entrepreneur and Civic Leader, 1905–1965* (College Station: Texas A&M University Press, 2001). For a contemporary take on the popularity of southwestern food, see Amy Bentley, "From Culinary Other to Mainstream America: Meanings and Uses of Southwestern Cuisine," in *Culinary Tourism*, ed. Lucy M. Long (Lexington: University of Kentucky Press, 2010), 209–25.

40. For Abarca, "sazón" is not only a literal flavoring or spice of a dish, but also women's "sensory way of knowing" and the "culinary discourse to conceptualize and articulate aspects of their personal and social cultural environment" as expressed in food. Abarca, *Voices in the Kitchen*, 50–51. Women add "chiste" when they add their own personal touches and creative expressions in their recipes, making them unique and original. Abarca, *Voices in the Kitchen*, 11.

41. Fabiola Cabeza de Baca Gilbert, "Boletin de Conservar," Extension Circular 106, May 1931, AES Circulars, NMSU; Fabiola Cabeza de Baca and Veda A. Strong, "Los Alimentos y su Preparacion," Extension Circular 129, April 1934, AES Circulars, NMSU.

42. Based on a review of similar English-language circulars. See, for example, Lilian Randall and W. T. Conway, "Preserving Food in the Home," Extension Circular 48, March 1919, AES Circulars, NMSU.

43. Cabeza de Baca Gilbert, "New Mexican Diets," 668.

44. Ibid.

45. In another example of perceived cultural condescension, *Alimentos* contained a lengthy illustrated section on manners and table settings. However, these lessons were reserved not only for a Spanish-speaking audience; the same images and lessons appear in English-language circulars, suggesting that the agency, born of middle-class reform efforts, also had problems with poor Anglo and Native American table manners. See Grace Long Elser and Dorothy Y. Hanny, "Family Meals," Extension Circular 110, revised June 1941, AES Circulars, NMSU.

46. Cabeza de Baca Gilbert, "New Mexican Diets," 668–69.

47. Reed, *A Woman's Place*, 142.

48. Ibid., 313 (see footnote 76). According to Reed, New Mexico governor Thomas Mabry was so convinced of *Historic Cookery*'s potential to attract visitors to the state that he sent a copy, and a bag of New Mexico frijoles, to every governor in the United States. Ibid., 123.

49. *Historic Cookery* fits into a much larger corpus of New Mexico writing that cultivated travel and tourism to the region during this era. See Genaro Padilla, "Imprisoned Narrative? Or Lies, Secrets, and Silence in New Mexico Women's Autobiography," in *Criticism in the Borderlands*, ed. Hector Calderon and José David Saldivar (Durham, NC: Duke University Press, 1991), 43–60; Writers' Program of the Work Projects Administration in the State of New Mexico, *The WPA Guide to 1930s New Mexico* (Tucson: University of Arizona Press, 1989). With Anglo New Mexicans largely controlling the state's historical preservation and cultural narrative, organizations like La Sociedad Folklorica de Santa Fe, founded by Cleofas Jaramillo (contemporary of Cabeza de Baca Gilbert and author of the 1942 *New Mexico Tasty Recipes*), sought to promote an alternate, Hispano-centered version of New Mexico through a variety of activities, including the publication of cookbooks privileging Hispano fare. On the Anglo control of heritage work, see Padilla, "Imprisoned Narrative?"

50. Fabiola Cabeza de Baca Gilbert, *Historic Cookery*, [1931?], p. 1, AES Circulars, NMSU. Emphasis mine. The earliest edition available is not dated, but one article dates its first publication in 1931. Lois Rudnick, "La Fabulosa Fabiola: First Lady of New Mexico Cuisine," *El Palacio* 117, no. 4 (Winter 2012): 72–75. For clarity and brevity, all subsequent references to *Historic Cookery* will be noted only by *HC* and date.

51. *HC* [1931?], 1.

52. *HC*, 1939, 7, 10, 15; *HC*, 1951, 16, 20.

53. *HC* [1931?], 2–3.

54. *HC*, 1951, 1, italics in original

55. *HC*, 1942, 5.

56. *HC*, 1939, 3.

57. *HC*, 1951, 1, emphasis mine.

58. Ibid., 3.

59. Edith M. Lantz, Helen W. Gough, and Mae Martha Johnson, "Nutritive Values of Some New Mexico Foods," Bulletin 379 (June 1953), 2–4, AES Circulars, NMSU. On pellagra in the US South, see Elizabeth S. D. Engelhardt, *A Mess of Greens: Southern Gender and Southern Food* (Athens: University of Georgia Press, 2011).

60. Lantz et al., "Nutritive Values," 1.

61. Ibid.

62. Ibid.

63. Ibid., 2, 16.

64. Ibid., 15–16.

65. Ruth Sneed, *Chile*, Circular 309 (August 1960), New Mexico State University Library Digital Collections, NMSU Cooperative Extension Service and Agricultural Experiment Station Publications, contentdm.nmsu.edu:2011/cdm/compountobject/collection/AgCircs/id/6425/rec/4, accessed April 10, 2014 (hereafter NMSU Digital Collections, NMSU CES-AES); Sneed, *Chile*, Circular 363 (August 1964), NMSU Digital Collections, NMSU CES-AES, contentdm.nmsu.edu:2011/cdm/compoundobject/collection/AgCircs/id/7290/rec/7, accessed April 10, 2014; Sneed, *Chile*, Circular 396 (October 1966), NMSU Digital Collections, NMSU CES-AES, contentdm.nmsu.edu:2011/cdm/compoundobject/collection/AgCircs/id/11552/rec/2, accessed April 10, 2014.

66. Sneed, *Chile*, 1960, 3. García began his chile research in 1907 and is recognized as the "father" of the New Mexico chile industry. David A. Fryxell, "The Red-or-Greening of New Mexico," *Desert Exposure* (December 2007), http://www.desertexposure.com/200712/200712_garcia_chile.php, accessed April 11, 2014.

67. *HC*, 1951.

68. Sneed, *Chile*, 1960, 5. Emphasis mine.

69. Sneed, *Chile*, 1966, 4.

70. Ibid., 4–5.

71. Sneed, *Chile*, 1960, 7.

72. On the kitchen as a space of female knowledge and empowerment, see Abarca, *Voices in the Kitchen*.

73. According to food studies scholar Charlotte Biltekoff, although "dietary ideals are generally presumed to be objective reflections of nutritional truths," they actually "reflect social ideals; they communicate profoundly important and widely shared . . . ideas about what it means to be a good person and, by extension, a good citizen." For Biltekoff, these ideals are shaped in large part by middle-class reformers and enforce a defining line between "good eaters" and irresponsible, lower class, and often minority eaters. See Charlotte Biltekoff, "Critical Nutrition Studies," in *The Oxford Handbook of Food History*, ed. Jeffrey M. Pilcher (New York: Oxford University Press, 2012), 173.

74. Dorothy B. Hacker, Marilyn S. Franks, Viola Fisher, Rebecca J. Grass, Marion Hotopp, MD, and Edith M. Lantz, "A Study of Food Habits in New Mexico (1949–1952)," Bulletin 384, March 1954, 3. NMSU Digital Collections, NMSU CES-AES http://contentdm.nmsu.edu: 2011/cdm/compoundobject/collection/AgCircs/id/25720/rec/2, Accessed April 10, 2014.

75. Arjun Appadurai, "How to Make a National Cuisine: Cookbooks in Contemporary India," *Comparative Studies in Society and History* 30, no. 1 (January 1988): 7.

Chapter 4: Food Gentrification in Downtown Puebla: UNESCO World Heritage Site

I would like to thank Priscilla Ybarra, Chad Pearson, Laila Amine, Michael Wise, Jennifer Wallach, the two anonymous reviewers, and the editors of this collection for their valuable suggestions.

1. Francine Prose, "Savoring the Pleasures of Puebla, Mexico," *New York Times*, September 10, 2013, accessed December 13, 2013, http://www.nytimes.com/2013/09/15/travel/savoring-the-pleasures-of-puebla-mexico.html?smid=fb-share&_r=1&.

2. A version of tacos árabes was introduced to Mexico in the 1920s by Middle-Eastern migrants; another version, tacos al pastor, was created by second-generation Lebanese. Jeffrey Pilcher, *Planet Taco: A Global History of Mexican Food* (Oxford: Oxford University Press, 2012), 155.

3. For a broader analysis of Puebla's gentrification, see Gareth A. Jones and Ann Varley, "The Reconquest of the Historic Center: Urban Conservation and Gentrification in Puebla," *Environment and Planning A* 31, no. 9 (1999): 1547–66.

4. Wahaca is a word that tries to imitate the sound of the Nahuatl-derived name for the state and state capital Oaxaca.

5. Wahaca's website features photographs of Mexican street vendors selling *antojitos* (little cravings) that the owners of this British chain took while living in Mexico. Wahaca Mexican Market Eating, accessed December 18, 2013, http://www.wahaca.co.uk/.

6. Food Carts Portland, accessed December 19, 2013, http://www.foodcartsportland.com/about-2/.

7. The historic downtown included La Victoria Market among 153 other buildings that experts considered of prime importance.

8. Puebla's dishes, as historian Jeffrey Pilcher notes, require a combination of pre-Columbian and Spanish/European ingredients that resulted in a Creole cuisine (cocina criolla) that was legitimized by Mexican elites in the nineteenth century as truly Mexican. For a discussion on the making of concepts of authenticity, see Pilcher, *Planet Taco*, especially chapter 3.

9. A synthetic history of La Victoria Market was produced by the municipal government ca. the mid-1980s based on archival documents. See Documento por el cual el municipio de Puebla se adjudica la posesión del inmueble del Mercado de la Victoria, Gobierno de Mariano Piña Olaya, Archivo Histórico Municipal de Puebla (hereafter AHMP).

10. Irma and Francisco Márquez de Jesús, conversation with author, January 8, 2014, Puebla, México.

11. Lists of products seized by inspectors, March 22 and April 21–23, 1971, expedientes de mercados, box 46, AHMP.

12. For instance, from a 1919 letter that a French immigrant baker sent to municipal authorities in 1919, we know that outside his bakery street vendors of enchiladas, beans, mole, and tacos set up their semi-fixed stalls to sell. The baker claimed that this food was "filthy merchandise," which caused "repulsion" to "Puebla's correct and educated classes" who shopped in his bakery. Letter from Enrique Belague to municipal authorities, June 13, 1919, expedientes de mercados, libro 630, file 318, AHMP. From petitions to expel vendors from the portales, we

learn that in the 1920s and 1930s, female, small-sized vendors sold *tortas compuestas*, cakes, and candy in fixed stalls. Letter from seventeen vendors to Presidente Municipal, October 25, 1923, libro 708, file 433, f. 241, and letter from fourteen women to Presidente Municipal, November 7, 1932, expedientes de mercados, libro 887, file 686, f.1, AHMP.

13. For a discussion of the "transgressive national rhythms" of Cuba, Brazil, and Argentina, see John Charles Chasteen, *National Rhythms, African Roots: The Deep History of Latin American Popular Dance* (Albuquerque: University of New Mexico Press, 2004).

14. The Archivo Histórico Municipal de Puebla houses hundreds of petitions written by sellers asking authorities for temporary permits, demanding lower fees for the use of public space, and demanding protection; see expedientes de mercados, AHMP.

15. Archival sources also indicate that some were very young, tending their own stalls as early as fourteen years old. Census, Secretaría del Trabajo y Previsión Social, Departamento de Registro de Asociaciones, expedientes de mercados, box 42, file 319, 1969, AHMP. According to secret police documents, by June 1970, street vendors were mostly women who sold fruits, vegetables, and legumes. They were all poor, "humildes," of humble backgrounds, and saw their work as a way to make their living in an honest way. Investigaciones Políticas y Sociales (IPS), Información de Puebla, Expediente 405, page 420 and 421, June 9, 1970, Archivo General de la Nación (hereafter AGN).

16. The Archivo Histórico Municipal de Puebla holds a photographic collection (*fototeca*) covering the political events in which Puebla's mayors and other politicians participated. This collection also includes pictures of Puebla's different public spaces such as markets and their surroundings. It is in these photographs where vendors appeared selling their wares. For a discussion on working-class women, see Joanne Hershfield, *Imagining la Chica Moderna: Women, Nation, and Visual Culture in Mexico, 1917–1936* (Durham, NC: Duke University Press, 2008), especially chapter 4.

17. Females who were mothers also used empty wood boxes as cribs to put their infants to sleep or as playpens. Photographs, Fototeca, AHMP.

18. Sandra Aguilar-Rodríguez mentions that in Mexico City construction workers were loyal customers of street vendors. "Cooking Modernity: Nutrition Policies, Class, and Gender in the 1940s and 1950s Mexico City," *The Americas* 64, no. 2 (October 2007): 177.

19. IPS, Información de Puebla, November 30, 1973, AGN.

20. City officials tried to expel street vndors from downtown public spaces since the early 1970s, but vendors organized a union and were able to stay on the streets until 1986.

21. Ingrid Bleynat, "Trading with Power: Mexico City's Markets, 1867–1958" (PhD diss., Harvard University, 2013), chapter 1.

22. Judith E. Marti, "Subsistence and the State: The Case of Porfirian Mexico," in *The Economic Anthropology of the State*, ed. Elizabeth M. Brumfiel (Lanham, MD: University Press of America, 1994), 319–22.

23. Letter to CANACO from Presidente Municipal, October 17, 1923, expedientes de mercados, box 708, file 436, p. 268, AHMP.

24. For a description of this violent removal, see Sandra C. Mendiola Garcia, "Vendors, Mothers, and Revolutionaries: Street Vendors and Union Activism in 1970s Puebla, Mexico," *Oral History Forum d'histoire orale* 33 (2013): 1.

25. In 1977, Puebla's city center became a "monumental zone" by a presidential decree. Decreto por el que se declara una zona de Monumentos Históricos en la ciudad de Puebla de Zaragoza, Estado de Puebla, Periódico Oficial del Gobierno Constitucional del Estado de Puebla, Tomo CCIX, No. 41, 18 de noviembre de 1977.

26. Nomination of Properties Proposal to UNESCO, ca. 1985–1986, Archivo del Patrimonio Mundial, Instituto Nacional de Antropología e Historia (INAH).

27. Martha Benítez, "El Retiro de los Ambulantes es Avance en Protección a la Salud Pública," *El Sol de Puebla*, August 1 1986, 1 and 9.

28. Since the 1970s and well into the 1980s, certain groups of people, among them business associations, city boosters, and journalists, talked about the rescuing and dignifying of the city. See, for example, newspaper articles published in the conservative and widely circulated newspaper *El Sol de Puebla*.

29. Gareth Jones and Ann Varley have suggested that this history can be "real, imagined, or recreated as a pastiche." Jones and Varley, "The Reconquest," 1548.

30. Ibid., 1547, 1548, 1560.

31. Carlos Flores Mancilla, "Histórica Reubicación: Ciudadanía," *El Sol de Puebla*, August 1, 1986, 2.

32. Customers had to walk some blocks north to the Cinco de Mayo Market.

33. "Esperan matar 50,000 Ratas en el Mercado La Victorira," *El Sol de Puebla*, February 3, 1971, 1.

34. Nomination of Properties Proposal to UNESCO, ca. 1985–1986, Archivo del Patrimonio Mundial, Instituto Nacional de Antropología e Historia (INAH).

35. Expdientes de mercados, box 15, file 3, AHMP.

36. For a flair of city boosters' intentions, see letter to Mayor Amado Carrillo from Colegio de Arquitectos de Puebla, October 27, 1986, box 15, file 4, pp. 1–6, AHMP.

37. Commodatum or Contrato de Comodato published in the Periódico Oficial, Puebla, July 3, 1992.

38. Decreto del H. Congreso del Estado que autoriza al H. Ayuntamiento del Municipio de Puebla, a celebrar contrato de Comodato con la Fundación Amparo, Periódico Oficial, Puebla, July 3, 1992, p. 5.

39. For a thorough analysis of the Jenkins Foundation and its most important players, see Andrew Paxman, "William Jenkins, Business Elites, and the Evolution of the Mexican State: 1910–1960" (PhD diss., University of Texas at Austin, 2008).

40. For a discussion of heritage tourism and its paradoxes, see Joseph L. Scarpaci, *Plazas and Barrios: Heritage Tourism and Globalization in the Latin American Centro Histórico* (Tucson: University of Arizona Press, 2005).

41. Chris Tilly, "Walmart in Mexico: The Limits of Growth," in *Wal-Mart: The Face of Twentieth-Century Capitalism*, ed. Nelson Lichtenstein (New York: New Press, 2006), 195–96. See also his "Wal-Mart goes South: Sizing Up the Chain's Mexican Success Story," in *Wal-Mart World: The World's Biggest Corporation in the Global Economy*, ed. Stanley D. Brunn (New York: Routledge, 2006), 357.

42. As per September 2013, Walmart sold its chain of restaurants to the Mexican group Alsea that owns Starbucks, Domino's Pizza, The Cheesecake Factory,

Chili's, and Burger King. Victor Cardoso, "Vende Walmart de México su división de restaurantes a Alsea," *La Jornada en línea* 11 (September 2013), accessed February 7, 2014, http://www.jornada.unam.mx/2013/09/11/economia/026n1eco.

43. Locales that used to house restaurants or mom-and-pop shops are now featuring nonprepared food shops such as OXXO convenient stores (the Mexican equivalent of Seven Eleven and largest store in Latin America). Only a couple of old-time restaurants survived: one that is attached to a hotel (Royalty) and another one that features pizzas and Italian food (Vittorio's).

44. This would have been culturally outrageous to residents of the city of Oaxaca who, since 2003, have been turning down the McDonald's application to open at the heart of the city center, another UNESCO World Heritage site. Reed Johnson, "McDonald's loses a round to Oaxacan cultural Pride," *Los Angeles Times*, January 3, 2005, accessed December 31, 2013, http://articles.latimes.com/2003/jan/05/entertainment/ca-johnson5.

45. Santa Clara, Historia, accessed February 15, 2014, https://www.santaclara.com.mx/historia1.asp.

46. The Italian Coffee Company, accessed February 6, 2014, http://www.italiancoffee.com/concepto.php.

47. In this article, Francisco Toledo is referring to changes occurring in Oaxaca, but here I am using his phrase because it also applies to Puebla. See Reed Johnson, "McDonald's loses a round to Oaxacan cultural Pride," *Los Angeles Times*, January 5, 2003, accessed December 31, 2013, http://articles.latimes.com/2003/jan/05/entertainment/ca-johnson5/2.

48. Nancy Churchill Conner, "El (re) desarrollo urbano neoliberal: El Paseo del Río San Francisco," in *Sujetos Neoliberales en México,* ed. Ricardo F. Macip (Puebla: BUAP, 2009), 149–50.

49. For a discussion of this kind of invisibility, see Irene Tinker, *Street Foods: Urban Food and Employment in Developing Countries* (New York: Oxford University Press, 1997), 15, 159.

50. Of course, some street vendors have managed to sell downtown, employing a number of strategies such as bribing police, hawking and hiding products, etc. And to this day, there are still a couple of tiny mom-and-pop food vendors in the Portales.

51. Pilcher, *Planet Taco*, 13.

52. Nomination File no. 00400 for Inscription on the Representative List of the Intangible Cultural Heritage in 2010, UNESCO, Fifth Session, Nairobi, Kenya, November 2010.

Chapter 5: From Working the Farm to Fast Food and Back Again: Rural Mexicans in the Neoliberal Food System

Many thanks to Sanjosepeños and valley residents for their hospitality and discussion over the years. A special thanks goes to Regino Melchor Jiménez Escamilla. I also thank Lindsay DuBois, Pauline Gardiner Barber, and the editors of this volume for their comments.

1. Teresa M. Mares, "Engaging Latino Immigrants in Seattle Food Activism

through Urban Agriculture," in *Food Activism: Agency, Democracy and Economy*, ed. Carole M. Counihan and Valeria Siniscalchi (London: Bloomsbury Publishing, 2014), 31.

2. Juan, in discussion with the author, June 8, 2005.

3. North America is used here to refer to Mexico, the United States, and Canada. This paper focuses primarily on valley workers in Mexico and the United States. Only a few residents discussed work in Canada, where Mexicans from other regions are employed in the Seasonal Agricultural Workers Program (see endnote number 5). In the US food sectors, Mexicans work alongside other Latin American immigrants, particularly Central Americans.

4. This paper is based on over seventy interviews with southern valley residents about their livelihoods, as well as participant observation in 2001–2002. I also conducted research during extended summer visits until 2008. My ethnography *The Struggle for Maize: Compesinos, Workers and Transgenic Corn in the Mexican Countryside* (Durham, NC: Duke University Press, 2011) is based on this fieldwork and interviews with participants in the GM corn debates. I remain in contact with several valley residents, receiving occasional updates, and plan to return to conduct a follow-up study.

5. Small and medium-sized farmers often identify as peasants or "campesinos." This has a complex political history in Mexico and other Latin American countries. Although the term carries a lot of conceptual baggage, including overgeneralized, reified, and romanticized notions of peasant and indigenous communities, I use it here because my interviewees use "campesino" to refer to themselves. I also use "campesino" to mean "petty commodity producer," which I discuss later in this chapter. For a more extensive treatment of the politicized concept and identity of "campesinos" in Mexico, see Christopher Boyer, *Becoming Campesinos: Politics, Identity, and Struggle in Postrevolutionary Michoán, 1920–1935* (Stanford: Stanford University Press, 2003), or my own research on the valley (*The Struggle for Maize*).

6. The concept of "food system" focuses our attention on policies and practices related to food—its production, provisioning, and consumption. Food systems are embedded in larger social, economic, and ecological contexts and can include alternative or counter practices. Here, for the sake of convenience, I use the term as shorthand to talk about food policies and practices under neoliberal capitalism.

7. Mexicans also work, to a lesser extent, in Canada, where there are important differences from the United States in policies and discourses around immigration. Under the Seasonal Agricultural Workers Program (SAWP), up to 26,000 contracted agricultural workers come to Canada annually, the majority of whom are Mexican. The program is open only to Mexicans and people from the Caribbean (CBC 2012). In the US food system, Mexicans work alongside other Latin American immigrants, particularly Central Americans. See recent research on the Canadian SAWP, such as Leigh Binford, *Tomorrow We Are All Going to Harvest* (Austin: University of Texas Press, 2013). For further reading on the anthropology of Mexican im/migrants working in different aspects of the US food system, see Steve Striffler, *Chicken: The Transformation of American's Favorite* (New Haven, CT: Yale University Press, 2005) on the poultry industry; Ruth Gomberg-Muñoz, *Labor and Legality: An Ethnography of Mexican Immigrant Network* (Oxford: Oxford University Press, 2011) on restaurant staff; and Patricia Zavella, *I'm Neither Here*

Nor There: Mexican Quotidian Struggles with Migration and Poverty (Durham, NC: Duke University Press, 2011), on Californian agriculture, especially strawberry production.

8. Native varieties of maize are "*maices nativos*" in Spanish. They are grown, selected, and improved by farmers in their fields, in contrast to scientifically improved or "modern" varieties. However, the term *criollo* is used by interviewees (and is popularly used in the countryside). *Criollo* refers to both native and creolized varieties. Creolized varieties are the result of intentional or unintentional mixing between native and scientifically improved varieties.

9. Less commonly, valley residents also move to urban centers in Mexico, sometimes as step-migration on the way to the United States. Unlike valley residents who went to the United States as Bracero farm laborers, recent migrants work in food processing and service sectors more frequently than in agriculture.

10. The romanticization of rural communities via calls for food self-sufficiency can be found among some of the En Defensa del Maíz network in Mexico. See Elizabeth Fitting, "The Political Uses of Culture: Maize Production and the GM Corn Debates in Mexico," *Focaal, Journal of Global and Historical Anthropology* 48 (2006): 17–34; Fitting, *The Struggle for Maize*; or Henry Bernstein, "Food Sovereignty: A Sceptical View" (Paper presented at the Agrarian Studies Conference, Food Sovereignty: A Critical Dialogue, September 14–15, 2013). http://www.yale.edu/agrarianstudies/foodsovereignty/pprs/1_Bernstein_2013.pdf.

11. Arturo Warman, *Corn & Capitalism: How a Botanical Bastard Grew to Global Domination*, trans. Nancy Westrate (Chapel Hill: University of North Carolina Press, 2003 [1988]): 20.

12. Ibid.

13. Jack Ralph Kloppenburg Jr., *The First Seed: The Political Economy of Plant Biotechnology 1492–2000* (New York: Cambridge University Press, 1988).

14. William Roseberry, introduction to *Coffee, Society and Power in Latin America*, ed. William Roseberry, Lowell Gudmundson, and Mario Samper-Kutschback (Baltimore: Johns Hopkins University Press, 1995), 1–37; Eric Wolf, *Europe and the People without History* (Berkeley: University of California Press, 1982).

15. Casey Walsh and Emma Ferry, "Introduction: Production, Power, and Place," in *The Social Relations of Mexican Commodities*, ed. Casey Walsh, Emma Ferry, Gabriela Soto Laveaga, Paula Sesia, and Sarah Hill (San Diego: Center for U.S.-Mexican Studies at the University of California-San Diego, 2003), 1–18.

16. Karl Marx, *Capital: Volume 1*, trans. Ben Fowkers (New York: Vintage Books, 1977 [1866–1867]), 163–77.

17. See Harriet Friedmann, "International Regimes of Food and Agricultural Since 1870," in *Peasants and Peasant Societies*, ed. Theodor Shamin (Oxford: Basil Blackwell, 1987), and Philip McMichael, *Food Regimes and Agrarian Questions* (Halifax: Fernwood Publishing, 2013), on the emergence of the first international food regime with capitalism and British colonialism, as well as for a discussion of the concept of food "regime."

18. Henry Bernstein, *Class Dynamics and Agrarian Change* (Halifax: Fernwood Publishing, 2010); Philip McMichael, "Peasant Prospects in the Neoliberal Age," *New Political Economy* 11, no. 3 (2006): 204–418; Philip McMichael, "A Food Regime Genealogy," *Journal of Peasant Studies* 36, no. 1 (2009): 139–69.

19. Gabriela Pechlaner and Gerardo Otero, "The Third Food Regime: Neoliberal Globalism and Agricultural Biotechnology in North America," *Sociologia Ruralis* 48, no. 4 (2008): 1–21.

20. Marx, *Capital*, part 8.

21. David Harvey, *The New Imperialism* (Oxford: Oxford University Press, 2003).

22. Discussed in Fitting, *The Struggle for Maize*, ch. 3; and Luis E. Henao, *Tehuacán: Campesinado e irrigación* (Mexico City: Edicol, 1980).

23. Farshard Araghi, "The Invisible Hand and Visible Foot: Peasants, Dispossession and Globalization," in *Peasants and Globalization*, ed. A. Haroon Akram-Lodhi and Cristóbal Kay (New York: Routledge, 2009), 111–47; Bernstein, *Class Dynamics*; McMichael, *Peasant Prospects*.

24. I expand on this argument elsewhere: Fitting, *The Struggle for Maize*.

25. This is known as nixtamalization, which releases the vitamin niacin and the amino acid tryptophan in the corn. Corn flour that is not nixtamalized lacks this nutritional benefit.

26. Interview, July 2, 2002.

27. Bernstein, *Class Dynamics*, 128.

28. David Harvey, "The Geopolitics of Capitalism," in *Social Relations and Spatial Structures*, ed. Derek Gregory and John Urry (London: Palgrave Macmillan, 1985), 128.

29. Warman, *Corn & Capitalism*.

30. This area is also one of the sites where the Mexican government found evidence of transgenes growing among native varieties of maize, contributing to the controversy over transgenic corn that made international headlines beginning in 2001–2002. Because the source of such transgenes is considered to be transgenic corn imported from the United States, this controversy illustrates the interconnectedness of our ostensibly national food systems. Elsewhere, I situate the GM corn controversy in relation to the food system (Fitting, "The Political Uses of Culture: Maize Production and the GM Corn Debates in Mexico," *Focaal, Journal of Global and Historical Anthropology* 48 (2006): 17–34; Fitting, *The Struggle for Maize*).

31. Richard S. MacNeish, "Summary of the Cultural Sequence and Its Implications for the Tehuacan Valley," in *The Prehistory of the Tehuacan Valley: Excavations and Reconnaissance*, ed. Richard MacNeish (Austin: University of Texas Press, 1972), 496–504.

32. Prior to Spanish conquest, the valley was settled by Nahua, Popoloca, Mixteca, Chocho, and Mazateca indigenous groups.

33. In the 1950s up to three dozen residents from San José left to work in the United States as temporary agricultural workers under the Bracero program, the binational treaty between the United States and Mexico, which ran from 1942 to 1964. There were local political struggles over water access during this period also (see Fitting, *The Struggle for Maize*, ch. 3). Close to five million Mexicans sought work in the United States under the program. As Gomberg-Muñoz explains, "As millions of Mexican workers became accustomed to employment practices, lifestyles, and consumption patterns in the United States, they established networks between jobs in the U.S. and friends and family members back home that allowed migratory flows to become self-sustaining in the decades that followed" (Gomberg-Muñoz, *Labor and Legality*, 31).

34. Fitting, *The Struggle for Maize.*

35. Interview, June 23, 2006.

36. Alejandro Nadal, "Corn and NAFTA: An Unhappy Alliance," *Seeding: The Quarterly Newsletter of Genetic Resources Action International* 17, no. 2 (2000): 10–17; Antonio Turrent-Fernández, Timothy A. Wise, and Elise Garvey, "Achieving Mexico's Maize Potential: Global Development and Environment Institute" (Working Paper, no. 12-03, Medford, MA: Tufts University, October 2012). http://www.ase.tufts.edu/gdae/Pubs/wp/12-03TurrentMexMaiz.pdf.

37. Hallie Eakin, Julia C. Bausch, and Stuart Sweeney, "Agrarian Winners of Neoliberal Reform: The 'Maize Boom' of Sinaloa, Mexico," *Journal of Agrarian Change* 14, no. 1 (2014): 26–51.

38. J. Samuel Barkin, *International Organization: Theories and Institutions* (New York: Palgrave Macmillan, 2006).

39. The Ejército Zapatista de Liberació Nacionel (EZLN), Zapatista National Liberation Army, made up largely of Mayans, declared war against the Mexican state on the first day of 1994, the day the NAFTA went into effect, from the Lacandon region of Chiapas. Although the movement began as an armed struggle, it became largely civil disobedience against the state's military excursions in the region and neoliberal globalization. This movement has generated enormous international and media attention on the struggles of indigenous peoples in Mexico and beyond, as well as discussions about participatory democracy and alter-globalization.

40. Philip Abram, *Historical Sociology* (Ithaca, NY: Cornell University Press, 1982), ch. 8.

41. Farmers from San José can be considered "petty commodity producers" in that they own or have usufruct rights to the land, irrigation water, and/or seed; they produce maize for consumption and sale, but the scale of production is relatively small; and they rely on unpaid labor or sharecropping. Those who can afford it hire local day laborers to help with the more arduous parts of planting and harvesting.

42. Boyer, *Becoming Campesinos.*

43. Explored further in Fitting, *The Struggle for Maize*, ch. 3 and 5.

44. Interview, June 20, 2006.

45. Jeffery Pilcher, "Taco Bell, Maseca, and Slow Food: A Postmodern Apocalypse for Mexico's Peasant Cuisine?" in *Fast Food/Slow Food: The Cultural Economy of the Global Food System*, ed. Richard Wilk (Lanham, MD: AltaMira Press, 2006).

46. Residents grow several varieties of maize. The most common are a rain-fed white corn—distinct from industrial, hybrid yellow corn—grown for human consumption and an irrigated white maize for sale on the cob, called elote. Residents have grown this commercial elote since the 1960s. Elote can be sold for a better price than grain because there is a market for it (both in the valley and beyond, in Mexico City), and it can be dried and eaten at home. However, elote requires irrigation water and therefore is more costly to produce than rain-fed corn, which means the poorer strata of households either grow rain-fed corn only or they sharecrop elote fields with a relative or neighbor who contributes the irrigation water or some other inputs.

47. Lourdes Flores Morales, *"No me gustaba, pero es trabajo": Mujer, trabajo*

y desechabilidad en al maquila (Mexico City: Instituto de Ciencias Sociales y Humanidades "Alfonso Vélez Pilego," BUAP/Plaza y Valdés S.A. de C.V., 2008).

48. Gomberg-Muñoz, *Labor and Legality*, 33–35.

49. Josiah Heyman, "Constructing a 'Perfect' Wall: Race, Class, and Citizenship in US-Mexico Border Policing," in *Migration in the 21st Century: Political Economy and Ethnography*, ed. Pauline Gardiner Barber and Winnie Lem (New York: Routlege, 2012), 153–74.

50. Interview with twenty-nine-year-old male migrant, June 8, 2005.

51. Luin Goldring, "Power and Status in Transnational Social Spaces," in *Migration and Transnational Spaces*, ed. Ludger Prier (Aldershot, UK: Ashgate, 1999), 162–86; María Leticia Rivermar Pérez, "La reconstrucción de las identidades sociales en el context de las migraciones," in *Conflictos migratorios transnacionales y respuestas comunitarias*, ed. Leigh Binford and María Eugenia D'Aubeterre (Puebla: Instituto de Ciencias Sociales y Humanidades, BUAP, 2000), 81–96.

52. Richard C. Jones, "U.S. Migration: An Alternative Economic Mobility Ladder for Rural Central Mexico," *Social Science Quarterly* 73, no. 3 (1992): 496–510, 507.

53. Flores Morales, *"No me gustaba."*

54. Nicholas De Genova, *Working the Boundaries: Race, Space, and "Illegality" in Mexican Chicago* (Durham, NC: Duke University Press, 2005).

55. Gomberg-Muñoz, *Labor and Legality*, 37.

56. Interview, November 12, 2001.

57. Rivermar Pérez, *La reconstrucción.*

58. Similarly, anthropologist Judith Friedlander found, in her study on indigenous ethnicity in Morelos forty years ago, that residents felt to a certain degree that "the more material symbols of Hispanic [mestizo] culture they obtain[ed], the less Indian they will become." Judith Friedlander, *Being Indian in Hueyapan: A Study of Forced Identity in Contemporary Mexico* (New York: St. Martin's Press, 1975), 131.

59. Interview, May 31, 2001.

60. Marx, *Capital*, part 26.

61. Fitting, *The Struggle for Maize.*

62. Delphine Thivet, "Peasants' Transnational Mobilization for Food Sovereignty in La Via Campesina," in *Food Activism: Agency, Democracy and Economy*, ed. Carole M. Counihan and Valeria Siniscalchi (London: Bloomsbury Publishing, 2014), 193–210, 193.

Chapter 6: *Las Gallinitas de Doña Luz*: Dominican Women Public Kitchens and Trans-Ethnic Networks in San Juan

I wish to thank Doña Luz, to whom this chapter is dedicated, for her collaboration and her delicious foods, and my sister Argen, through whom I first tasted the gallinitas. Thanks to the editors and two anonymous reviewers, whose comments helped greatly to improve the coherence of this chapter. I am also grateful for my food survival networks, locally and abroad.

1. Meredith E. Abarca and Nieves Pascual Soler, "Introduction," *Rethinking Chicana/o Literature through Food: Postnational Appetites*, ed. Nieves Pascual Soler and Meredith E. Abarca (New York: Palgrave Macmillan, 2013).

2. Doreen Massey, *Space, Place, and Gender* (Minneapolis: University of Minnesota Press, 1994); Doreen Massey, *Spatial Divisions of Labor: Social Structures and the Geography of Production* (New York: Palgrave, 1995); Dolores Hayden, "Urban Landscape History: The Sense of Place and the Politics of Space," in *Understanding Ordinary Landscapes*, ed. Paul Groth and Todd W. Bress (New Haven, CT: Yale University Press, 1997), 111–33; Dolores Hayden, *The Power of Place: Urban Landscapes as Public History* (Cambridge, MA: MIT Press, 1997).

3. Neoliberal re-structuring refers to a series of measures managed by international organizations and G8 countries, which impose challenging measures to continue lending to underdeveloped countries (or, in some cases, simply to stop prosecution for not paying old debts). In a way, this has been a project to repurpose ex-colonies, now called the Global South, and push countries at the periphery of capital to integrate into the global marketplace. The SAPs (structural adjustment programs) impose on national budgets significant costs to social public services as well as subsidies to health, education, and welfare protection for workers. They also affect the privatizing of national resources and services and the closing of government offices. Deregulation of lands and eviction of peasants without land titles is balanced with free-trade zone corporations' need for cheap labor. The corporations invest foreign capital, yet do so free of taxes, labor, and environmental regulations. Furthermore, these corporations' profits are not invested locally. Such measures cripple the country's ability to improve social welfare and promote both labor migration (legal and illegal) and brain drain. See Jorge Duany, "El Sector Informal y la Migración Internacional: El Caso de los Dominicanos en Puerto Rico," *Nueva Sociedad* 113 (1991): 16–27, 21.

4. We stopped in front of an AMA bus terminal where a loudspeaker voice of a mulatto preaching Bible verses about doomsday and salvation filled the area. Luz said that she did not like all that shouting and the harassment of giving *papelitos* (leaflets). She said that she is Catholic and they do not go out looking to harass people. As a Catholic, she attends Nuestra Señora del Carmen on Sunday, which is in Obrero Barrio. The priest is from PR, but Luz said he served in DR and most in attendance are Dominicans. I share this anecdote to show how her religious identity is significant for Luz, but is not her way of making local community.

5. Juan A. Giusti Cordero, "Afro-Puerto Rican Cultural Studies: Beyond Cultura Negroide and Antillanismo," *Centro: Journal of the Center for Puerto Rican Studies* 8, no. 1–2 (1996): 56–77.

6. Kamala Visweswaran, "Histories of Feminist Ethnography," *Annual Review of Anthropology* (1997): 591–621.

7. Chandra Talpade Mohanty, *Feminism without Borders: Decolonizing Theory, Practicing Solidarity* (Durham, NC: Duke University Press, 2003).

8. Stuart Hall, *Critical Dialogues in Cultural Studies* (New York: Routledge, 2006).

9. Abarca and Pascual Soler, "Introduction."

10. Kirin Narayan, "How Native Is a 'Native' Anthropologist," in *Feminist Postcolonial Theory: A Reader*, ed. Reina Lewis and Sara Mills (New York: Routledge, 2003), 285–305.

11. For a more detailed description of *foodmaps*, see Lidia Marte, "Foodmaps: Tracing Boundaries of 'Home' through Food Relations," *Food & Foodways* 15, no. 3–4 (2007): 261–89.

12. See Psyche Williams-Forson and Carole M. Counihan, *Taking Food Public: Redefining Foodways in a Changing World* (New York: Routledge, 2013); Sidney W. Mintz, "Food and Its Relationship to the Concepts of Power," in *Tasting Food, Tasting Freedom: Excursions into Eating, Culture, and the Past* (Boston: Beacon Press, 1996), 17–32; Cruz Miguel Ortíz Cuadra, *Eating Puerto Rico: A History of Food, Culture, and Identity*, trans. Russ Davidson (Chapel Hill: Univeristy of North Carolina Press, 2013); David Sutton, "A Tale of Easter Ovens: Food and Collective Memory," *Social Research: An International Quarterly* 75, no. 1 (2008): 157–80.

13. Sutton, "A Tale of Easter Ovens."

14. For the significance of mangú as a mark of Dominicanness, see Lidia Marte, "Versions of Dominican Mangú: Intersections of Gender and Nation in Caribbean Self-Making," in *Food and Identity in the Caribbean*, ed. Hanna Garth (New York: Bloomsbury Academy, 2013), 57–74.

15. Cruz Miguel Ortíz Cuadra has a discussion of PR cuisine and its diluting *criollicidad* in "Ayer, hoy, mañana" in *Puerto Rico en la olla, ¿Somos aún lo que comimos?* (Aranjuez: Doce Calles, 2006), 313–26.

16. Gustavo Setrini, "Agriculture Policies in Puerto Rico and the Limits of Industrial Agriculture," in *Cultivating New Development Paths: Food and Agriculture Entrepreneurship in Puerto Rico* (Presentation, Dept. of Political Science, Massachusetts Institute of Technology, Cambridge, MA, 2012), 11–14.

17. Nelson Alvarez Febles, "Serie Ecológica y Soberania Alimentaria en Puerto Rico Partte 4: Apuntes sobre la Historia de la Agricultura Agricultura," *80 Grados*, November 2011, http:// www.80grados.net/apuntes-sobre-la-historia-de-la-agricultura-y-la-alimentacion/; Setrini, "Agriculture Policies in Puerto Rico and the Limits of Industrial Agriculture."

18. Setrini, "Agriculture Policies in Puerto Rico and the Limits of Industrial Agriculture."

19. Dagmar Guardiola Ortíz, "Los Derechos Humanos en Puerto Rico: Pobreza, Desigualdad y Políticas Sociales," in *Puerto Rico y los Derechos Humanos: Una Intersección Plural*, ed. Colón Morera, José Javier, y Idsa E. Alegría Ortega (San Juan: Ediciones Callejón, 2012).

20. Cruz Miguel Ortíz Cuadra, "Nación-ald's? Y las Culturas Alimentarias Contemporáneas," *80 Grados*, October 2001, http://www.80grados.net/fast-foods/.

21. Ibid.

22. Meredith E. Abarca, "*Charlas Culinarias:* Mexican Women Speak from Their Public Kitchens," *Food & Foodways* 15 (2007): 183–212.

23. This concept is similar to the "loyalty of palate" that Abarca (2007) spoke about in relation to Mexican women's public kitchens.

24. Isar P. Godreau, "Scripts of Blackness and the Racial Dynamics of Nacionalism in Puerto Rico," in *Cuadernos del Instituto de Investigaciones Interdisciplinarias*, Universidad de Puerto Rico, en Cayey 6 (2009), http://webs.oss.cayey.upr.edu/iii/sites/webs.oss.cayey.upr.edu.iii/files/ u1/Cuaderno_6. pdf; Safa, Helene, "Women and Globalization: Lessons from the Dominican Republic," in *The Spaces of Neoliberalism: Land, Place and Family in Latin America* (2002): 141–58.

25. Godreau, "Scripts of Blackness and the Racial Dynamics of Nacionalism in Puerto Rico."

26. Duany, "El Sector Informal y la Migración Internacional: El Caso de los Dominicanos en Puerto Rico," 16–27.

27. Patricia R. Pessar, "The Role of Households in International Migration and the Case of US-Bound Migration from the Dominican Republic," *International Migration Review* (1982): 342–64.

28. Jorge Duany, "Racializing Ethnicity in the Spanish-Speaking Caribbean: A Comparison of Haitians in the Dominican Republic and Dominicans in Puerto Rico," *Latin American and Caribbean Ethnic Studies* 1, no. 2 (2006): 231–48.

29. Yolanda Martínez-San Miguel, "De Ilegales e Indocumentados. Representaciones Culturales de la Migración Dominicana en Puerto Rico," *Revista de ciencias sociales* 4 (1998): 147–72.

30. Ruth Nina-Estrella, "Immigración, Discriminación y Educación Intercultural," in *Puerto Rico y los Derechos Humanos: Una Intersección Plural*, ed. Colón Morera, José Javier, y Idsa E. Alegría Ortega (San Juan: Ediciones Callejón, 2012); K. Weyland, "Dominican Women 'con un pie aqui y el otro alla': International Migration, Class, Gender and Cultural Change" (PhD diss., New School for Social Research, 1998).

31. Williams-Forson, in her historically rich examination of Black women and chicken, helps to tell a counter-story to dislodge mindsets of food only as sites of oppression. Her analysis of racialization through food reminds us of the necessity of including intersections of race, class, and gender in analytic accounts. Psyche Williams-Forson, "Epilogue: From Train Depots to Country Buffets," in *Building Houses out of Chicken Legs: Black Women, Food, and Power* (Chapel Hill: University of North Carolina Press, 2006), 1–12.

32. The impossibility of claiming a proper "Latino" label in PR reveals Doña Luz's invisibility in the local PR food system, but it does not produce it. That is to say that the racism does not come alone, but aligned with the class categories of the majority of Dominican immigrants to PR. Institutional discrimination, the conditions of labor migration, and stereotypes about Dominicans' stigma of arrival by sea, *en yolas*, or makeshift boats, exposes an internalized racism already present in PR society since colonial times when dark-skinned Afro-Puerto Ricans had to endure a long history of struggles for equal citizenship and cultural recognition. The prevalent narratives of Dominicans in relation to the fraught PR nation claims renders them, in ethnic or nationality terms, as an image of foreign nationals: a term never applied to Cuban immigrants even if they are uneducated, do not speak proper Spanish, or do not use sophisticated household and work tools.

33. Godreau, "Scripts of Blackness and the Racial Dynamics of Nacionalism in Puerto Rico."

34. Samuel M. Wilson, "The Prehistory and Early History of the Caribbean," in *Biogeography of the West Indies: Patterns and Perspectives*, ed. Charles A. Woods and Florence E. Sergile (London: CRC Press, 2001), 519–27.

35. Helene Safa, "The Transformation of Puerto Rico: The Impact of Modernization Ideology," *Transforming Anthropology* 19, no. 1 (2011): 46–49.

36. The modification to a verb is done with permission from Ortiz.

Chapter 7: Queering the Chili Queens: Culinary Citizenship through Food Consciousness in the New Borderlands

I am grateful to Nancy Barbour for generous feedback and critical comments on this essay. Thank you to Meredith E. Abarca, Consuelo C. Salas, and the two anonymous reviewers for their suggestions for revision. I also thank Ana Fernández for allowing me to interview her in San Antonio.

1. Suzanne Bost, "Women and Chile at the Alamo: Feeding U.S. Colonial Mythology," *Nepantla: Views from South* 4, no. 3 (2003): 493–522; Donna R. Gabaccia and Jeffrey M. Pilcher, "'Chili Queens' and Checkered Tablecloths: Public Dining Cultures of Italians in New York City and Mexicans in San Antonio, Texas, 1870s–1940s," *Radical History Review* 110 (2011): 109–26; Marci R. McMahon, *Domestic Negotiations: Gender, Nation, and Self-Fashioning in US Mexicana and Chicana Literature and Art* (New Brunswick, NJ: Rutgers University Press, 2013); Adán Medrano, *Truly Texas Mexican: A Native Culinary Heritage in Recipes* (Lubbock: Texas Tech University Press, 2014); Nikki Silva and Davia Nelson, *Hidden Kitchens: Stories, Recipes, and More from NPR's The Kitchen Sisters* (New York: Rodale Books, 2005); Robb Walsh, *The Tex-Mex Cookbook: A History in Recipes and Photos* (New York: Broadway Books, 2004).

2. Meredith E. Abarca, "*Los Chilaquiles de mi 'amá*: The Language of Everyday Cooking," in *Pilaf, Pozole, and Pad Thai: American Women and Ethnic Food*, ed. Sherri Inness (Amherst: University of Massachusetts Press, 2001), 119–44; Meredith E. Abarca, "*Charlas Culinarias*: Mexican Women Speak from Their Public Kitchens," in *Taking Food Public: Redefining Foodways in a Changing World*, ed. Psyche Williams-Forson and Carole M. Counihan (New York: Routledge, 2001), 94–114; Carole M. Counihan, "Mexicanas Taking Food Public: The Power of the Kitchen in the San Luis Valley," in *Taking Food Public: Redefining Foodways in a Changing World*, ed. Psyche Williams-Forson and Carole M. Counihan (New York: Routledge, 2011), 491–509; Chrystel Pit, "Tortillas to Riches: Ninfa Laurenzo, Houston, and the Business of Food and Culture 1973–98," *Food, Culture & Society* 12, no. 2 (2014): 245–60.

3. Meredith E. Abarca in "*Charlas Culinarias*: Mexican Women Speak from Their Public Kitchens," defines "familial wealth" as "a model that defines a business' success in terms other than capital gain [and] undeniably requires a paradigm shift that moves beyond the principles of market economy.... The concept of familial wealth does not ignore the importance of financial gain. However, the social as well as cultural advantages of owning a business can carry more weight, especially as the fruit of such profits are enjoyed not only by family members but also by other members of the community" (185).

4. Meredith E. Abarca and Nieves Pascual Soler define "food consciousness" as an embodied theory of cognitive and emotional knowledge that interconnects food's production, distribution, and consumption, as well as cultural and historical politics and policies. See introduction in Abarca and Pascual Soler, *Rethinking Chicana/o Literature through Food: Postnational Appetites* (New York: Palgrave Macmillan, 2013), 2, 7.

5. Alicia Arrizón, *Queering Mestizaje: Transculturation and Performance* (Ann Arbor: University of Michigan Press, 2006); Adela C. Licona, *Zines in Third Space: Radical Cooperation and Borderlands Rhetoric* (Albany: State University of

New York Press, 2012); Emma Pérez, "Queering the Borderlands: The Challenges of Excavating the Invisible and Unheard," *Frontiers: A Journal of Women Studies* 24, no. 2 & 3 (2003): 122–31; Sandra Soto, *Reading Chican@ Like a Queer: The De-Mastery of Desire* (Austin: University of Texas Press, 2010).

6. Richard R. Flores, *Remembering the Alamo: Memory, Modernity, and the Master Symbol* (Austin: University of Texas Press, 2002), 55.

7. Nikki Silva and Davia Nelson, *Hidden Kitchens*, 47.

8. Bost, "Women and Chile at the Alamo: Feeding U.S. Colonial Mythology," 506.

9. Marci R. McMahon, *Domestic Negotiations: Gender, Nation, and Self-Fashioning in US Mexicana and Chicana Literature and Art* (New Brunswick, NJ: Rutgers University Press, 2013).

10. During the 1940s, anti-Mexican xenophobia led to the deportation of Mexicans and Texas Mexicans. José Angel Hernandez, *Mexican American Colonization during the Nineteenth Century: A History of the U.S.-Mexico Borderlands* (Cambridge: Cambridge University Press, 2012).

11. Working in unsanitary conditions was prevalent for female cigar workers and pecan shellers in San Antonio during the time.

12. Lewis F. Fisher, *Chili Queens, Hay Wagons and Fandangos: The Spanish Plazas in Frontier San Antonio* (San Antonio: Maverick Publishing Company, 2014).

13. Laura Hernández-Ehrisman, *Inventing the Fiesta City: Heritage and Carnival in San Antonio* (Albuquerque: University of New Mexico Press, 2008).

14. Linda Heidenreich, "Me and Betty Crocker, or from WASPy White to Mestiza: 75 Years of General Mills," *Reconstruction: Studies in Contemporary Culture* 10, no. 4 (2010).

15. In 2005, the Dutch oven, a cast-iron pot, was named the official cooking pot of Texas, which was "used extensively by Spanish explorers, early settlers, ranchers, and chuck wagon cooks." The oven was brought to the United States by Dutch traders. It won over the barbeque pit. Melissa Block, "Texas Pays Tribute to Dutch Oven," *NPR*, April 22, 2005, http://www.npr.org/2005/04/22/4616266/texas-pays-tribute-to-the-dutch-oven.

16. The Frito, meaning fried in Spanish, or corn chip recipe was purchased by Elmer Doolin in 1932 for $100 from Gustavo Olguín, who had placed an ad in the *San Antonio Express*. Doolin, whose family owned the Highland Park Confectionary, partnered with Herman W. Lay to distribute Fritos in 1945. Kaleta Doolin, "DOOLIN, CHARLES ELMER [C. E.]," *Handbook of Texas Online*, last modified on August 27, 2013, http://www.tshaonline.org/ handbook/online/articles/fd073.

17. Retired editor of the *San Antonio Express-News* and current director of the *Rivard Report*, Robert Rivard, worked the First Friday shift at the Institute of Chili. Robert Rivard, "A Night with Ana and Jenn Working at the Institute of Chili Food Truck at the Alamo Street Eat-Bar," *Rivard Report: Urban. Independent. All About San Antonio*, July 12, 2012, http://therivardreport.com/a-night-with-ana-and-jenn-the-chili-queens-working-the-alamo-street-eat-bar/.

18. Award-wining chef and author Marcus Samuelsson commissioned a set of these miniature knife pendants.

19. I argue "food consciousness," as presented by Abarca and Pascual Soler,

Rethinking Chicana Literature through Food, combines theory in the flesh, based on Tex-Mex food production and consumption, to achieve culinary citizenship. Cherríe Moraga and Gloria Anzaldúa, *This Bridge Called My Back: Writings by Radical Women of Color* (Watertown, MA: Persephone Press, 1981), 23.

20. Jeffrey M. Pilcher, "Who Chased Out the 'Chili Queens?' Gender, Race, and Urban Reform in San Antonio, Texas, 1880–1943," *Food & Foodways* 16, no. 3 (2008): 173–200; Jeffrey M. Pilcher, "José Cuervo and the Gentrified Worm: Food, Drink, and the Touristic Consumption of Mexico," in *Holiday in Mexico: Critical Reflections on Tourism and Tourist Encounters,* ed. Dina Berger and Andrew Grant Wood (Durham, NC: Duke University Press, 2009), 221–40; Jeffrey M. Pilcher, *Planet Taco: A Global History of Mexican Food* (Oxford: Oxford University Press, 2012).

21. Gary Paul Nabham, *Cumin, Camels, and Caravans: A Spice Odyssey* (Berkeley: University of California Press, 2014).

22. Juana Maria Rodriguez, *Sexual Futures, Queer Gestures, and Other Latina Longings* (New York: New York University Press, 2014).

23. Pilcher, "José Cuervo and the Gentrified Worm," 225.

24. Francisco J. Santamaria, *Diccionario de Mejicanismos* (Mexico City: Editorial Porrua, 1959), 385.

25. Rosa Linda Fregoso writes an exemplary genealogy of Lupe Vélez as "Queen of the Bs," who starred in feature films known as the Mexican Spitfire series. Hollywood western films mirrored the racial tensions by portraying an Anglo cowboy hero against a Mexican "greaser" set in frontier towns. The militarism was usually inspired by Teddy Roosevelt's cowboy persona. Rosa Linda Fregoso, *MeXicana Encounters: The Making of Social Identities on the Borderlands* (Berkeley: University of California Press, 2003), 298.

26. Clara Lomas, "The Articulation of Gender in the Mexican Borderlands, 1900–1915," in *Recovering the U.S. Hispanic Literary Heritage, Volume I,* ed. Ramón A. Gutiérrez and Genaro Padilla (Houston: Arte Público Press, 1993), 298.

27. In contrast, the segregated Ladies LULAC chapter displayed a feminist politics in regard to female participation, but patriarchal family ideology remained intact. Appeals from the West Side Improvement and Taxpayers Association tried to counter Mexican American whiteness; however, it was met with resistance. Cynthia E. Orozco, "Alice Dickerson Montemayor: Feminism and Mexican American Politics in the 1930s," in *Writing the Range: Race, Class, and Culture in the Women's West,* ed. Elizabeth Jameson and Susan Armitage (Norman: University of Oklahoma Press, 1997), 435–56.

28. Ana Fernández, Facebook post, July 15, 2014, https://www.facebook.com/ChamoyCityLimits?ref=br_tf.

29. "The Roosevelt" is a combination of the Frito pie and tamale pie.

30. The Texas Rangers, a paramilitary group who lynched Mexicans indiscriminately, also propagated the white masculinist cowboy image.

31. "Food consciousness" reimagines postnational identities with gender and sexual desires and remaps the borderlands to find spaces of inclusion and healing, as argued by Abarca and Pascual Soler (*Rethinking Chicana Literature through Food*). Having embodied knowledge of Tex-Mex food production, distribution, and consumption, Fernández creates dishes that bring her pleasure as well as serves a food consciousness that awakens individual and collective subjectivities in her customers.

32. The "210" was also the title of Fernández's first painting of a bungalow and a car with a 210 stickered on the back.

33. Richard R. Flores, *Remembering the Alamo: Memory, Modernity, and the Master Symbol* (Austin: University of Texas Press, 2002).

34. Fiesta San Antonio, "Chili Queens Chili Cook-Off," *Fiesta San Antonio*, April 12, 2014, http://www.fiesta-sa.org/events/2014/chili-queens-chili-cook-off.

35. Sandip Roy, "Curry Queens and Other Spices," in *Q & A: Queer in Asian America*, ed. David L. Eng and Alice Y. Hom (Philadelphia: Temple University Press, 1998), 257.

36. Ramón García, "Against Rasquache: Chicano Camp and the Politics of Identity in Los Angeles," in *The Chicana/o Cultural Studies Reader*, ed. Angie Chabram-Dernersesian (New York: Routledge, 2006), 211–23, 211.

37. Fiesta San Antonio, "Chili Queens Chili Cook-Off."

378.Fernández could not disclose details of the case as it is confidential. The Institute of Chili, "For Immediate Release: 'Chili Queen' Good Truck Re-launches as 'The Institute of Chili,'" July 30, 2012, http://www.instituteofchili.com.

39. Camilla Fojas, *Border Bandits: Hollywood on the Southern Frontier* (Austin: University of Texas Press, 2008), 65.

40. Antje Lindenmeyer, "'Lesbian Appetites': Food, Sexuality and Community in Feminist Autobiography," *Sexualities* 9, no. 4 (2006): 469–85, 478.

41. Institute of Chili, "Motochefs Aaron Sanchez & Aquiles visit the Institute of Chili," *YouTube*, April 25, 2013, https://www.youtube.com/watch?v=OFWZG1Z-B2Lo.https://www.youtube.com/watch?v=OFWZG1ZB2Lohttps://www.youtube.com/watch?v=OFWZG1ZB2Lo

42. Institute of Chili, "Local Favorite The Institute of Chili Tops Food & Wine Magazine's List of Best Chili in the U.S.," *Press Release*, November 26, 2013, www.pr.com/press-release/529622.

43. Institute of Chili, "Chamoy City Limits, the Chili Queens Ice Cream Truck," *Press Release*, April 28, 2014, http://www.instituteofchili.com/for-immediate-release-chamoy-city-limits-the-chili-queens-ice-cream-truck-launches.

44. Alison Cook (@alisoncook), Twitter post, May 28, 2014, http://bit.ly/1E1hqAn.

45. Chamoy City Limits (@HouseOfChamoy), Twitter post, June 24, 2014, https://twitter.com/houseofchamoy.

46. Chamoy City Limits (@HouseOfChamoy), Twitter post, May 31, 2014, https://twitter.com/houseofchamoy.

47. Chamoy City Limits (@HouseOfChamoy), Twitter post, May 22, 2014, https://twitter.com/ houseofchamoy.

48. Chamoy City Limits, "Signature Shaved Ice," chamoycitylimits.com.

49. Chamoy City Limits (@HouseOfChamoy), Twitter post, June 28, 2014, https://twitter.com/ houseofchamoy.

50. Kogi BBQ, a Korean-Mexican taco truck in Los Angeles, was made famous for using Twitter to advertise and connect with customers; see Oliver Wang, "Learning from Los Kogi Angeles: A Taco Truck and Its City," in *Eating Asian American: A Food Studies Reader*, ed. Robert Ji-Song Ku, Martin F. Manalansan, and Anita Mannur (New York: New York University Press, 2013), 78–97. According to Gustavo Arellano, "If it wasn't for the years of legal fights these loncheros engaged in—without Twitter, Facebook or much start-up cash—you wouldn't have these big

festivals, or young chefs dreaming of amazing fusions within the confines of move-able metal"; see Gustavo Arellano, "Where Are the Loncheras at the Luxe-Lonchera Fests?" *OC Weekly Blogs*, September 1, 2010, http://blogs.ocweekly.com/stickafork init/2010/09/where_are_the_loncheras_at_the.php.

51. Richard Gambitta, "Development, Renewal, and . . . Displacement," *San Antonio Express-News*, August 2014.

52. Amanda Reyna (@optimistic_hthm), Twitter post, June 23, 2014, http://bit.ly/1mRTkCy.

53. Adela C. Licona, *Zines in Third Space: Radical Cooperation and Borderlands Rhetoric* (Albany: State University of New York Press, 2012), 166n13.

54. Institute of Chili (@TheChiliQueens), Twitter post, April 2, 2013, https://twitter.com/thechiliqueens.

55. Alison Caldwell, "Will Tweet for Food: Microblogging Mobile Food Trucks—Online, Offline, and In Line," in *Taking Food Public: Redefining Foodways in a Changing World*, ed. Psyche Williams-Forson and Carole M. Counihan (New York: Routledge, 2001), 306–21, 311.

Chapter 8: More Than "Just a Waitress": The Waitress as Artist and Activist in Contemporary Chicana Literature

1. Denise Chávez, *A Taco Testimony: Meditations on Family, Food and Culture* (Tucson: Rio Nuevo Publications, 2006), 61.

2. For a further exploration on the mother's culinary talent influencing a daughter's writing and artistic development, see Cristina Herrera, "'Delfina, ¡más tacos! Food, Culture, and Motherhood in Denise Chávez's *A Taco Testimony*," *Food, Culture and Society: An International Journal of Multidisciplinary Research* 13, no. 2 (June 2010): 241–56.

3. Vicki Ruiz, *Las Obreras: Chicana Politics of Work and Family* (Los Angeles: Regents of the University of California, 1993, 2000); María A. Gutiérrez Soldatenko, "ILGWU Labor Organizers: Chicana and Latina Leadership in the Los Angeles Garment Industry," *Frontiers: A Journal of Women Studies* 23, no. 1 (2002): 46–66; Patricia Zavella, *Women's Work and Chicano Families: Cannery Workers of the Santa Clara Valley* (Ithaca, NY: Cornell University Press, 1987).

4. Denise Chávez, *Face of an Angel* (New York: Warner Books, 1994), 215.

5. Ana Castillo, *So Far from God* (New York: Plume, 1993), also *The Guardians* (New York: Random House, 2008); Bárbara Renaud González, *Golondrian, why did you leave me?* (Austin: University of Texas Press, 2009); Sandra Cisneros, *Caramelo* (New York: Vintage, 2002).

6. Gloria Anzaldúa, *The Gloria Anzaldúa Reader*, ed. AnaLouise Keating (Durham, NC: Duke University Press, 2009), 31.

7. Virginia Woolf, *Room of One's Own* (New York: Mariner Books, 1988 edition).

8. For a study that examines the "negotiation" of domestic space, see Marci McMahon, *Domestic Negotiations: Gender, Nation, and Self-Fashioning in US Mexicana and Chicana Literature and Art* (New Brunswick, NJ: Rutgers University Press, 2013); also see Mary Romero, *Maid in the USA* (New York: Routledge, 1992, 2002).

9. Tey Diana Rebolledo, *The Chronicles of Panchita Villa and Other Guerrilleras: Essays on Chicana/Latina Literature and Criticism* (Austin: University of Texas Press, 2006), 141–42.

10. Tey Diana Rebolledo, *Women Singing in the Snow: A Cultural Analysis of Chicana Literature* (Tucson: University of Arizona Press, 1995), 202.

11. Karen Kovacik, "Between L=A=N=G=U=A=G=E and Lyric: The Poetry of Pink-Collar Resistance," *NWSA Journal* (Spring 2001): 34–35.

12. González, *Golorinda, why did you leave me?*

13. Meredith E. Abarca, *Voices in the Kitchen: Views of Food and the World from Working-Class Mexican and Mexican American Women* (College Station: Texas A&M University Press, 2006).

14. Dorothy Sue Cobble, *Dishing It Out: Waitresses and Their Unions in the Twentieth Century* (Urbana: University of Illinois Press, 1991), 2.

15. Greta Foff Paules, *Dishing It Out: Power and Resistance among Waitresses in a New Jersey Restaurant* (Philadelphia: Temple University Press, 1991), 137.

16. Jan Whitaker, "Domesticating the Restaurant: Marketing the Anglo-American Home," in *From Betty Crocker to Feminist Food Studies: Critical Perspectives on Women and Food*, ed. Arlene Voski Avakian and Barbara Haber (Amherst: University of Massachusetts Press, 2005), 101.

17. Sherrie A. Inness, *Secret Ingredients: Race, Gender, and Class at the Dinner Table* (New York: Palgrave Macmillan, 2006), 107.

18. Víctor M. Valle and Rodolfo D. Torres, *Latino Metropolis* (Minneapolis: University of Minnesota Press, 2000), 92.

19. Cobble, *Dishing*, 2.

20. Paules, *Dishing*, 7, 9.

21. Leon Elder and Lin Rolens, *Waitress: America's Unsung Heroine* (Santa Barbara: Capra Press, 1985), 16.

22. Sharlene Nagy Hesse-Biber and Gregg Lee Carter, *Working Women in America: Split Dreams* (New York: Oxford University Press, 2005), 164.

23. Ibid., 165.

24. Marlen Kanagui-Muñoz et al., "Latina/o Food Industry Employees' Work Experience: Work Barriers, Facilitators, Motivators, Training Preferences, and Perceptions," *Journal of Career Development* 39, no. 1 (2012): 121.

25. Kovacik, "Between L=A=N=G=U=A=G=E," 31.

26. Diana López, *Sofía's Saints* (Tempe, AZ: Bilingual Press, 2002), 13.

27. Ibid., 15.

28. Ibid., 25.

29. Ibid., 29.

30. Ibid., 34.

31. Ibid., 61.

32. Ibid., 88.

33. Demetria Martínez, *The Block Captain's Daughter* (Norman: University of Oklahoma Press, 2012), 4.

34. Ibid., 4.

35. Lisa Heldke, "Let's Cook Thai: Recipes for Colonialism," in *Pilaf, Pozole, and Pad Thai: American Women and Ethnic Food*, ed. Sherrie A. Inness (Amherst: University of Massachusetts Press, 2001), 184.

36. Martínez, *The Block Captain's Daughter*, 49.

NOTES TO PAGES 146–55

37. Ibid., 58.

38. Ibid., 71.

39. Ibid., 72–73.

40. Ibid., 94.

41. Linda Naranjo-Huebl, "Faith, Hope and Service in Denise Chávez's *Face of an Angel*," *Rocky Mountain Review of Language and Literature* 61, no. 1 (Spring 2007): 53; Maya Socolovsky, "Narrative and Traumatic Memory in Denise Chávez's *Face of an Angel*," *MELUS* 28, no. 4 (Winter 2003): 187–205.

42. Maya Socolovsky, "Narrative and Traumatic Memory in Denise Chávez's *Face of an Angel*," *MELUS* 28, no. 4 (Winter 2003): 200.

43. Chávez, *Face of an Angel*, 107.

44. Ibid., 108.

45. Ibid., 110.

46. Ibid.

47. Ibid., 148: Larry refers to himself as a "Spanish white man," not a Mexican American or Chicano.

48. Ibid., 150.

49. Ibid., 271.

50. Ibid., 451.

51. Ibid., 305.

52. Ibid., 381.

53. Rebolledo, *The Chronicles*, 149.

54. Other women characters in the novel, such as Chata and Oralia, are similarly described by Soveida as divine or holy because of their service and work.

55. Chávez, *Face of an Angel*, 270.

56. Ibid., 343.

57. Ibid., 171.

58. Ibid., 451.

Chapter 9: Conspicuous Consumption?: Eating Disorders as Nervous Immigrant Conditions in Contemporary Latina Fiction

1. Paul Rozin, "Food Is Fundamental, Fun, Frightening, and Far-Reaching," *Social Research* 66, no. 1 (Spring 1999).

2. For detailed historical information, see Anthony Bourdain, *Typhoid Mary: An Urban Historical* (New York: Bloomsbury, 2001), and Judith Walzer Leavitt, *Typhoid Mary: Captive to the Public's Health* (Boston: Beacon Press, 1996). It is noteworthy that Mary Mallon, an asymptomatic carrier of the disease, infected most people with typhoid as a result of her work as a cook.

3. For a historical account of the surveillance and linking of Haitian immigrants to the HIV/AIDS crisis in the United States, see, for example, A. L. Fairchild and E. A. Tynan, "Policies of Containment: Immigration in the Era of AIDS," *American Journal of Public Health* 84, no. 12 (December 1994): 2011–22.

4. For the full text of AZ SB 1070, see http://www.azleg.gov/legtext/49leg/2r/bills/sb1070s.pdf. For the full text of AZ HB 2281, see http://www.scribd.com/doc/125653774/Arizona-House-Bill-2281.

5. For the full text of First Lady Michelle Obama's speech, see http://www.whitehouse.gov/the-press-office/2013/07/23/remarks-first-lady-national-council-la-raza.

6. Psyche Williams-Forson connects "food shaming" to racialized food controlling and closely relates it to body shaming and the omnipresent privileging of thin, white, androgynous bodies in the advertising industry and other media. Psyche Williams-Forson, *Don't Yuck My Yum: Food Shaming, Food Policing, and Other African American Food Dilemmas* (Forthcoming).

7. Tsitsi Dangarembga, *Nervous Conditions* (London: Women's Press, 1988), 1. In her 1988 novel *Nervous Conditions*, Zimbabwean novelist and filmmaker Tsitsi Dangarembga created a postcolonial, feminist bildungsroman in which two cousins, one a remigrant from the UK, the other a daughter of a schoolmaster in rural Rhodesia, function as foils that represent different stages of the colonization of the mind, which manifests itself in the protagonists' eating habits, as well as in other forms. Nyasha, who returns from London at the age of thirteen, expresses her rebellion against traditional values of femininity and motherhood in Rhodesia by starving herself and, subsequently, developing an *anorexia nervosa* that almost kills her. Her cousin, Tambu, chooses the healthier, if less radical, route of fighting her way through the educational system in the hope of challenging sexism from within. Nyasha's radical rebellion is linked literally and metaphorically to her illness.

8. Psyche Williams-Forson, *Don't Yuck My Yum*; see Psyche Williams-Forson and Abby Wilkerson, "Intersectionality and Food Studies," *Food, Culture & Society: An International Journal of Multidisciplinary Research* 14, no. 1 (2011): 12–14.

9. Ellen McCracken, *New Latina Narrative: The Feminine Space of Postmodern Ethnicity* (Tucson: University of Arizona Press, 1999).

10. Adrienne Rich, "Notes towards a Politics of Location," in *Women, Feminist Identity and Society in the 1980s: Selected Papers*, ed. Myriam Díaz-Diocaretz and Iris M. Zavala (New York: John Benjamins Publishing Co., 1985), 7–15.

11. Nestor García Canclini, *Consumers and Citizens: Globalization and Multicultural Conflicts* (Minneapolis: University of Minnesota Press, 1995), 42, quoted in Raphael Dalleo and Elena Machado Sáez, *The Latina/o Canon and the Emergence of Post-Sixties Literature* (New York: Palgrave Macmillan, 2007), 113.

12. Deane W. Curtin, "Food/Body/Person," in *Cooking, Eating, Thinking: Transformative Philosophies of Food*, ed. Deane W. Curtin and Lisa M. Heldke (Bloomington: Indiana University Press, 1992), 11.

13. Ibid.

14. The term consumption itself carries a curious double meaning. Once associated with the "wasting away" of malnourished and overworked immigrants in tenements in nineteenth-century urban America, "consumption," a colloquial reference to bacterial tuberculosis, has a longstanding history linked to nativist and racist anxieties over foreign contamination in the United States since the late eighteenth century.

15. Warren J. Belasco, *Appetite for Change: How the Counterculture Took on the Food Industry: 1966–1988* (Ithaca, NY: Cornell University Press, 2007), 10.

16. Cristina García, *Dreaming in Cuban* (New York: Ballantine, 1992), 73.

17. Ibid., 18.

18. Anita Mannur, "Culinary Nostalgia: Authenticity, Nationalism, and Diaspora," *MELUS* 32, no. 4 (2007): 12.

19. Rozin, "Food Is Fundamental, Fun, Frightening, and Far-Reaching," 10.

20. Fred L. Gadarphé and Wenying Xu, "Introduction: Food in Multi-Ethnic Literatures," *MELUS* 32, no. 4 (2007): 7.

21. García, *Dreaming in Cuban*, 20.

22. Ibid., 21.

23. Laura Esquivel, *Como agua para chocolate* (New York: Vintage Español, 2001).

24. These phenomena are, of course, not unique to Latina/o and Latin American fiction. The recent film *Labor Day* (2013), based on the eponymous novel by Joyce Maynard, for example, never shows an actual sexual encounter between the agoraphobic housewife and her convict-on-the-run lover; instead, their sensual encounter climaxes in the shared baking of a perfect summer peach pie. Joyce Maynard, *Labor Day* (New York: William Morrow and Co., 2009).

25. García, *Dreaming in Cuban*, 142–43.

26. Ibid., 18.

27. Ibid., 223.

28. Ibid.

29. Rozin, "Food Is Fundamental," 23.

30. García, *Dreaming in Cuban*, 223.

31. Horatio Alger was the author of widely available young adult novels in the late nineteenth century, which exemplify the "from-rags-to-riches" myth and helped popularize the American Dream narrative for immigrants during this period.

32. Meredith E. Abarca and Nieves Pascual Soler, "Introduction" in *Rethinking Chicana Literature through Food* (New York: Pelgrave, 2013), 7.

33. Helena María Viramontes, *Under the Feet of Jesus* (New York: Plume, 1995), 177–80.

34. Lisa M. Heldke, "Food Politics, Political Food," in *Cooking, Eating, Thinking: Transformative Philosophies of Food*, ed. Deane W. Curtin and Lisa M. Heldke (Bloomington: Indiana University Press, 1992), 311.

35. Ibid., 15.

36. Viramontes, *Under the Feet of Jesus*, 12.

37. Ibid., 16.

38. Ibid., 63.

39. Ibid., 18.

40. Ibid., 32.

41. For more information on the working conditions of farmworkers, see Laura-Anne Minkoff-Zern and Christy Getz, "Farmworkers—The Basis and Bottom of the Food," *Race, Poverty and the Environment* 18, no. 1 (2011): 17–19, and Linda Nash, "The Fruits of Ill-Health: Pesticides and Workers' Bodies in Post–World War II California," *Osiris* 19 (2004): 203–19.

42. It is worth mentioning here as well that lard was not introduced to the cuisine of the Americas until the arrival of the Spaniards, hence the very notion of the "authenticity" of Mexican American cuisine is problematic from the very onset.

43. Psyche Williams-Forson, *Building Houses out of Chicken Legs: Black Women, Food, and Power* (Chapel Hill: University of North Carolina Press, 2006), 3–5.

44. Viramontes, *Under the Feet of Jesus*, 119.

45. Gadarphé and Xu, "Introduction: Food in Multi-Ethnic Literatures," 6.

46. Jonna Barszewska Marshall, "'Boast now, chicken, tomorrow you'll be stew': Pride, Shame, Food and Hunger in the Memoirs of Esmeralda Santiago," *MELUS* 32, no. 4 (2007): 9.

47. Ester Hernández, "Sun Mad," 1982.

48. Viramontes, *Under the Feet of Jesus*, 49–50.

49. Ibid., 31.

50. Ibid., 110.

51. Ibid., 9.

52. Ibid., 105.

53. Ibid., 18.

54. Ibid., 31.

55. Ibid., 98.

56. Jean Anthelme Brillat-Savarin, *The Physiology of Taste: or, Meditations on Transcendental Gastronomy*, trans. M. F. K. Fisher (New York: Heritage Press, 1949), 1.

57. Lázaro Lima, *The Latino Body: Crisis Identities in American Literary and Cultural Memory* (New York: New York University Press, 2007), 9.

Chapter 10: Writing against Food-Based Aesthetics of Objectification: The Work of Judith Ortiz Cofer

1. Trope is from the Greek meaning "turn" and refers to a figurative, rather than literal, use of language.

2. Born in the town of Hormigueros, Puerto Rico, in 1952, she and her family migrated to Paterson, New Jersey, in 1956. In 1967 they relocated again to Augusta, Georgia, where the family remained until her father's untimely death, and her homesick mother returned to Puerto Rico shortly thereafter. Ortiz Cofer has resided in Georgia for decades now. She currently teaches at the University of Georgia in Athens, and was inducted into the Georgia Writers' Hall of Fame in April of 2010. She is widely anthologized: her novel *The Line of the Sun* (1989) was nominated for a Pulitzer Prize.

3. See Sherrie A. Inness, *Cooking Lessons: The Poltics of Gender and Food* (Boulder, CO: Roman & Littlefield Publishers, 2001); Arlene Voski Avakian and Barbara Haber, eds., *From Betty Crocker to Feminist Food Studies: Critical Perspectives on Woman and Food* (Amherst: University of Massachusetts Press, 2005); Elspeth Probyn, *Carnal Appetites: Food Sex Identities* (New York: Routledge, 2001).

4. Psyche Williams-Forson, *Building Houses out of Chicken Legs: Black Women, Food and Power* (Chapel Hill: University of North Carolina Press, 2006), 1.

5. In another example, Williams-Forson describes how chicken traveled in what African Americans called "a shoe box special": a package that made for hearty fare on tiresome journeys. The strategic dimension is disturbing, as part of the rationale was to avoid potentially dangerous encounters. Williams-Forson explains, "The experience of freedom brought on by mobility is momentarily disrupted to include an understanding of how many aspects of the American travel landscape —restaurants, rest areas, and gas stations—were harbingers of hostility for black

people." Thus, Williams-Forson's careful analysis dismantles the racist system of representation that deploys the trope of African Americans as mindless eaters of fried chicken. Williams-Forson, *Building Houses out of Chicken Legs*, 132.

6. Esmeralda Santiago, *When I Was Puerto Rican* (New York: Random House, 1994), 4.

7. Ibid., 3–4.

8. Indeed, numerous examples of food relating to self-knowledge appear in Santiago's memoir, including *pasteles* on Christmas as they relate to nostalgia, or the attempt by the US government officials to "improve," read Anglicize, the Puerto Rican diet, as well as Negi's subsequent rejection of the US food by vomiting.

9. Meredith E. Abarca and Nieves Pascual Soler, introduction in *Rethinking Chicana/o Literature through Food: Postnational Appetites*, ed. Nieves Pascual Soler and Meredith E. Abarca (New York: Palgrave Macmillan, 2013), 2.

10. Carole M. Counihan, *The Anthropology of Food and Body* (New York: Routledge, 1999); Carole M. Counihan, "Female Identity, Food, and Power in Contemporary Florence," *Anthropological Quarterly* 61, no. 2 (April 1988): 51–62, 2.

11. And while not dehumanizing, Ortiz Cofer even cites an incident with an Anglo-American woman regarding the ways in which ethnic assumptions relating to food all too readily locate Latinas in positions of servitude. While at one of Ortiz Cofer's poetry readings, a white woman mistakes the author for a waitress and attempts to order a cup of coffee. "The Myth of the Latin Women: I Just Met a Girl Named Maria," in *The Latin Deli: Telling the Lives of Barrio Women* (New York: Norton, 1993), 153.

12. To note, citizenship was conferred on Puerto Ricans with the Jones Act of 1917.

13. Judith Ortiz Cofer, "Rituals: A Prayer, a Candle and a Notebook," in *Woman in Front of the Sun* (Athens: University of Georgia Press, 2000), 26.

14. Judith Ortiz Cofer, "Woman in Front of the Sun," in *Woman in Front of the Sun* (Athens: University of Georgia Press, 2000), 48.

15. Ibid., 48.

16. Ibid., 53.

17. Cruz Miguel Ortíz Cuadra, *Eating Puerto Rico: A History of Food, Culture, and Identity*, trans. Russ Davidson (Chapel Hill: University of North Carolina Press, 2013), 255.

18. A common Puerto Rican experience, *el vaivén*, refers to the movement back and forth from the mainland to the island. For more on *el vaivén*, see Jorge Duany, *The Puerto Rican Nation on the Move* (Chapel Hill: University of North Carolina Press, 2002).

19. From the "Song of Songs" in the Old Testament to contemporary culture, women are often represented as items for consumption. For instance, in "Song" the lover rejoices in the female beloved as he exclaims, "Your lips distill nectar, my bride / honey and milk are under your tongue / ... your channel is an orchard of pomegranates with all the choicest fruits." See *The Holy Bible containing the Old and New Testaments with the Apocryphal/Deuterocanonical Books (New Revised Standard Version)*, Song of Songs 4:11–13. The type of Bible translation should be indicated. Later, in the Renaissance, writers often used a catalogue of beauty, or the blazon, which dissects the woman and sometimes depicts her physical qualities as food.

Authors such as Spenser in his *Amoretti* sonnet cycle writes of "two golden apples, Her brest, that table was, so richly spredd." *Edmund Spenser's Poetry: Authoritative Texts and Criticism,* 3rd ed., ed. Hugh Maclean and Anne Lake Prescott (New York: W. W. Norton & Co., 1993), 618. In *Astrophel and Stella,* Sidney's famous sonnet cycle that is also of the Renaissance, after the speaker's Platonic contemplation of Stella's virtues, he offers his famous exhortation, "'But, ah,' Desire still cries, 'give me some food.'" *The Poems of Sir Philip Sidney,* ed. William A. Ringler Jr. (Oxford: Oxford University Press, 1962), 201. Even in the twentieth century, there are famous literary utterances such as Prufrock's timid inquiry if he should "dare to eat a peach" and "force the moment to its crisis." T. S. Eliot, "The Love Song of J. Alfred Prufrock," in *Prufrock, and Other Observations* (Charelston, SC: Booksearch, 2002), 26.

20. Ernesto Quiñonez, *Bodega Dreams* (New York: Random House, 2000), 213.

21. Junot Díaz, *The Brief Wondrous Life of Oscar Wao* (New York: Penguin, 2007), 123–24.

22. Judith Ortiz Cofer, "The Myth of the Latin Women: I Just Met a Girl Named Maria," in *The Latin Deli: Telling the Lives of Barrio Women* (New York: Norton, 1993), 148–54, 150.

23. Ibid., 150.

24. Regarding gender, Svedka Vodka ads depict women as sexy robots, or femme-bots, who are high-heeled automatons that serve men cocktails made with Svedka Vodka. Femme-bot debuted in 2005, but the campaign has ended as the Swedish vodka's new ads focus on the outdoors and the various flavors of the vodka. See E. J. Schultz, "Svedka Pulls the Plug on Its Sexy Robot for New Campaign," *Advertising Age,* March 20, 2013, accessed March 11, 2015, http://adage.com/article/news/svedka-pulls-plug-sexy-robot-campaign/240435/.

25. Foot Hills Brewing, "Sexual Chocolate," *Foot Hills Brewing,* January 21, 2015, accessed March 11, 2015, http://www.foothills brewing.com/brews/sexual-chocolate/.

26. bell hooks, "Eating the Other," in *Black Looks: Race and Representation* (Boston: South End Press, 1987), 21.

27. Lisa Heldke, *Exotic Appetites: Ruminations of a Food Adventurer* (New York: Routledge, 2003), xiii.

28. Ibid., xvi.

29. hooks, "Eating the Other," 21.

30. Ortiz Cofer, "The Myth of the Latin Women: I Just Met a Girl Named Maria," 151.

31. Ibid., 151.

32. For a sustained analysis of the representational process by which women are represented as meat, see Carol Adams, *The Politics of Meat,* rev. ed. (New York: Bloomsbury, 2010).

33. Peter Chapman, *Bananas: How the United Fruit Company Changed the World* (New York: Canongate, 2007), 15.

34. Eleanor Ty, *The Politics of the Visible in Asian North American Narratives* (Toronto: University of Toronto Press, 2004), xii.

35. Ortiz Cofer also recounts another unfortunate meeting, this time when a white, middle-aged man "half-bellowed 'Don't Cry for Me, Argentina.'" She muses that the ignorant crooner would likely not have behaved in this manner with a white woman. See "The Myth of the Latin Woman: I Just Met a Girl Named Maria," 151.

36. Ibid., 148.

37. Judith Ortiz Cofer, "Corazon's Café," in *The Latin Deli: Telling the Lives of Barrio Women* (New York: Norton, 1993), 93–118.

38. Carmen S. Rivera, *Kissing the Mango Tree: Puerto Rican Women Rewriting American Literature* (Houston: Arte Público Press, 2002), 151.

39. Ortiz Cofer, "Corazon's Café," 95.

40. Ibid., 93.

41. Ibid., 97.

42. Ibid., 100.

43. The blazon is a literary technique whereby the physical attributes of a woman are listed in a manner that focuses on her various parts. It is a strategy something akin to a dissection and sometimes it describes those various parts of her body as food, as in the example mentioned above in footnote 19 with Spenser and the "two golden apples, Her brest."

44. Ortiz Cofer, "Corazon's Café," 94.

45. Frances Aparicio and Susana Chávez-Silverman, introduction to *Tropicalizations: Transcultural Representations of Latinidad*, ed. Frances Aparicio and Susana Chávez-Silverman (Hanover, NH: University Press of New England, 1997), 2.

46. Ortiz Cofer, "Corazon's Café," 102–3.

47. Ibid., 103.

48. Ibid.

49. Arjun Appadurai, "Gastro-poetics in Hindu South Asia," *American Ethnologist* 8 (1981): 494–511.

50. Renato Rosaldo, "Imperialist Nostalgia," *Representation* 26 (1989): 107–22, 108.

Chapter 11: Food Marketing Industry: Cultural Attitudes Made Visible

1. W. B. Park, The New Yorker Collection: www.cartoonbank.com, quoted in Priscilla Parkhurst Ferguson, *Word of Mouth: What We Talk About When We Talk About Food* (Berkeley: University of California Press, 2014).

2. Quoted in Victor M. Valle and Mary Lau Valle, *Recipe of Memory: Five Generations of Mexican Cuisine* (New York: New Press, 1995), 170.

3. Ibid., 170.

4. While traveling through Santa Fé, New Mexico, just at the onset of the US-Mexican war, in her diary covering the years of 1846–47, *Down the Santa Fé Trail and into Mexico*, Susan Shelby Magoffin records some of these early attitudes. Susan Shelby, *Down the Santa Fé Trail and into Mexico: The Diary of Susan Shelby Magoffin* (Lincoln, NE: Bison Books, 1982).

5. Katherine Massoth, "Making Tortillas, Making Southwest: Blurred Boundaries of Food, Identity, and Citizenship in the 'American' Southwest, 1846–1945" (np).

6. Charles Fletcher Lummis, *Letters from the Southwest, September 20, 1884 to March 14, 1885*, ed. James W. Byrkit (Tucson: University of Arizona Press, 1989), 118.

7. Ibid., xxiii.

8. This is a mythology that Taco Bell has tried to capitalize on with its mission bell towers as an iconic symbol—but as Mexican food, not Spanish.

9. Valle and Valle, *Recipe of Memory*, 171.

10. Ibid., 132–33.

11. In Ferrero's analysis, she demonstrates that restaurants have become a site of cultural affirmation. Syvlia Ferrero, "Comida sin par. Consumption of Mexican food in Los Angeles: 'Foodscapes' in a Transnational Consumer Society," in *Food Nations: Selling Taste*, ed. Warren Belasco and Philip Scranton (New York: Routledge, 2002), 194–222.

12. Robb Walsh in *The Tex-Mex Cookbook: A History in Recipes and Photos* shows this commercializing process of altering Mexican food's appeal by way of appropriation and modification of recipes, and by the displacements of actual Mexican people from the realm of selling food, as was the case of the famous Chili Queens. The commercialization of Mexican-based food was such that eventually even its name changed to Tex-Mex. Rob Walsh, *The Tex-Mex Cookbook* (New York: Ten Speed Press, 2004).

13. Judith Williamson, *Decoding Advertisement* (London: Marion Boyard, 1994).

14. For an extensive discussion on advertiser's use of images to interact with consumers, refer to Williamson, *Decoding Advertisement*.

15. Roland Barthes, "Toward a Psychosociology of Contemporary Food Consumption," in *Food and Culture: A reader*, 3rd ed., ed. Carole M. Counihan and Penny Van Esterik (New York: Routledge, 2013), 29.

16. There are two scholars that influence our understanding of "node" and "web of meaning." They are Bruno Latour and Clifford Geertz. The concept of "node" derives from Latour's definition of "networks" as "a concept, not a thing out there. It is a tool to help describe something, not what is being described. It has the same relationship with the topic at hand as a perspective grid to a traditional single-point perspective painting: drawn first, the lines might allow one to project a three-dimensional object onto a flat piece of linen; but they are not *what* is to be painted, only what has allowed the painter to give the impression of depth before they are erased. In the same way, a network is not what is represented in the text, but what readies the text to take the relay of actors as mediators" (131). Within networks, Latour explains, "Action is not done under the full control of consciousness; action should rather be felt as a node, a knot, and a conglomerate of many surprising sets of agencies that have to be slowly disentangled" (43). Therefore, in our use, a node represents the "conglomerate" of "agencies" that have to be "disentangled." Also, continuing with the metaphor of untangling, "webs of meaning" derives from Clifford Geertz's definition of culture. Clifford Geertz argues, "Believing, with Max Weber, that man is an animal suspended in webs of significance he himself has spun, I take culture to be those webs, and the analysis of it to be therefore not an experimental science in search of law but an interpretive one in search of meaning" (5). Looking at images presented by food advertisements, it becomes clear that there is much to be untangled when looking at the single actor of food images embedded within already constructed understandings of what the images mean and represent to certain groups (cultures). Our analysis attempts to do a portion of the untangling

for each of the images we highlight. Bruno Latour, *Reassembling the Social: An Introduction to Actor-Network-Theory* (Oxford: Oxford University Press, 2005); Clifford Geertz, "Thick Description: Toward an Interpretive Theory of Culture," *Interpretation of Cultures: Selected Essays* (New York: Basic Books, 1973).

17. Meredith E. Abarca introduces the concept of "holistic culinary approach" in "Culinary encounters in Latino/a Literature." Meredith E. Abarca, "Culinary Encounters in Latino/a Literature," in *Routledge Companion to Latino/a Literature*, ed. Suzanne Bost and Frances R. Aparicio (New York: Routledge, 2013) 251–60, 252.

18. Consuelo Carr Salas proposes this theoretical concept in her dissertation, "Commodified Perceptions of Culture: A Rhetorical Inquiry of Food Advertisement."

19. Donna R. Gabaccia, *We Are What We Eat: Ethnic Food and the Making of Americans* (Cambridge, MA: Harvard University Press, 1998).

20. Arjun Appadurai, "Global Ethnoscapes: Notes and Queries for a Transnational Anthropology," *Recapturing Anthropology: Working in the Present*, ed. Rechard G. Fox (Seattle: University of Washington Press, 1991), 195.

21. Juan Manuel Mendoza Guerrero, in this collection.

22. Chimamanda Ngozi Adiche, "The Danger of the Single Story." *TED* video. July 2009 www.ted.com/talks/chimamanda_adiche_the_danger_of_a_single_story.

23. Pancho Villa and Emiliano Zapata were leading figures in the Mexican Revolution. Pancho Villa led his revolt against Porfirio Díaz in northern Mexico; Emiliano Zapata led a revolt in central Mexico that later became known as the Zapatistas.

24. Gabaccia, *We Are What We Eat*.

25. While we are focusing on male objectification, female commodifed perception of culture also applies to Latin@s, as seen in chapters 7 (Cárdenas) and 10 (Cruz).

26. Maribel Alvarez, quoted in Gustavo Arellano, *Taco USA* (New York: Scribner, 2012), 272.

27. The investigative reporting by John Kenneth Turner conducted during the Porfiriato in 1910; *Barbarous Mexico: An Indictment of a Cruel and Corrupt System* (Chicago: Charles Kerr and Company, 1910).

28. David J. Weber provides his readers with a history of the "Black Legend" in "Scarce More than Apes," in *Myth and the History of the Hispanic Southwest* (Albuquerque: University of New Mexico Press, 1990), 159.

29. Charles Phillips Jimenez, *Sleeping Mexican Phenomena* (Whittier: C. P. Jimenez Pub., 1990); Maribel Alvarez, quoted in Gustavo Arellano, *Taco USA* (New York: Scribner, 2012), 272.

30. Nevin O. Winter, *Mexico and Her People Of Today: An Account of the Customs, Characteristics, Amusements, History, and Advancement Of the Mexicans, and the Development and Resources of Their Country* (Boston: L. C. Page and Company, 1913), 117.

31. Ibid., 185–86.

32. Alvarez, quoted in Gustavo Arellano, *Taco USA*, 273.

33. Our use of the terms "icon" and "symbol" derives from C. S. Pierce's theory of semeiotics. See C. S. Pierce, *The Writing of Charles C. S. Pierce: A Chronological Edition*, ed. Pierce Edition Project (Bloomington: Indiana University Press,

1982); Stanford Encyclopedia of Philosophy, "Pierce's Theory of Signs," *Stanford Encyclopedia of Philosophy,* November 2010, http://plato.stanford.edu/entries/peirce-semiotics/#SigEleSig.

34. C. Allan Jones, *Texas Roots: Agriculture and Rural Life before the Civil War* (College Station: Texas A&M Press, 2005), 15.

35. Richard W. Slatta, "Hat," *The Cowboy Encyclopedia* (Santa Barbra: ABC CLIO, 1994), 171–72.

36. For the complexity of this term, see Fitting in this volume.

37. Slatta, "Hat," 171.

38. Kathleen M. Sands, *Charrerías Mexicana: An Equestrian Folk Tradition* (Tucson: University of Arizona Press, 1993), 285.

39. William Wroth, *Sarape Textiles from Historic Mexico* (St. Louis: St. Louis Art Museum, 1999), 11; Ramon Mena, "El Zarape," *Mexican Magazine* 11, no. 4 (1926).

40. Wroth, *Sarape Textiles from Historic Mexico,* 19–20.

41. Ibid., 26.

42. Marie Sarita Gaytán, "Tequila Shots," in *Taking Food Public,* ed. Psyche Williams-Forson and Carole M. Counihan (New York: Routledge, 2012), 439.

43. Pulque is "a beverage fermented from the agave (maguey) plant and similar to beer in its low alcohol content and high number of nutrients." Ibid., 438.

44. Ibid., 438.

45. These five states are Tamaulipas, Nayarit, Jalisco, Guanajuato, and Michoacán.

46. Gaytán, "Tequila Shots," 438.

47. For an extensive collection and analysis of images that have been used in advertisements and other media, refer to William Anthony Nericcio, *Tex{t} Mex: Seductive Hallucinations of the "Mexican" in America* (Austin: University of Texas Press, 2007).

48. Mendiola García, in her chapter in this collection, addresses the same issue of *commercialización salvage.* While Toledo uses this term in regard to the gentrification of Oaxaca's city center, we feel that the statement is applicable to the "cultural hijacking" that the use of the image of the sleeping Mexican man has created. See Reed Johnson, "McDonald's loses a round to Oaxacan cultural Pride," *Los Angeles Times,* January 5, 2003, accessed February 5, 2015, http://articles.latimes.com/2003/jan/05/entertainment/ca-johnson5/2.

49. Marie Sarita Gaytán, "From Sombreros to Sincronizadas: Authenticity, Ethnicity and the Mexican Restaurant Industry," *Journal of Contemporary Ethnography* 37, no. 3 (2008): 314–41, 323.

50. Maribel Alvarez's work on souvenirs found on the Arizona US/Mexico border and the sleeping Mexican complicates the notion that the image always has a derogatory association. Within her work Alvarez discusses the concept of "kitsch." She defines "kitsch" as "the term used in aesthetic criticism to refer to objects that emulate or copy the styles and tastes of the educated, sophisticated class, resulting in an inevitable caricature or 'bad taste'" (44). While there is a long history on the evolution of the term "kitsch," we use the term to mark that the image's presence should not be taken seriously. Maribel Alvarez, "Made in Mexico: Souvenirs, Artisans, Shoppers and the Meaning of Other 'Border-Type-Things'" (PhD diss., University of Arizona, 2003).

51. Mexi-Snacks Las Cruces brand tortilla chips is owned and operated out of El Paso, Texas. It is unclear if there is an affiliation with other "Mexi-Snax" products.

52. Theodor Adorno and Max Hokeimer, *Dialect of the Enlightenment* (Palo Alto: Stanford University Press, 1979).

53. Gaytán, "From Sombreros to Sincronizadas," 338.

54. Weber, "Scarce More than Apes," 161.

55. Ibid., 166.

56. David Domínguez, *Work Done Right* (Tucson: University of Arizona Press, 2003).

57. Carol J. Adams, *The Sexual Politics of Meat: A Feminist-Vegetarian Critical Theory* (New York: Continuum International Publishing Group, 1990).

58. Del Sol Foods, "Product Packaging," *DelSoldfoods.com* 2013, accessed October 15, 2014, http://delsolfoods.com/delsolcompany/our-company/product-packaging.

59. Michael Pollan, *Omnivorous Dilemma: A Natural History of Four Meals* (New York: Penguin Press, 2006); Karl Webber, *Food Inc: A Participant Guide: How Industrial Food Is Making Us Sicker, Fatter, and Poorer—And What You Can Do about It* (Los Angeles: Participant Media, 2009); Eric Schlosser, *Fast Food Nation: The Dark Side of the All-American Meal* (New York: First Mariner Books, 2001).

60. Lorraine Collette Peterson, according to Sun Maid Raisin's website, was discovered in 1915 in Fresno, California. For a detailed history of Lorraine Collete Peterson and the creation of the Sun Maid image, refer to http://www.sunmaid.com/the-sun-maid-girl.html. Sun Maid, "The Sun Maid Girl," *Sun Maid*, 2014, accessed October 15, 2014, http://www.sunmaid.com/.

61. Therese Thau Heyman, *Posters American Style* (New York: Harry N. Abrams, 1998), as qtd. in "Del Corazón: Latino Voices in American Art," *Smithsonian American Art Museum*, accessed October 15, 2014, Americanart.si.edu./education/Corazon/galleria_06.cfm.

62. Abarca and Pascual Soler, in their introduction to *Rethinking Chicana Literature through Food,* define food consciousness as "a theory of pragmatic embodied epistemology wherein knowledge is acquired through the sensations and emotions that food awakens in the body." Meredith E. Abarca and Nieves Pascual Soler, "Introduction," *Rethinking Chicana Literature through Food*, ed. Nieves Pascual Soler and Meredith E. Abarca (New York: Pelgrave, 2013), 2.

63. Ibid.; Thau Heyman, *Posters American Style*. For more information farming conditions, see Pollan, *Omnivorous Dilemma*; Webber, *Food Inc*; Schlosser, *Fast Food Nation*.

64. Seth Holmes's *Fresh Fruit, Broken Bodies: Migrant Farmworkers in the United States* (Berkeley: University of California Press, 2013) is a good source to refer to for more information on the working conditions of farmworkers.

65. Elizabeth Fitting, "The Political Uses of Culture: Maize Production and the GM Corn Debates in Mexico," in *Taking Food Public: Redefining Foodways in a Changing World*, ed. Psyche Williams-Forson and Carole M. Counihan (New York: Routledge, 2012).

66. Abarca and Pascual Soler, "Introduction," 2.

67. National Center for Farmworker Health, Farmworker health fact sheet: demographics (National Center for Farmworker Health, 2012), 1.

68. Anthony Bourdain, "Under the Volcano," *Food Travel Anthony Bourdain Parts Unknown* (blog), May 3, 2014, http://anthonybourdain.tumblr.com/post/84641290831/under-the-volcano.

69. Alvarez, "Made in Mexico: Souvenirs, Artisans, Shoppers and the Meaning of Other 'Border-Type-Things.'"

70. Williamson, *Decoding Advertisement*, iv.

71. *Representations and the Media*, directed by Sut Jhally (1997; Northhampton: Media Education Foundation: Documentary Films, Challenging Media, 2002), DVD.

CONTRIBUTORS

MEREDITH E. ABARCA is an associate professor in the Department of English at the University of Texas at El Paso. At the undergraduate level she teaches Chicana/o literature, Mexican American folklore, and women in literature. She also teaches graduate courses that examine the intersection of literature and globalism, cosmopolitanism, and food as cultural and theoretical discourses. She is the author of *Voices in the Kitchen* (2006) and coeditor of *Rethinking Chicana/o Literature through Food* (2013). Her work has appeared in *Food & Foodways*, *Food, Culture & Society*, and in edited collections such as *Taking Food Public: Redefining Foodways in the Changing World* (2011) and *The Routledge Companion to U.S. Latino Studies* (2013).

NORMA L. CÁRDENAS joined the Chicano Education Program at Eastern Washington University from her position as assistant professor in ethnic studies at Oregon State University. She received her PhD in culture, literacy, and language from the University of Texas at San Antonio. Her research has been supported by fellowships from the USDA and the Center for Humanities at OSU. Cárdenas's research explores food, identity, and representation. She is presently working on a manuscript titled *Forgetting Tex-Mex: San Antonio's Culinary Borderlands* that traces the cultural history of Tex-Mex food. Her publications have appeared in edited collections.

KAREN CRUZ is a visiting lecturer of continuing education at University of North Carolina-Chapel Hill, and a lecturer at North Carolina State University in the English Department with a specialization in twentieth- and twenty-first-century American literature. In 2014, she designed and taught the first ever Latina/o literature course at NC State, as well as hosted a Latina/o Speaker series. Her current research interests focus on contemporary Latina/o literatures and cultures, women's studies, food studies, and critical race and ethnic theory. In particular, her work examines aspects of food culture and how they relate to constructions of Latina/o identity. She also teaches independent classes on wine appreciation.

ELIZABETH FITTING is an associate professor in the Department of Sociology and Social Anthropology at Dalhousie University in Halifax, Canada. She has looked at the impact of neoliberalism and water shortages on the livelihoods of Tehuacán Valley residents, and how the experiences of *campesinos, maquiladora* workers, and transnational migrants are generational and gendered. Additionally, she has researched anti-GM movements that value and promote the use of traditional seed varieties in both Mexico and Colombia. Her ethnography, *The Struggle for Maize: Campesinos, Workers and Transgenic Corn in the Mexican Countryside* (2011), was recently translated into Japanese.

CRISTINA HERRERA is an associate professor of Chicano and Latin American studies at California State University, Fresno. She holds a PhD in English from Claremont Graduate University, specializing in Chicana/Latina literature. Her work has appeared in journals such as *Food, Culture & Society, Chicana/Latina Studies*, and *Journal of Caribbean Literatures*, among others. Herrera is author of *Contemporary Chicana Literature: (Re)Writing the Maternal Script* (2014). Currently, she is working on several projects in Chicana/Latina literature.

LIDIA MARTE is an assistant professor at the University of Puerto Rico-Rio Piedras campus; she received her PhD in cultural anthropology from the University of Texas at Austin. She is a critical ethnographer and food studies scholar interested in researching and documenting place-memory in the Dominican diaspora and in the Caribbean experience.

JOSIE MÉNDEZ-NEGRETE is a sociologist who teaches Mexican American Studies in the Department of Bicultural-Bilingual Studies at the University of Texas at San Antonio. She is the author of *Las hijas de Juan: Daughters Betrayed.* Her upcoming book, *A Life on Hold*, which is an examination of schizophrenia in the context of the lived experience of a Chicano family, will be published by the University of New Mexico Press (2015). From 2009 to 2014, Méndez-Negrete served as lead editor of *Chicana/Latina Studies: The Journal of Mujeres Activas en Letras y Cambio Social.*

SANDRA C. MENDIOLA GARCÍA is an assistant professor of Latin America history at the University of North Texas. She has also taught at the University of Alabama in Huntsville. She received her PhD in history from Rutgers University. She is completing a book-length study on street vendors' independent unionization efforts and the use of public space in Mexico from the 1970s to the mid-1990s. She has recently begun researching a new project on a mining community in central Mexico.

JUAN MANUEL MENDOZA GUERRERO received his PhD from the Borderlands History Program at the University of Texas at El Paso. He won the national award for research on foreign trade (Mexico, 2003) and the Fellowship Mexico-North Research Network. He has taught at the Monterrey Institute of Technology. He currently teaches at the Autonomous University of Sinaloa, Mexico. He is a member of the National System of Researchers. His areas of interest are migration, ethnic businesses, and studies of food and poverty.

MONICA PERALES is associate professor of history at the University of Houston and associate director of the UH Center for Public History. She received her PhD in history from Stanford University in 2004, and holds a BA in journalism and an MA in history from the University of Texas at El Paso. Her book *Smeltertown: Making and Remembering a Southwest Border Community* (2010) received the Kenneth Jackson Award for Best Book in North American Urban History from the Urban History Association. She is codirector of the Gulf Coast Food Project at UH, a public history project that promotes the scholarly study of food in southeast Texas. She is presently working on a book on Mexican women, labor, and foodways in San Antonio in the twentieth century.

MARION CHRISTINA ROHRLEITNER (PhD University of Notre Dame, 2007) is associate professor in the Department of English at the University of Texas at El Paso, where she researches and teaches contemporary American Literature with an emphasis on Chicana/o, Latina/o, and Caribbean diasporic fiction. She is coeditor of *Dialogues Across Diasporas: Women Writers, Scholars, and Activists of Africana and Latina Descent in Conversation* (2013), and her scholarship has appeared in *American Quarterly, Antípodas, Callaloo, Interdisciplinary Humanities*, and *Latino Studies*. She is a contributor to the Oxford Bibliographies in Latino Studies. Her current book project, Transnational Latinidades, explores the production, translation, and marketing of Latina/o narratives outside of the United States, specifically in Canada and the European Union.

CONSUELO CARR SALAS is a doctoral candidate in the Rhetoric and Composition program at the University of Texas at El Paso. She is coauthor of "*De aquí y de allá*: Changing Preseptions of Literacy thought Food Pedagogy, Asset-Based Narratives, and Hybrid Spaces" (2015). She is the inaugural recipient of the Outstanding Doctoral Student Strauss Research Fellowship for the 2014–2015 academic year. Her research explores the rhetorical use of images on food advertisements. She is presently working on her dissertation titled "Commodified Perceptions of Culture: A Rhetorical Inquiry of Food Advertisement."

INDEX